GUERRILLA FILM SCORING

GUERRILLA FILM SCORING

PRACTICAL ADVICE FROM HOLLYWOOD COMPOSERS

JEREMY BORUM

ROWMAN & LITTLEFIELD
Lanham • Boulder • New York • London

Published by Rowman & Littlefield
A wholly owned subsidary of
The Rowman & Littlefield Publishing Group, Inc.
4501 Forbes Boulevard, Suite 200, Lanham, Maryland 20706
www.rowman.com

Unit A, Whitacre Mews, 26-34 Stannary Street, London SE11 4AB

British Library Cataloguing in Publication Information Available

Library of Congress Cataloging-in-Publication Data

Borum, Jeremy.
  Guerrilla film scoring : practical advice from Hollywood composers /
Jeremy Borum.
    pages cm
  Includes index.
  ISBN 978-1-4422-3728-5 (hardback : alk. paper) — ISBN
978-1-4422-3729-2 (pbk. : alk. paper) — ISBN 978-1-4422-3730-8 (ebook)
  1. Motion picture music—Vocational guidance. 2. Film composers—
Interviews. I. Title.
  ML3795.B73 2015
  781.5'4213—dc23   2014040899

Printed in the United States of America

CONTENTS

ACKNOWLEDGMENTS

TO ALL THE BRILLIANT COMPOSERS who are part of this book, thank you for sharing your time and wisdom. Mark Abel and Stephen Ryan, thank you for your editorial support. Marty Borum, you have edited everything I have ever written. You are one of my biggest fans and harshest critics. I couldn't have done this without you. I love you, Dad. Viola Steffens, my muse, you inspired me to write this book by simply sharing your life with me. You inspire me in countless ways every day. I adore you.

INTRODUCTION:
THE NEW SCORING
LANDSCAPE

WHY ANOTHER BOOK?

THERE IS A REAL need for taking a fresh look at the modern-day scoring process. From the very beginning, music has been used in movies, television, video games, and advertisements, and all the while, the film and music industries have been in a constant state of change. Because of shifts in styles and innovations in technology, scoring today is completely different from the way it was twenty or even ten years ago. The art and craft of scoring needs to be reevaluated and reexamined, since, like all forms of art, it is a living thing that grows and evolves.

In the last decade there have been major and irreversible changes in the music industry. Adaptation and rapid learning are required when industries go through radical change. Companies and individuals that can't adapt fall away and are replaced. Those who fight to keep things the same usually lose. Composers need to adapt to this new environment and learn new skills.

The film and music industries have both made a dramatic shift toward independent productions with smaller budgets. Indie films, labels,

VIDEO: THE NEW SCORING LANDSCAPE. Pictured: Miriam Cutler. www. vimeo.com/guerrillafilmscoring/introteaser

and game productions used to be only for beginners, but those days are now history. Independent artists are increasingly respected, artful, productive, and profitable. Despite that fact, to date there are very few books, university courses, or trade schools that focus specifically on creating high-quality professional scores on a limited budget. Limited-, low-, or no-budget scores are the norm, and a field manual of guerrilla film scoring techniques is greatly needed.

The vast majority of books and university film scoring programs focus almost exclusively on the well-funded Hollywood machine—and for good reason. It is the established and traditional method of creating commercial music for film and television. The structure of studios, unions, contractors, players, and careful division of labor is well known and well documented. Teaching a composer about that system can be likened to teaching a performer classical music. It is the foundation out of which other things arise. It is a shrinking system, however, and newer methods are replacing it.

As with all things academic and theoretical, these same books and programs talk about film scoring in idealized ways. It is almost always assumed that budgets are adequate, schedules are reasonable, resources are available, players are good, studio equipment functions as expected, and the composer is artistically fulfilled. These things rarely happen at once, and many projects provide none of them. Although a study of the Hollywood machine is interesting, it's ultimately not very useful. A skeleton of the Hollywood music machine still exists, but the once-pervasive model now only applies to big-budget productions. In today's industry the composer is the whole machine. Studying the Hollywood machine is like studying frictionless surfaces in physics. It is valuable as a learning tool but doesn't apply directly to the real world.

This is a major indictment against the available learning resources. Most talk about an industry model that is increasingly obsolete, and they discuss it in theoretical terms that are impossible to apply in a direct manner. The massive transition toward independent productions and smaller budgets is quite recent, so the myriad problems and solutions have yet to be thoroughly explored or codified. Composition students are basically trained in formal combat and then sent into the music industry to do battle guerrilla-style.

A more realistic model involves independent productions, limited money, short schedules, minimal resources, malfunctioning equipment, high expectations, and artistic conflict or frustration. Budgets that are too small for comfort are the rule, and well-funded music budgets are the exception. More attention must be paid to the modern, real-life constraints of film scoring and the harsh realities of the film scoring industry at large.

The traditional division of labor in the film scoring process has eroded completely. Long ago, composers were just one part of a large music machine. They put notes on paper and attended recording sessions, with few other responsibilities. Those duties have steadily increased. Today's film composer is responsible for each step of the music team's process, and oftentimes a guerrilla composer is the entire team. Modern composers must have a good balance of artistry, craft, and business, wearing all hats and managing many disparate tasks single-handedly.

Guerrilla Film Scoring is the first book of its kind, a practical field manual for film scoring soldiers. It is not about the art of writing music, the Hollywood music system, or the politics and interpersonal obstacles that come naturally when working in the arts. Composers everywhere and at each level need more ways to create a great film score quickly and inexpensively. This is a book for them: The craft of guerrilla film scoring.

VOICES FROM THE TRENCHES

Throughout this volume you will find advice, techniques, shortcuts, and secrets from successful composers who are in the trenches every day. They are influential pillars of the industry within their niches. Appendix B contains bios and websites for additional information on each one. This book follows the film composing time line, dividing the process by task. As you move through each step, seasoned professionals will explain how they manage to survive, meet the demands of the modern film scoring process, and excel. This book features information not available in other sources. It is not taught systematically at any university or trade school and is not mainstream knowledge. It is not intuitive. These insider tips and tricks will reveal how today's successful composers do it with guerrilla film scoring techniques.

THE INDUSTRY HAS CHANGED

Like many other revolutions in history, the changes in the film and music industries were brought about by improvements in technology. Films and music are significantly easier to produce and distribute than they were just ten years ago. It is now possible to obtain affordable, high-quality equipment, and substantial changes in content distribution models have made self-publishing simple and accessible to everyone. Lest we forget how recent these changes are, remember that Apple's fledgling MP3 player iTunes was first introduced in 2001, and YouTube didn't launch until 2005. The digital revolution that gave us increased ease of production and distribution is brand new, and like a tsunami it quickly changed everything.

As a result, the number of films produced each year has skyrocketed. Between 1940 and 2000, the number of film productions roughly doubled. By 2010, only ten years later, that number had doubled yet again. Since then the rate of production has continued to accelerate. During the same time, however, the number of films made by major studios has been in decline. The industry is clearly in a state of flux, but despite its growing pains there are far more opportunities for film composers than ever before.

Music production has changed in a similar way. Studio equipment is consistently getting better and cheaper, and computers are ever more powerful. This paves the way for project studios to spring up every-where, and it now takes only a minimal investment in equipment to get good recordings from a home studio. The number of independent bands, labels, and album releases has climbed sharply, as has the number of people doing guerrilla film scoring.

Media delivery methods are changing rapidly as well, and as new formats grow up, old ones die. As CDs, DVDs, and Blu-rays wane in popularity, streaming and download formats are coming into favor. The older formats were dependent on a physical product, and the cost of a physical product was always prohibitive to smaller artists and productions. Since digital distribution is essentially free and unlimited, product scarcity no longer exists. The entire approach to distribution and delivery has changed. All artists and products are not equally visible, but they are now equally accessible.

A complicating factor, of course, is that many of the new digital distribution channels do not pay royalties to composers. The download and streaming services that do pay royalties to composers pay very little compared to physical sales. There are still few rules governing digital distribution, and any rules created in the future may be impossible to police. Media loses value the moment it is digitized because it can be copied and shared infinitely. People do not expect to pay for data,

I've been able to watch the entire evolution of the industry because when I started out the composer's tool set was pretty much just pencil, paper, metronome, and stopwatch. I think there were roughly 250 working film composers at that point, it was pretty small. The advent of computers democratized everything and spread everything so wide that the supply and demand ratio is extremely different. Now there are probably tens of thousands of film composers throughout the world as opposed to several hundred, and because of supply and demand economics you can get people to score cheaply. The democratization is both positive and negative. One of the negative effects is that it brought the price down. But one of the main reasons why we have so many film composers is that it's just easy and fun. Who wouldn't want to score films in these conditions?—**Charles Bernstein** so the perceived value of any form of media has been all but totally destroyed.

Whether we are talking about a film, recording, or photo, if the finished digitized product has little inherent value, then the best way to make a profit from it is to keep the production costs low. The digital demonetization of media is upon us (or perhaps behind us), and this new reality is significantly impacting the industry. Composers were once appreciated for their sophistication and scarcity. Now they are so ubiquitous that it's difficult to differentiate oneself from the crowd enough to justify a premium price. The industry has completely changed, and the low-budget model is here to stay. The composers quoted in this book confirm that those who adopt guerrilla film scoring techniques are more likely to survive.

THE OLD INDUSTRY DIES

One obvious result of the digital revolution is the death of film studios, record labels, and retailers. Film studios and labels have progressively gotten smaller, and many have gone out of business. Those remaining have slashed their budgets considerably. They are increasingly particular and cautious about which projects they take on because, more so now than ever, their profits must be essentially guaranteed if they are to survive. The days of gambling on a little-known director or artist are in the past, and most take only the sure bets.

In the golden era of Hollywood filmmaking, the major studios were self-sufficient moviemaking factories. They had their own dedicated resources from concept to delivery, from scriptwriters to theaters. Movies were imagined, created, and projected to viewers completely in-house. The technology of television was instrumental in toppling this system, and the work that used to be done in the confines of a studio was dispersed. The work continued, but it was distributed amongst numerous companies and organizations.

The last half of the twentieth century can be called the silver era of Hollywood. Filmmaking was still highly specialized, difficult, expensive, and exclusive. The big studios no longer had a monopoly, but they still had enormous influence and control. Many guilds and unions were founded to protect employees who were suddenly on their own. Filmmaking remained almost exclusively the right and privilege of large companies with deep pockets. The industry reorganized itself and was reasonably stable for many decades, but the technology of digital media has toppled this system too.

Film composers and filmmakers are now back in the bronze age. The industry is suddenly unrefined, uncontrolled, unforgiving, and unorganized. The remains of the major film studios are hanging on, but large companies almost always adapt slowly and much of the productivity has moved elsewhere. It is increasingly common for major studios to buy films that are already completed, their role increasingly becoming limited to advertising, sales, and distribution. Music labels are going through the same process, often only signing established acts with an existing audience and completed albums that are ready for sale.

Naturally, the retailers that were dependent on the corporate business model of physical media production have also had a difficult time and face an irreversible changing tide. Companies that once boasted enormous influence and market share disappeared rapidly, examples being Columbia House, BMG Music Service, Wherehouse, Blockbuster, Tower Records, and Borders Books and Music, to name just a few. These were big names that disappeared almost overnight because of digital distribution. The studios, labels, and retailers that have endured are far less influential than they once were, resulting in a less organized media industry that must be navigated intuitively and guerrilla-style.

FILM AND MUSIC GO INDEPENDENT

The aforementioned technological developments have caused more than just changes in the cost of production. Today a cell phone video can be as globally accessible as a major motion picture. The two are not equally publicized, but each film and each recording can have equal accessibility. The reason for this is the method and cost of distribution. Digital delivery makes distribution essentially free. The rise of infinite accessibility and zero-cost distribution has allowed the independent market to explode. The shift of power is self-perpetuating. As the market becomes friendlier to independent artists, the big studios suffer. As the studios suffer, they make fewer and fewer deals with artists and filmmakers. As the number of deals decreases, the number of independent artists necessarily increases, and so the market fuels its own irreversible change.

Film composers are now often working under package-deal agreements where the budgets tend to be small, and the composer is in charge of everything and paying all the bills. The majority of working bands are now heavily involved in or totally responsible for the production of their own albums. The majority of films are now funded by private investors instead of big studios. It is an independent, do-it-yourself landscape populated by people who are simultaneously reinventing the industry.

In the new industry landscape, being independent no longer means being a beginner or being unsuccessful. Being backed by a major studio or label used to be an indicator of success, and although this can still be true, it is much less significant than it once was. Film scores for large and visible projects are more frequently being recorded outside of the Hollywood union system, with orchestras in Europe or elsewhere. A growing number of film scores are forgoing the orchestral sound altogether. Online stores like Amazon and iTunes are equally accessible to indie artists and major studios. There are substantial financial and artistic benefits to being independent, and self-publishing today is easier and better business than in the past. The value of being backed by studios, labels, and publishers has been substantially diminished.

BUDGETS SHRINK CONSISTENTLY

Newton's third law of motion says that for every action there is an equal and opposite reaction. He certainly wasn't talking about the movie industry, but the axiom fits. The production of films and music is no longer completely dominated by large corporations and conglom-

The middle of the budget landscape has disappeared. Films with budgets between $5 and $20 million aren't made much anymore. The majority of films are either small or blockbusters. That has impacted every aspect of film making, including music. Composers need to make sure the budget will allow them to write the score that the movie needs. In cases where this isn't possible, they have to be creative to get more out of few forces. It's important to be up front with directors and producers early on if they haven't budgeted for what the film requires.—**Peter Golub**

From 1967 through 1977, I worked for CBS Television Music Operations. After that time, I was freelancing as a television composer, so I'm well acquainted with the fees, which were stable during that period. CBS paid composers $2,000 for their services on a one-hour television show. This was a fee, not a package deal. Other studios, like Universal, paid as much as $2,500 for an hour show. Some smaller, independent producers paid $1,800. The deal was essentially similar everywhere. Adjusting for inflation and using two different inflation guides on the web, $2,000 in 1970 was worth approximately $12,055.52 in today's dollars.—**Bruce Broughton**

erates. Media production and commercial art forms are now in the hands of the people. While this is enormously empowering, in this case the opposite reaction is connected to funding. When creativity moved toward individuals, the funding for that creativity was scattered to the four winds, forcing the average budget for films and film scores steadily downward.

According to the Berklee College of Music Career Development Center, an hour-long medium- to small-budget television show pays about $2,000 per episode today. Adjusted for inflation, production companies are paying a mere 16 percent of what they paid forty-five years ago. To make things worse, the deals today are package deals, meaning that the composer has to spend part of that money to pay for the music production. In the past, the composer received a creative fee that was pure income. To be fair, the decrease in music budgets is also fueled by decreased budgetary needs. The tools available to composers are increasingly sophisticated in sound and function, and with ever-decreasing cost. The resources required to produce film music are more modest than before, so it is a reasonable reality that budgets would shrink accordingly.

Nonetheless, film music budgets are not shrinking accordingly. They are shrinking at a much faster rate, and the downward pressure on the composer's income is great. Unlike most other film-related professions, there is no union for composers. As a result, composers have been undercutting one another for decades just to get work, and it's a self-perpetuating cycle. The more composers are willing to cut their fees, the less reason there is to pay them well. The greater the supply

Film music budgets have come down, which is a tragedy, but the technology has gone up, which is a great leveler. There was once a time when the equipment to make a film score was very expensive. The fact that you can now do the same thing and more, much more, on a laptop is a great leveler, which means that that kid with the cool ideas has the same wherewithal to do a score as somebody with all that gear.

People with orchestral chops to write for orchestra, the John Williamses of the world, will never be threatened because there are certain types of movies that will only use that kind of music. But this is about guerrilla composing. Setting orchestral scores aside, the industry is actually in a great place at the moment because you can survive on the basis of your talents and your skills, not on the basis of the head start that you have.—**Stewart Copeland**

of available composers, the more supply and demand will force wages downward. The number of hopeful composers hitting the streets grows each year. The market is completely saturated, the competition is fierce guerrilla warfare, and the rules of supply and demand still apply. The baselines of fair wages, fair working hours, and health care do not exist for composers. Film music budgets are moving inexorably downward, and film composers enter into the budget crisis at a disadvantage compared to other film professionals.

RESPONSIBILITIES MOVE TO INFINITY

As film score budgets march toward zero the responsibilities of composers are approaching infinity, and composers no longer have the luxury of being specialists. They are expected to own and operate their own studios and perform a multitude of other tasks not expected of them ten or twenty years ago. They used to be just one part of a team, an important element of a larger moviemaking machine. Today they are increasingly the CEOs of small music businesses, responsible for every aspect of music production.

Low budgets naturally mean less money to hire help. Package deals are now common, and they also give composers added incentive to hire less help: The less they spend the more they get to keep. With a package deal, the most financially rewarding approach is typically the hermit method, where the composer hides away in a dark studio doing everything himself and keeping the cash. Without adequate funding, the music team shrinks.

Although the music team shrinks, the workload doesn't. The guerrilla film composer has the job description of each team member he doesn't hire. One-man bands used to be a novelty. They were quirky gypsy types that walked the streets with instruments tied to their person in all sorts of creative ways. Today every film composer is, in a way, a one-man band, because frequently the composer must also be the orchestrator, copyist, studio owner, producer, performer, conductor, recording engineer, music editor, and mix and mastering engineer. These are just some of the music-related tasks. Composers are also the janitor, tech support, administrator, lawyer, contract negotiator, publicist, and project manager, to name a few others. The skill set required is enormous and cannot be overstated. A thorough blend of art, craft, and business must be juggled at all times.

Successful modern-day composers are not artists as we might like to imagine them. The antithesis of pure creativity, commercial film composing is really a chaotic collision of business administration, technical knowledge, marketing savvy, objective process-oriented craft, and subjective art. It is the rare person indeed who can be pulled in numerous different directions and bear the infinite responsibilities, while enjoying and succeeding in the work at the same time. Being a film composer is more like being in a street fight than running a business, and it's definitely not for the faint of heart.

We are seeing mostly package deals with diminishing resources for live players, mixing, and music editing. Many composers, including myself, have used our entire composer's fee to hire live players in order to produce the sound the film deserves. We hope for residuals or back-end, but many times it never happens. The landscape is changing toward exactly what this book is about, the "do-it-yourself" composer.—**Bill Brown**

If you understand that film composing is a craft, not pure art, you'll be more effective as a composer. Even though it's only craft, the film composer can hold his head up high, because the film composer has a wider skill set than any other kind of musician. More than a rock band musician, a songwriter, a symphonic composer, you name it. There is no other musician in the world of music that has more of a skill set than the film composer.

He has to write music for every instrument, every genre, every time period, every cultural environment: wild western, space fiction, period drama, ethnic adventure. The film composer has to go into all types of music that a pure artist would never go into. The film composer has to address a director's very specific emotional message and to be able to create that, exactly that. A film composer needs a lot of skills.—**Stewart Copeland**

COST-EFFICIENT SOLUTIONS ARE NECESSARY

While today's composers are expected to do monumental amounts of work with minimal budgets, often with short schedules, everyone involved also wants the highest production values on a consistent basis. This is now the rule, not the exception, and a huge arsenal of cost-efficient solutions is necessary if composers are to win their battles. They must single-handedly find ways to simultaneously be fast, good, and inexpensive.

Guerrilla film scoring is now the norm. It is an irreversible reality imposed by the relentless progression of technology and massive surge in independent film production. A lucky handful of composers on the A-list still have the luxury of working within a Hollywood system that is well funded with a clear division of labor. The rest must fight through the wild jungle of the music industry like guerrilla warriors. What you hold in your hand is the first of its kind, a field manual for the guerrilla film composer founded on the expert advice and battle scars of many successful composers.

I

PREPRODUCTION

EDUCATION

PREPARE YOURSELF TO BE LUCKY

ALMOST ANY CAREER in the arts can be traced back to at least one stroke of luck. If you talk to successful creatives, no matter what the medium, you will find that somewhere in their past there was something beyond their control that contributed to a snowball effect, helping their career pick up speed and grow. Every working artist has a story about a serendipitous event, a fortuitous meeting, or some other chance opportunity. Unfortunately, simultaneously being a brilliant composer, orchestrator, performer, conductor, engineer, producer, and mixer is not usually good enough to bring success. Success in the music industry requires more than being a multifaceted genius. It appears that little moments of magic are still required in which fate chooses to provide good fortune. The need for luck is extremely frustrating for artists who are developing their careers.

What you can control, however, is how prepared you are to accept opportunities when they present themselves. Only when you are prepared to grab an opportunity and use it for all it's worth are you truly lucky. If the same chance appears but you don't know what to do with it, it becomes a missed opportunity. It follows, then, that there are guerrilla tactics you can use to put yourself in luck's path and control your luck when it comes. In business, luck is actually just the alignment of opportunity with solid preparation and planning. When you have spe-

VIDEO: EDUCATION. Pictured: Laura Karpman. www.vimeo.com/
guerrillafilmscoring/educationteaser

cific goals and are prepared to succeed, you will not miss opportunities.
In other words, you can convert your bad luck into good luck through
preparation.

Preparation must come in two different forms in the music industry:
knowledge and experience. Knowing how to do something and actu-

> A very common question is, "How did you get your break?" No matter
> who you ask the answer is a circuitous series of seemingly random
> connections. It's intangible. It's hard to say when you're first starting
> out how that's going to happen to you.—**Timothy Andrew Edwards**

> What I always say to people is that successful careers are a function
> of luck. Most people hear that and they shut off. They think, "That
> sucks. I just have to get lucky." Except, you can manifest luck by
> being in the right place at the right time. Being in the right place is
> easy. The right place is mainly a state of mind, but it is also actively
> engaging in the industry, going to events, constantly meeting peo-
> ple, and just projecting outward in all directions that you give a damn
> about all of this, because people are drawn to passion. The right
> time, as in an opportunity, happens constantly.—**Austin Wintory**

ally having experience doing that same thing are completely different. Knowledge without experience isn't very useful because music is a practical applied art form. Experience without knowledge isn't very useful because the experience can easily become misdirected or unproductive. The best way to put yourself on a sure path in the music industry is to pursue a combination of the two.

CULTIVATE KNOWLEDGE

If you are going to be a guerrilla composer you must always be battle ready, so musical preparedness and consistent continuing education are essential. Every time you get a gig, the reason behind it is that somebody believes in you and believes that you have the ability to pull it off. On a practical level, the responsibilities of working musicians, the things expected of them, and the depths of artistic expression are all seemingly endless. The art itself is infinite as well and limited only by the artist. The only way to march in lockstep with the practical and artistic demands of the music industry is to constantly educate yourself.

When scoring for films, television, or video games your collaborators will assume that you have deep knowledge and expertise. You need to understand everything from music theory to compression ratios to business management, and you must definitively be an expert in everything that you do. Your writing and production values might be compared to any other music in the world. Thus, each step of the way you need to be imagining and creating your scores in the most high-end professional manner possible. Since composers are now wearing all the hats, it is usually assumed that they have all the specialized skills that, in years past, were dispersed amongst the various teams of people that made up the Hollywood music machine. Acquiring expertise in all of these skill areas is a massive undertaking, but one you must pursue.

Music is one part learned skill and one part intuition. Techniques are learned from focused work, so you can learn them just as quickly as you are able to retain information and build habits. The intuitions and talents develop more slowly, and they only come by cultivating a meaningful relationship with music. Your connection to music needs to be fostered daily through practicing, writing, studying, or listening—the only way to truly gain the technical and artistic proficiency that directors will assume you have. After a lifetime of study, we might be able to

> How much did you pay for your education? How many years did you spend practicing your instrument? It's a lifetime of study. I joke with my friends who are doctors and lawyers that I have a much, much deeper education than any of them. How long was med school? I started seriously studying music when I was seven or eight, and I'm still at it.—**Craig Stuart Garfinkle**

> The number one thing I would say to composers is to continue honing your craft. You don't know much. I don't know anything about composing. I'm always learning, and in order to do that you have to do it regularly, all the time.—**Yoav Goren**

master one instrument in one genre, but as composers we need not look far to find things that we don't know. Music is a demanding muse, and keeping up with her needs is definitely a life's work. Education is not something you go through once. It must be a way of life.

KNOW THE VALUE OF EDUCATION

The words *music education* imply a formal study of music and evoke images of private lessons, books, and university programs, but none of those things are strictly necessary. Degrees and diplomas in music have little intrinsic value unless you intend to pursue even higher education or become a professor of music at a university. From time to time people may ask out of curiosity where you studied, but the real currencies in the music industry are what you have done in the past, what you can do now, and what you can do by Monday morning.

Nevertheless, it is not music education that is worthless. On the contrary, music education is not only valuable, it's essential. Since composers also need to be artists, craftsmen, and businessmen, there is an endless queue of things to learn. Composers must be constantly educating themselves about new trends, styles, tools, techniques, strategies, and market conditions. The industry demands a deep and proactive approach to learning, and those who are better educated will have greater success in both art and business.

> A director who is considering hiring you as a composer is not go-
> ing to evaluate you based on your education. He's going to listen
> to the music. A demo reel. A show reel. That's it. I can say I was
> a member of the Police and that might move my music to the top
> of the pile so they'll listen to it first. But they don't give a rat's ass
> what our credentials are, they're listening to the music. If it rings for
> them, you're in. If it doesn't, it doesn't matter what your credentials
> are.—**Stewart Copeland**

One of the things that makes the music industry unique is that proof of education does not come in the normal way. When musicians and directors are evaluating their peers or considering hiring new team members, they look at experience and credits. Past work demonstrates a musician's depth of knowledge and artistry far better than any certificate, so a collection of movie posters and album covers on the wall is far more impressive and functional than an expensive diploma.

The fact that composers can acquire knowledge of music in whatever way suits them best is one of the great luxuries of the industry. You are free to forge your own path through the jungle. Some learn from study, some from doing, some from listening, some from mentors, some from peers, some from mistakes, and some from success, and all are equally valid. You are judged not by what books you have read or what classroom you sat in, but by your abilities and talent.

> A person is the sum of their experiences, and there are innumer-
> able ways to get great learning experiences outside of a university
> setting. In more than three decades of professional work I have not
> once been asked if I have a university degree, although I do have
> one. I did, however, learn an enormous amount while I attended
> university, and I always try to learn new things daily.—**John Rodd**

LEARN HOW TO LEARN

Music can be learned in an infinite number of ways, so the cost of music education depends entirely on how you pursue it. Like all other things in art there are an endless number of starting and ending points. You might be a purely self-taught guerrilla composer without any mentors whose education is experience based, or you might choose the opposite route and pursue extensive private lessons, university study, and apprenticeship experience. Everything within this spectrum is capable of producing extremely talented and successful composers.

Since a degree in music is not valued in the way that degrees are valued in most other fields, the educational path can be unique and different for everyone. It's up to you to create your own goals and also to decide for yourself how you want to invest your time and money into your education. Your education will shape you, but you can also shape your education. You may learn well in a structured, formal setting and decide to engage in private lessons and university, but you could quit halfway through and get an internship. You could change your battle plan again and form a business, learning as you go. Another composer could approach it in the reverse order, and a third composer could do nothing but jam to recordings in his bedroom. All three paths could garner equal opportunity for success as a commercial composer.

To decide if university education is the right approach for you, you need to decide what you want to learn and how best to learn those things. Some elements of music can be learned in both formal and informal settings, while others must come from direct experience no matter how the concepts are initially presented. In many cases a teacher can point out what needs to be learned, but the learning has to come from within the student. The various aspects of music are very different from one another and benefit from diverse educational approaches. Thus, thinking about these categories may be helpful as you plot your route.

Notes: This encompasses music theory, reading, writing, and learning pieces, and playing them correctly. This category can be learned in many ways, but because of its deep history and precise methodical nature it is probably best initially learned from a teacher. Improvisation and composition, however, are intangible and more difficult to teach.

Technique: This could be technique of performance, composition, orchestration, recording, software, and so forth. There is also deep history and tradition of technique, making experienced teachers quite useful, but artists often create their own unique techniques too. The best plan of action is probably getting a head start with a teacher and then pursuing mastery of technique on your own.

Phrasing: Phrasing can be the shape of an individual note, a group of notes, a section, or an entire piece. While phrasing can have a lot to do with the notes on the page, it also involves communicating emotion, which must be learned through experience and practice.

Articulation: This is about the attack, duration, and release of notes. It's also about the manner in which they are attacked and released, and the expressive reasons for that. Articulation is one of the more expressive elements of music, so although a teacher can demonstrate articulations it's something that you ultimately have to discover, experiment with, and take ownership of on your own.

Dynamics: These are the subtleties of loud and soft, but even more important is the emotional motivation behind the changes. Dynamics are a core part of the expressive art of music. They can be demonstrated, but they must be felt deeply and learned through experience.

Groove: Groove is all about how the music feels to the listener and how the performer or writer feels when actively making music. It's also about the subtle ways one part interlocks with another, because no two instruments put a beat in exactly the same place. A teacher can point out groove and comment on it, but groove is best learned collaboratively with other musicians.

Rhythm: This encompasses reading rhythms, rhythmic patterns, and tempos. Formal study of how rhythms and tempos work and intertwine is helpful, but musicians must experience rhythm and connect with it on a gut level to master it.

Emotion: The fundamental reason for music is that it makes the listener feel something, so emotion is the most important element of music. There is little a teacher can do to transform a student into a sensitive and emotive person who expresses his feelings fluently. At best a teacher can only help the student to simulate emotionality. True expression must come from within.

Tone: Tone is the range of timbres an instrument is capable of creating, and for composers, arrangers, and orchestrators it is the type of sounds used in writing. This is a subjective aspect of art closely related to emotion, requiring dedicated listening and individual exploration.

Space: The absence of notes can be just as powerful as the notes themselves but in an arbitrary and subjective way that is much more difficult to codify. Music is abstract, and empty space is one of the most abstract elements of it. Thus, an understanding and mastery of space must come from experience and from within.

Listening: There are myriad ways to focus attention when listening. Ear-training classes can help musicians to listen to notes, harmony, and rhythms more intelligently; however, only a mature musician can connect deeply with the aforementioned elements at will. True listening can't really be taught, it's a function of time and experience.

LEARN FROM FORMAL STUDIES

No matter what the field, no degree guarantees job opportunities. The real value of a degree is the education that you get. A university music education gives you valuable tools for life as a musician. You can gain techniques, insights, methods, and intuitions that can be used throughout your career. It also provides a framework and methodology for music learning. Since music education needs to be a lifelong journey, one of the most important things you can take away from formal study is knowledge about the ways in which you learn best.

When you have a formal education you are better prepared to benefit from practical experience in the real world. You have a solid foundation that allows you to better assimilate and grow from new experiences. You speak, read, and write the language of music, which allows you to connect with other musicians more easily. You have studied under masters, which helps you relate to the other great musicians you encounter. Most importantly, you can hold your head high and carry yourself with confidence because you are an expert. An educated, self-confident person is prepared to benefit from real-world experience.

One major advantage to formal university education is the focus and structure that it brings. While in school your full-time job is to study, learn, and become a master of your subject. You devote a huge amount of time to your own improvement and the development of expertise. The routine is helpful, and discipline and self-improvement become a habit. Immersion is the best way to learn any subject, and you reap large benefits quickly. Of course, it's possible to accomplish extremely focused learning without a university, but formalized education exists because it makes it easier and works well for the vast majority of people.

At a university you are also surrounded by people in your age group who are doing exactly the same thing, making the learning process easier and more fun. When you are surrounded by a culture of curiosity and learning, it's much easier to be in that space yourself. Having a large group of peers with common goals has another advantage. The music industry is heavily based on relationships, and the connections you build in college can sometimes last throughout your career. Once you are out of college those friends and acquaintances will be guerrillas fighting their way through the music industry either with you or against you, but at school you are friends and allies. The opportunities and connections that can come from university communities will never appear if you are learning on your own.

Another substantial advantage is the fact that the material you're trying to learn is organized and presented in a way that is intended for easy digestion. Professors break the information up into methodical, bite-sized pieces and spoon-feed them to you, making learning immensely easier. When you enter a degree program information is continuously pushed to you for four years, requiring a lot less discipline than teaching yourself. Few people can sustain such a level of active learning autonomously.

Many universities do their utmost to stay connected to the music industry, which can have a tangible value as well. They try to bridge the gap between the academic world and the music industry in numerous ways. There may be internship opportunities, master classes with professionals, courses taught by industry leaders, career advisers, access to industry organizations and events, and many other connections. The two worlds are very different, and there will always be gaps between them. The first goal of any music program is focused study purely for the sake of learning and art. A university's first priority is not job placement; however, many universities try to maintain helpful connections to the industry.

University study is valuable, but the cost is a clear disadvantage. There is an undeniable need for the study of art only for art's sake, but film and game composers aim to be in the business of music. This is a different context than pure art, and a cost benefit analysis is worthwhile. The best music schools in the United States charge about $40,000 per year, but recent graduates can anticipate their first occasional gigs to pay only hundreds of dollars at a time. The numbers just don't add up, particularly when attending the more expensive and well-known music schools.

The cost to become a veterinarian, lawyer, or biologist makes sense because those professions have stable career paths with predictable incomes that justify the cost of education. Compared to other career paths, the cost of a university music education is wholly impractical. A music degree is not as reliable a financial investment as other types of degrees. It might pay off, but from a practical business perspective an expensive music degree is a high-risk investment.

That doesn't mean the cost is inappropriate or not worthwhile, but there are no reliable numbers for expected wages or estimated annual income after graduation. Most music graduates don't even start earning their first income after college with music. Most go directly from their universities to some kind of day job. This is fine for people who are interested in music purely as an art form, but it's not for those who hope to have a music career. The comparison between the price tag on a university music education and its potential payoff in the real world must be considered.

There are a lot of music schools churning out students and releasing them into an industry that does not have ample opportunity to support them all. It's not ideal for the students nor is it ideal for the industry

> I don't see the long-term value in the formal education system. It costs a lot of money, and that puts you deeply in the red when you enter the real world. I'm also incredibly skeptical about a university's capability of keeping their finger on the pulse of how things are done in the real world. The technology and the music evolve too quickly. I don't think university education is a good option for composers. Education, certainly, but it doesn't have to be formal. I'm not the personality type to sit through an education. I'd rather crash and burn a dozen times than learn something formally.—**Nathan Furst**

> I believe one can benefit even more from their practical experience if they already have a solid musical foundation to build upon, so I would highly recommend starting with formal education first, if possible. Ultimately, however, success and growth will come from what is learned and applied. If a formal education isn't possible, that shouldn't preclude one from pursuing their goals and learning from practical experiences.—**Ryan Shore**

at large because it puts enormous downward pressure on the value of composers. Self-motivated learners who inject themselves into the music scene might be justified in saying that an expensive university degree does not have enough value. A huge amount of the learning material is available from any library, and the rest can be learned from experience. Proactive and internally driven learners do not necessarily need the structure and faculty that a university provides to grow. In the community of working composers, the experiences of music education are as wild and varied as you can imagine. As a result, there are many strong and varied opinions about the value of a formal education.

> Why do formal education and experience have to be in opposition? Get as much education as you can. I have a doctorate from Juilliard, and that education I use every second of every day. I have also taught at several universities. As educators we want to think the tuition is fair. I have been inside of that system, and I know that they really care about that deeply. The fees are not charged lightly. They care about what the value is, what the students are getting, what the curriculum is, and justifying that huge expense. Do graduates keep learning from working? Of course. Does that go 100 times beyond what I or anybody else could have taught them? Absolutely. That's just the way it is.—**Laura Karpman**

> One of the things I would say to the younger composers is that you really need to get involved with the composer community. It's the best supplement I know to formal education.—**Craig Stuart Garfinkle**

LEARN FROM EXPERIENCE

The alternative to a university education is a self-directed one, and it's a very viable option. Most self-taught musicians usually begin in the same way: They dig in and start doing things that they don't know how to do. It is the most natural learning method in the world. We start trying to walk and speak long before we know about athletics or languages. We play games and coerce our parents long before we know about strategy. When we travel, it's often specifically because we don't know what to expect and we're curious. We do these things and countless others because they look like fun and we want to experience them. That natural fun-filled curiosity is the most fertile soil imaginable for learning. One of the most effective and instinctive ways to learn music is to start doing something you like even though you don't have a clue how it's done.

The biggest advantage of that approach, of course, is the inherent individuality in being self-taught. You can learn the things you want to learn, and you can also choose when, where, why, how, and from whom. You can go at your own speed. You're free to redirect yourself at any time because you never really have to commit to anything. You can also mold your education to fit your schedule so that it doesn't interrupt or deprioritize other things that are important in your life. When you're self-taught you're always in control, and there are definite advantages to this method.

The funny thing is, it's not hard to make a counterargument that these advantages are actually educational disadvantages. Most students do not have the same big-picture view as the teacher. When you have the freedom to learn only the things you want to learn you may not pursue a well-rounded learning path. Without being challenged to learn at a certain pace, you may move slowly. Being able to change course at will can challenge your commitment. Oftentimes the things you don't enjoy learning at first are valuable. And, certainly, without the support structure of accountability, many never reach their goal.

The secret to success is simple: Get up early and work all day. The best resources for becoming an accomplished self-taught musician are no secret. You can learn from textbooks, YouTube, scores, practice, ensembles, private lessons, friends, concerts, lesson books, biographies, software manuals, trial and error, workshops, and so on. It doesn't matter which items from this list you use. Try them all and stick with the ones you like. The secret, or rather the part that most people find diffi-cult, is the constant self-discipline required to stretch yourself beyond what you know and your comfort level.

There are still costs associated with education even if you are self-taught, but they are small compared with the cost of university educa-tion. You'll still buy books, instruments, equipment, and other learning aids. You may hire teachers or coaches from time to time. The largest cost is probably in time. Self-taught musicians don't stop everything in their lives for four years to study music full-time, so they have a much more gradual climb toward expertise. Even if you're diligent it may take two to three times longer to gain the same expertise that a university program can provide, and most people are not diligent part-time stu-dents for ten consecutive years on their own. It can take a long time to teach yourself the equivalent of a university education, and opportuni-ties can be lost during that period of time, as you are operating with less knowledge than your competition. Hence, you may lose opportunities to people who appear to be more qualified or better educated than you.

However, this can work the other way around. Another luxury of the music industry is that there is the possibility of being paid to learn through internships and assistant positions. How do you get your education fast, good, and cheap all at once? On the job. On-the-job

I think one of the best ways to learn recording, mixing, and mas-tering, which all composers need to know, is to find an opportunity to assist highly skilled engineers (or composers who happen to be great engineers) and learn from them. Unfortunately, those men-torship opportunities are few and far between. Critical listening skills take years to develop, but you also need an enormous amount of technical knowledge to do great work. I recommend this to all com-posers, in addition to educational facilities.—**John Rodd**

I got really serious about studying music only when I was in the Mystic Knights of the Oingo Boingo. I was in a band with really great players, and I realized I needed to supplement my experience with knowledge.—**Miriam Cutler**

> The skills to score a film can be arrived at very quickly. You just have to be good with computers and you have to do a lot of it, and you'll pick it up really quickly. I don't think you need to go to college for that.—**Stewart Copeland**

training is always completely relevant, not theoretical. Practical experience quickly demonstrates what knowledge is essential and what is secondary, because the focus tends to be on immediate needs and not on peripheral or background knowledge. Having exposure to people working in your chosen line of work will also help you decide whether it's actually a career you want.

Working as an apprentice under a successful composer can provide wonderful learning and career opportunities. There are many stories in Hollywood of people who began answering phones and getting coffee and went on to build successful music careers. Most industries tend to hire from the inside before they begin a search for unknown qualified people, and since the music industry is so collaborative and based on relationships, this tendency is especially prevalent. If an overworked composer already knows and trusts you, he's much more likely to give you an opportunity than start a search for a new collaborator. Every job you do is also an audition. In the right context, getting coffee can lead to a job as tech support, then studio managing, then MIDI wrangling, then orchestration, then ghostwriting, and then feature film scoring gigs.

Experience as an apprentice has the potential to be more impressive and noteworthy than formal education. In a university you spend four

> I know plenty of successful composers who never went to college. By successful I don't mean financially successful, though they may be. I mean people that are happy with the course their life has taken.—**Austin Wintory**

> I think one is very fortunate to find mentors that inspire you, and the best education is a combination of study and trial and error. You don't really learn it until you try it.—**Peter Golub**

The composer has to do everything, and that's not going away. The only thing that will adapt is how a composer accomplishes those things, and that's changing constantly. I believe that baptism by fire is the best way to go in this industry, whether that means that you just try to make it on your own or whether that means you become an apprentice or an assistant to a bigger-name composer who knows the ropes. You'll learn more in two months doing that than you will attending four years at a university. Universities can't keep up with how things are actually happening.—**Nathan Furst**

years learning from experts. In an apprenticeship you might spend the same four years learning from experts, plus you get real-world experience, coupled with credits and connections. You also meet people who are at the same stage in their careers as you are, and you have the opportunity to both learn from and teach them. This is a clear advantage that self-taught musicians have over university students. In the right apprenticeship situation, such a combination can put you miles ahead of a college grad.

There is no such thing as too much education. For one individual, university study may be the only path to success. For another, it may be the grim reaper coming to take his passion for music. There is disagreement and debate about the monetary value of degree programs, but every seasoned composer confirms both the unquestionable value of education and the need for practical, real-world experience. Different people have different learning styles, so there is no one, ideal learning context for everyone. You need to decide for yourself what resources of time and money you want to invest. Still, there is no question that if you want to have a career in music you must gain practical experience. Whether your music education comes before or after you start working is entirely up to you.

As with all the arts, I think it is better to go out and *do*, even if it means that you're going to spend eight years in a lowly position somewhere. You need exposure to the environment and to the connections. You need to be out in the real world doing it as opposed to being in a university laboratory, which is a bubble.—**Yoav Goren**

TEAM BUILDING

BE BUSINESS MINDED

IF YOU WANT MUSIC to be your business, you should treat it like a business. There is a big difference between a sole proprietor and a small business owner, and most composers operate more like sole proprietors. Sole proprietors' businesses begin organically. They take a liking to a certain type of work and begin to charge money for it. As they get more and more successful, they get busier and busier. When they start to get very busy, their career begins to own them, not the other way around, because they are time poor and yet want to do everything themselves. The need for total control is a common malady amongst composers, and it often limits their professional growth.

On the other hand, if you are a composer with a small business owner mentality, then you probably have a better plan for future growth. Small business owners are more prepared to build a team and are always looking for good help. They try not to do work unnecessarily and recruit more troops instead of indefinitely increasing their personal time commitment. Concert hall composers can take two years to complete a piece and boast about how they used their own hands for everything. Commercial composers can't be that precious when it comes to their music because the industry doesn't have that luxury of time. There is no shame in getting good help. On the contrary, a team of people helping you is an admired and respected asset that converts easily into

VIDEO: TEAM BUILDING. Pictured: Charles Bernstein. www.vimeo.com/guerrillafilmscoring/teambuildingteaser

income. It is possible for you to be successful as a sole proprietor artist, but you will have better chances if you think like a business owner.

Although it may feel like you always need to work alone, it's often possible to build a team. There are always people working at your level, and you can usually find mutually beneficial ways to team up with them. Even if you're a new composer with no budget who is trying to break into the industry, you could team up with a new sound engineer who also needs credits. If you're creative and you reach out to other people in the industry you can always find a way to collaborate and build a team.

The wonderful thing about teamwork is that one plus one can equal three. The end product can often have a certain magic that is more than

We often work by ourselves. I find that the more I open up my circle the more fulfilling it is, the more fun it is, the more I can do, the more I can create, and the more interesting the results are. It becomes effortless, actually. It becomes easier to do more, and I love that. When you bring more people into the mix, suddenly one plus one is larger than two. When you see what your part is in that it becomes really satisfying and fun.—**Jack Wall**

> You can find all the help you need, you can build a team around you, you can bring on freelance composers, and you can hire an orchestra in Budapest to do a remote session overnight. We're in L.A., so we're privy to some of the world's best session musicians. Nothing is impossible these days, and anything can be had.—**Yoav Goren**

the sum of the team members' skills. A great team has a great synergy, and great synergy inspires creativity. As creative people gather, work toward a common goal, and inspire one another, the collaboration can become a fertile creative soil. Wonderfully artistic things can result that could not have been imagined by the individuals on their own.

If there is one common thread between successful modern composers it's that when push comes to shove, they can work as guerrillas and deliver a high-quality product. Even at the very high end of the market, the A-list composers do a large percentage of their work in their personal studios with few people around them; however, no man is an island. You have strengths and weaknesses like everyone else, and your product will be better if you get some help. The set of skills required for scoring is so vast that it's impossible for one person to completely master

> When you're starting out you truly have to do everything alone, but that's not always a bad thing. Quite the opposite, it can be invaluable. Working as a guerrilla composer gives you skills you didn't possess before and insight on how to be more effective when managing team members later on.—**Timothy Andrew Edwards**

> I'm used to doing it all myself—writing, recording, conceptualizing, demoing. It feels like it's all part of the same thing and I find it really hard to delegate, but I admit that it's the wrong way to do it. The proper way to work is to have a team. All good composers have a team, from John Williams on down. A good team is crucial. As I hear myself talking, I'm talking myself out of the way I've been doing business.—**Charles Bernstein**

When I'm deciding how much I do myself versus delegating, it all comes down to quality of life. When you have to do everything yourself it means you're not sleeping. You can play in all the parts of a symphony orchestra, but think of the time for one person to play eighty parts versus an eighty-piece orchestra playing one part per person. Do the math. It's a lot more complicated when you're alone, and it takes a lot more time. Time is money, so sometimes the key to getting fast, good, and cheap is to avoid doing it alone.—**Craig Stuart Garfinkle**

them all. When you score in do-it-yourself mode you limit both yourself and the finished product.

ASSESS YOUR NEEDS

When an opportunity is presented there is always a hesitancy to say no, but sometimes saying yes can be a dangerous thing. There are lots of horror stories about bad work experiences in the scoring world, and they often involve projects that overwhelm the available resources. Most of the stories boil down to insufficient time, inadequate money, or too little artistic consensus. Successful composers assess the requirements in advance and call for backup to avoid a horror story.

When you know your team and their capabilities, costs, and limits, you will be able to properly assess jobs and better decide whether to take the gig. The best way to avoid a bad experience is to practice prudent planning, which means clearly assessing the needs of the project

You have to be able to assess things properly when you're going into a project because you don't want to end up with your own personal horror story. You have to lay it all out in front of you, see what's coming in, and decide what you'll be able to put out in return. You need to have a solid battle plan so everyone you are directly working with benefits, whether it's the post house or the director. You want to limit your horror story exposure.—**Timothy Andrew Edwards**

I will only take a job if I know I can deliver on time and on budget and high quality. The work will expand or contract to fill the time allotted, and sometimes a schedule is really short. When that happens I'll bring assistants in and get as much help as I need to get the job done. When it comes down to it you have a limited amount of time, and there's no choice but to get the job done.—**Jack Wall**

and comparing them with the capabilities of your team. You need to build a network of collaborators beforehand, because by the time you realize you need help it's too late to look for it. You must maintain your connections with your musician community and keep your team loosely bound together so that when the jobs come you can pick up the phone and swiftly mobilize your team.

HAVE YOUR TEAM READY

A collection of skilled people isn't necessarily a team. When you assemble a group of people and work with them for the first time it may work out wonderfully. If they are seasoned professionals, they will surely get the job done; however, a team is something more than a highly functioning assembly line. A team has a connectivity and synergy that generates energy, ideas, and superior results. A newly assembled group might work like a team, but you may get a collection of impassive service providers instead.

The only way to know a team's dynamics is to test its ability to function, which is why it's important to have your team in place before you need to rely on it. To find team members, get recommendations, meet new people, see how individuals work on small jobs, or do any number of other things to test the waters. This will give you experience with prospective teammates, which is important. A highly skilled individual still might not be the right fit for your music or personality. If you explore your options and try working with lots of people, you'll know whether you want to keep those freelancers in your back pocket. Then, when you need your team, you'll be able to pull everyone together, and the team dynamics will be based on the relationships you have already built, a situation much more likely to produce the desired results.

The deadlines and pressures of the scoring world can sometimes make scoring feel like a battle. Once you have experience with trusted collaborators, you will be better prepared to go into battle together. When you have some history with people, they are more likely to want to see you succeed, so you can more easily trust your team and put your reputation into their hands. When they are invested in you to the point that your goals become their goals, the team's effectiveness rises to a new level and carries your music much further, which means the final product is stronger and you effectively become a better composer as a result.

One great luxury of today's music industry is that teams are almost always fluid. It's an industry full of freelancers, and people come together and move apart cyclically. Composers have ample opportunity to experiment with new team members because they are always forming and then disbanding their teams. A huge benefit of the freelance industry is that you can contract wonderful expertise when you need it, and you have no commitment to those people during your quiet seasons. When you encounter individuals who aren't a good fit for whatever reason, you're never bound to them. The next time you need to gather your troops, you can use a different lineup. Music teams are fluid, allowing you to refine them until you have formed your ideal creative squad.

It's very important to have a community of composer friends and other music people. You need that support. The industry tends to foster a fluid community of people who have different skills and are available to one another. You pull people in for one project and then you let them go when it's done, and you hope that they're available the next time that you need them.—**Miriam Cutler**

You need to know your team in advance. I've had experiences working with people who have a good reputation, and I've found it to be a great frustration because I still have to micromanage. It's important to find the right people for you.—**Garry Schyman**

For me personally, the most valuable thing in this industry, as a composer but also across the board in my opinion, is loyalty. If you have a creative team in which there's a sense of loyalty, your success is important to those people as well. If I'm just using a random music editor, a random engineer, a random orchestrator, then I'm just another job. If I'm using people that I have history with, that I have a trusted relationship with, and I'm loyal to those people and I feel that they do right by me, then it becomes mutual and we all want the same thing. I firmly believe that creates a better product and creates better people at the same time. That's how you build your team.—**Nathan Furst**

PREPARE FOR VICTORY

Many composers like to keep their teams small so that they can maximize their profits, but that's not always possible. More than anything else, your schedule will dictate the size of your team. Delivery dates are usually nonnegotiable because a composer's work fits into a much larger production time line. Even if you have the expertise to do all things well, when you don't have the time to do them you need to find help to be successful. The majority of composers hiring help in Hollywood do so not because they're unable to do things, but because they don't have the time to do them alone.

Second, your weaknesses dictate what you must outsource because they are the bottlenecks in your schedule and the limitations in your production value. Begin by delegating the tasks that are the most tedious or unfathomable to you. They will be the easiest to let go of, and you will be more willing to trust in the expertise and authority of your colleagues in those areas. In the long chain of scoring production tasks, from the first concept to the last cue, identify your weakest links and get help with them. It's a smart way to begin building your team and the fastest way to strengthen your position.

Third, your budget dictates the size of your team. Once you are confident that you will meet your schedule and quality goals you can assess your budget and decide if it can support additional team members.

You may want to get additional help for creative reasons, for example, hiring more live players or freeing up more time. If your budget won't allow it, then you have to take care of everything yourself. Because composers feel attached to their work it is a consistent temptation to use all of the available money to make the best product possible, but if you do so your career quickly becomes a hobby. There are times when that investment is appropriate for your business, but unless you have a clear business plan that requires investment your budget should limit your team size and you should take some profits.

Guerrilla film scoring forces you to learn constantly, learning that helps prepare you to be the leader of a music team. When you are delegating your work it's extremely helpful if you know how to do what your partners or employees are doing. Even a rudimentary knowledge is helpful, but the more you know the better you can direct them. Being capable of doing all the tasks of scoring makes you better equipped to bring people into your projects and build a team. The do-it-yourself scoring that is almost mandatory early in your career will pay dividends later on.

Another important factor when it comes to deciding which tasks you can do yourself and which to delegate is the kind of experience you want to have. Musicians get into the music industry because they have a passion or longing for something in particular, which means that most people have an idea of what they want their future success to look like. You should be doing whatever you want to be doing in your ideal future, because work brings more work and success breeds success. Try to delegate anything that gets in the way of the work you want to do.

For maximum success you should spend the majority of your time on the things at which you excel. Everyone has different strengths and weaknesses, and the scoring process requires so many different types of skills that there is room for all types of musicians and skill sets. If you focus on your strengths and exploit them consistently, you will become known for those things and get even better at them. That is how people build niches for themselves. If you are a jack-of-all-trades you have no niche, you have no differentiation, and you will not stand out in people's minds. If you are extremely good at just one thing it will stand out and can become your brand. No matter what your musical strength is, you should set your sights on it and do that thing relentlessly. People will remember you and come to you for it.

The other side of that coin is that you should identify your weaknesses and get help with them. You don't want to become known for subpar work, so always try to avoid doing tasks that you know you can't pull off very well. If you're not great with string arrangements and can't afford an orchestrator then write for other instruments. If you need to write in a genre that you have trouble connecting with, get some authentic players. If you don't understand a contract, find someone who does. You will be asked to do things that are not your forte, both in art and business, and instead of saying yes and attempting them you should stay focused on your strengths and get help with your shortcomings whenever possible.

GATHER YOUR TROOPS

There are as many methods to building a team as there are composers, but talking to other people in the trenches is usually the most effective. The music industry is highly interpersonal and relationship based, and personal recommendations carry a lot of weight. Music is very subjective and working relationships can profoundly affect art, so when composers are building teams they don't typically do broad searches by simply calling anyone who has adequate credentials. Composers usually build their teams by asking trusted colleagues for recommendations, and there are several good reasons for that.

A personal recommendation from a trusted source is a valuable insight, and it tells you a lot more about that person than a simple resume or conversation. But more importantly, the industry is so saturated with people looking for work that you could spend days interviewing potential candidates and not get anywhere. There simply isn't time to do a true evaluation of all the options. The best way to begin building your team is from within the network of musicians that you already have. You won't really know if someone's skill and personality is a good fit for you and your team until you try that individual out, but personal recommendations are a fantastic filter and starting point.

When trying to build a good team without spending a lot of money, alternative currencies are sometimes a viable option. There is a certain amount of trading favors that is common in the music industry, and it is valid to engage in some form of bartering. In the beginning of your career you may need to rely on favors or the mutual passion of others just to get things done, and in the right context such a practice can persist throughout your career. It's common for people to have complementary skills, for instance, a sound engineer and an arranger/composer who often team up and hire one another back and forth. If the work relationship is mutually beneficial, there is nothing wrong with bartering or trading favors from time to time. It can make a big difference in both your budget and the final result, and as long as those favors are balanced on each side it's a good possibility for team building. Be sure to pay back the favors, however, or you will suffer the consequences in the long run.

Although bartering is always possible, most working professionals prefer to pay their peers. The best way to show appreciation and respect for another person's expertise and artistry is through fair pay, because money is the most widely agreed upon measurement of value. It feels good to pay people well, and most working composers would take a pay reduction themselves before shortchanging their team members. This is as it should be, because the music production budget is not the responsibility of the individual team members. More importantly, you will not be able to keep your team together if you shortchange them. If you make sure your team members feel appreciated and pay them fairly, they will be much more likely to work with you again. Most of the time you aren't able to survive without your team members, so they're worth every penny you can spare. If your team is carefully chosen and feels appreciated, your odds of success are greatly enhanced.

When you bring people onto your team, either for a single recording session or in a more sustained role, team leadership skills become important. Being a manager of tasks is not your main job. Music is

> Each person's individual style will dictate how they build their team, but the best team building happens by word of mouth. When I'm looking for people I always go through other people I know, often other composers. We composers talk to one another, and we share a lot of musicians. You need to be part of the community, I highly recommend that. That's what's so great about the Society of Composers and Lyricists. It creates a space where composers can meet other people at all phases of their careers and interact, giving you access to a wealth of resources. It's very important.—**Miriam Cutler**

> I always try to be budget conscious in the reverse. I don't want to have to ask people to do me a favor. I always want to pay something that, if it's not great it at least shows that I respect that person and that I'm making an effort to say, "You're of value to me." If I can't do that financially then I try to do everything myself. I start by thinking about everybody I want to bring onto a project, but then I look at the budget. Can I afford a music editor? Can I afford a mixer? And then I take everybody that I'd love to have on my team and I start red inking names.—**Nathan Furst**

collaborative, so it's never just a boss and employee context. You need to be a strong leader of people. You need to use good communication to motivate and coach your team members to achieve your artistic vision. You must give them adequate space to contribute so it becomes a collaboration and not a dictatorship. You need to ensure that the critiques you give are not personal and the praise is. You must set ambitious but attainable goals and keep everyone focused on them. You need to be ready to teach and learn at all times.

First and foremost, you need to build a rapport with your team. You might be a guerrilla composer, but you can't be a drill sergeant. You should always think about the team members' experience when they're working with you. Create an atmosphere in which they are happy to work. Money is one way to get someone to want to be there, but the money's not always good. Even if it is, that doesn't mean you'll get the best performance out of them. When you cultivate your team as individuals and make them feel genuinely appreciated you will get better results, and good leaders can do that while pushing their team hard when necessary.

DELEGATE EFFECTIVELY

A lot of composers do things incorrectly when trying to delegate. Delegation is not giving instructions and monitoring the result. That is supervision, and it is what most composers do. The reason most composers supervise instead of delegate is that they don't correctly transfer authority. Supervision is very involved, and the people under you need to check in with you continuously to stay on track. Delegation requires

> Delegating responsibility applies to all businesses; however, for me, the biggest reason I delegate responsibility amongst my team is so that I can keep my focus on the creative aspects of the work and to free up as much of my time for composing as possible.—**Ryan Shore**

authority to be transferred to your team members, enabling them to take the actions necessary for accomplishing their task autonomously. Only then are you truly free to focus on other things. When you bring someone onto your team you should focus on the result that you want, not the process that your team members use to get there. When you micromanage their process you are not giving them the freedom and authority to help you in the best way possible.

When delegating you should let go of the details and embrace the value of your team members. Give people credit for their work, even if it's just through verbal affirmation, and adequate space to do that work to maximize their potential. If you're working with a mix engineer you should give him as much authority over the specifics of the mixing process as possible. If you have an orchestrator doing something for you, let that person revoice your ensembles and just check it at the end. You should arm your team with information about your goals and artistic intent, but you should also empower them to make their own decisions and accomplish your goals their way. Maintain a guiding force but refrain from being in the middle of what they are doing.

Delegation allows you to focus on the important things and equips you to do the things you need and want to do. Perhaps you want to be free to write every single note yourself, but maybe you want to be free

> I think there are questions that each composer needs to answer for themselves. What do they do best and what is best to delegate to somebody else? What is going to maximize their efficiency? I quickly realized that it was not efficient for me to try to do everything—to sketch, orchestrate, find all the sounds, do all the overdubbing, and do the mixing—because that was a very inefficient way for me to work.—**Ron Mendelsohn**

> The way I delegate is very simple. I have never had anybody in my studio, never throughout my entire career (except for musicians, of course). I don't like people around. To me it's all about the first thing, which is the creative thing. So much of the composition happens in different phases of the work that I'm not comfortable delegating. Everybody I know has a better life in that regard than I do. I like the idea of having helpers, but I can't seem to let go well enough.—**Charles Bernstein**

to focus on publicity and marketing strategy instead. No matter where you want to focus your energies, proper delegation can make it happen, but only if you consciously delegate both the tasks and the authority instead of simply supervising tasks.

Learning to delegate is sometimes difficult. You typically start out as a composer doing everything on your own, and all composers are opinionated artists. Your name is going on everything that leaves your studio. It can be a scary thing the first few times you put your art, reputation, and success into another person's hands. It is common to believe that no one else can perform a particular task as well or as efficiently as you. That's a struggle that most small business owners in most industries

> When I am working at my commercial studio, Clearstory Sound, I work alone and never delegate. When people hire me to work for them they know that they will get my ears on every sonic decision that is made.—**John Rodd**

> I know there are guys who insist on writing every single note. I feel very strongly about what I do, but I believe when I work with somebody else they're going to bring another dimension to the music, which actually adds more to the project. If the schedule is really tight and I have to bring in somebody to help me write something, I will do that. Creatively I'd rather not, because I love writing music; however, sometimes time will dictate that you must have help.—**Jack Wall**

> I will never let go of composition. It was really hard for me to let
> go of orchestration. I'm still mixing everything myself. I still use
> engineers on projects during recording because I never want to mic
> an orchestra myself, and when I'm in a recording studio I also don't
> want to push the buttons. I want to be focused on the performance
> and not worry about which tracks are armed. Sure, I engineer for
> smaller projects, but if it's not small I don't do it.—**Craig Stuart
> Garfinkle**

have. It will serve you well to remember the humbling fact that everyone in the music industry is highly replaceable. There is a huge world full of musicians, and very little of what you do is actually unique to you. That's a bit depressing for the individualist in every artist, but it can also reassure you that there is plenty of good help out there. When you find good help you are free to let go.

The best way to make the process of delegation easier is to work with people who have expertise that surpasses your own. You have excellent reason to trust them, it's much easier to let go, and the end product is better as a result. Many composers begin their team building by going in the other direction and finding younger, inexpensive helpers. This is a good way for you to get help, but it is difficult to truly delegate because you need to supervise and educate. If instead you look up the experience ladder and find ways to collaborate with people whose skills surpass your own, delegation becomes a real pleasure. It also becomes

> Usually I have a music editor and a mixer. I have faith in them, and I
> hand it over to them. I have never been in a situation where I didn't
> do the writing for myself. Even if I, on occasion, had an assistant
> flesh something out, it's still my music, and of course I give com-
> ments and notes and fixes, so I'm deeply involved.—**Peter Golub**

> When projects are busy I bring synthestrators on board my team
> (people who orchestrate and perform the music on their rigs with
> samples) so that I can spend more time composing.—**Ryan Shore**

Mixing, without a doubt, is an area in which it's very important for me to collaborate. When I mix a piece of music by myself I'm never happy with it. When I give it to a mixer and don't interact with them I'm never happy with it either. I'm only happy with a mix when I've been involved and yet I'm not the one doing it.—**Nathan Furst**

We have a person in our company that is the marketing director, and she does all of the liaising with the clients. It's not that I don't like to talk to them, but it's just another thing that takes me away from what I'm trying to get to, which is the music.—**Yoav Goren**

a situation in which you can learn and grow, and that has great benefits as well. It may cost you more to do so, but it may be well worth it.

With good delegation it shouldn't take long until you are a more focused composer, are more productive, have more free time, and are creating a product of much higher quality. There is a wide spectrum of the ways in which people delegate, ranging from not delegating at all to team composing. The choice of what to delegate and what to control directly is individualistic and personal, so don't be afraid to try many approaches until you find your way.

BEFORE YOU BEGIN

SET YOURSELF UP FOR SUCCESS

OF ALL THE THINGS that need to be in place before you begin a project, your contract is the most important one. There should always be a contract in place for the protection of both the client and the composer. It is always wise to have a written agreement, even if you are just making custom demos in hopes of landing a job. It needs to be clear who owns the music and has rights to its use. A contract establishes parameters for payment and ownership, and it determines how the business relationship will function. Every element in a contract can be negotiated or changed, so until your contract is signed your focus needs to be on your business, particularly on getting the best terms that you can. Only after signing are you free to focus your energy on the artistic side of composing.

One of the most important elements in a composer's contracts is the writer's rights. You should always, under all circumstances, keep your writer's rights and the royalties associated with them. They are your legal right, and no library or production company should take them away from you. The only exception is in the video game world, where there are never any "performances" that generate royalties, and total buyouts of the music are the norm.

Whenever possible you should retain your publishing rights as well (appendix A contains sample contracts that can facilitate this).

Composers retaining publishing rights used to be unheard of, but now it's quite common. If the production doesn't have enough of a budget to make the work lucrative for you, then you can license the music to the film instead of using a work-for-hire contract. The filmmakers will have all the rights they need to use the music, and you will have the freedom to license it to other projects in the future. If you surrender your publishing rights, make sure you are well paid for them and that your contract addresses the rights associated with soundtrack releases as well.

Your payment schedule should be clearly stated, and landmark events in your work should be accompanied with payments. Small projects may have only a single payment at the end, but incremental payments are common as the total budget increases. There is oftentimes a payment after execution of the contract, one at the beginning of production, and one at final delivery. The payment schedule is always negotiable, but it should be very clear.

Your contract should also stipulate the delivery expectations. You need to know the amount of music, the delivery date, and any other schedule landmarks that you need to hit along the way. Although contracts almost always state an approximate amount of music, that number is rarely accurate. If possible, get additional clauses stating that if you go over the estimate by a certain amount you will be paid more. If you give the production a carte blanche price for a complete score you may find the workload increasing without additional compensation.

There are several aspects that will not appear in your contract but must be made clear-cut. The collaborative work flow is important, and you and your client should have a mutual understanding of what you want that to look like. This includes the time frame in which demos can be produced and shown, the manner in which they will be shown, and the process for revisions and approval. Many filmmakers don't fully understand the work involved in prepping cues for recording sessions and putting music onto paper. It's usually helpful to educate the filmmaker about the processes that go into preparing a cue for recording after it has been approved to help ensure that you get locked picture and cue approvals in a timely manner.

The specs for your audio deliverables need to be clearly stated. You should know from the beginning what sample rate to work in, what stereo or surround format to use, what bit depth is needed, how many music stems are wanted for the final dub, and how the music will be delivered. The range of requirements can be enormous. For a little mobile platform game you might only need to e-mail a few MP3s. For a big film you might be delivering many cues with many surround stems for each. The needs and expectations vary wildly based on the context, particularly with video games.

Once you have a contractual delivery date you can begin to make a schedule for yourself, and you will know very quickly whether it is achievable on your own. If you're going to need help, it is important to assemble your team before doing anything else. If you're uncertain, have some help on call just in case you need it. You must always deliver a great product on time and on budget, so plan ahead and make sure you have the necessary resources.

KNOW YOUR FRAME RATE

The frame rate is the most important specification to clarify. Because there are so many esoteric variations, it's not uncommon for video shooters and directors to give out bad information. You must, without fail, triple confirm the frame rate. It may look like your video is running at one rate but could actually be running at a slightly different one. It is possible to work in the wrong frame rate throughout the duration of a project only to find at the end that your Quicktime videos at home were running at a different rate than they should have been. If you get it wrong you'll be time stretching your music or editing frantically at the last minute. This is a problem most composers are forced to address at some point in their careers, and it's not one you want to deal with.

In brief, the reason there is so much confusion surrounding frame rates is because of color television. The National Television System Committee (NTSC) video standard began in the 1940s in black and white, and in the 1950s it was expanded to include information for the new technology of color televisions. Due to limitations of frequency divider circuits at the time, the NTSC standard had to be modified, and they reduced the frame rate from 30 frames per second (fps) to 29.97 fps. In summary, this was the only way to broadcast a single signal that would work for both color and black-and-white TVs and avoid the forced obsolescence of black and white.

Other countries were not in favor of this change, nor did they like some of the other weaknesses in the NTSC broadcast standard, so they developed Phase Alternating Lines (PAL), which runs at 25 fps. This is the frame rate used in Europe, Australia, and parts of Asia and Africa. North America and a few other countries use NTSC. The NTSC frames are numbered from 0 to 29, but they run just slightly slower than 30 fps. As a result, over time the frame counter drifts out of sync from the real-time clock. Sometimes this is compensated for by skipping over specific numbers in the frame counter, enabling the clock and the frame counter to agree. This system is called drop-frame. When it is not used it's called nondrop.

Theatrical film reliably runs at 24 fps everywhere; however, there is a relatively new frame rate that is increasingly affecting composers now that digital cameras have propagated so widely. If a digital camera shoots 24 frames but plays back at the NTSC clock speed, it ends up at 23.976 fps. The time code will be numbered from 0 to 23, and there is no drop-frame equivalent here, so when working in 24 frames you really need to know if your 24-frame video is true 24. Always triple-check with the technical people on the production team.

In video games the frame rate isn't relevant most of the time. Games are generally not scored to picture, and the people implementing the audio are the ones responsible for good synchronization with game play, not the composer. Cinematics are film sequences between levels or at crucial points of game play, and in those cases the frame rate does matter. Nevertheless, they're typically short enough that it's unlikely your music will drift out of sync in any significant way. Game composers are much more sheltered from the idiosyncrasies of frame rate issues.

KNOW YOUR DELIVERY REQUIREMENTS

Delivering audio for film, television, and commercials is fairly simple. First, the audio almost always runs at 48k. Second, unlike video games, they are fixed-form mediums without dynamic elements. If you got your frame rates right, the audio will end in the right spot if you started in the right spot. Third, it's easy to move audio from one platform to another. Getting audio from a recording studio into a movie used to be a fairly technical process, but now it's almost as easy as dragging and dropping files.

Organizing the files can be a challenge since there are typically lots of them, and the best methods will depend on how the final audio mix of the project is going to be done. If you are working at a proper dubbing stage you can drop your music into a Pro Tools session and deliver that session to the stage. If it's a smaller indie film or show you may need to export an OMF or AAF for your picture editor, which are file formats for delivering multitrack audio. For commercials or less sophisticated film and television productions, you can send just the audio files. No matter what context you're in, whatever the process, it's a no-brainer as long as your files are well organized and properly named.

You should decide at the beginning of the process how much control of the music you want to give the people who are doing the final dub. If you deliver only final music mixes without any splits, your mixes are static and protected. It will sound exactly as you left it, and all they can do is to turn the volume up or down; however, when music is turned up or down the balances change. A cue that is turned down because of distracting percussion may have all of its low end buried under sound effects once the percussion is at an acceptable level. Commercials tend to be finished mixes, but in film and television it's more customary to deliver the music in stems or submixes. In the aforementioned example, if the mixer had the ability to turn down only the percussion, he'd be leaving the rest of the music untouched. If the dialogue and sound effects are simple, stems may not be necessary, but the more complex the overall audio gets the more valuable it is to have your music split into stem mixes.

It is important to think about this in preproduction because it could affect how you set up your writing template. If you plan to mix to stems, you may want to set up your template that way from the beginning. Depending on your writing, the mix process, and the amount of live recording, this could be a big time saver. The composition process no longer has clear-cut demo and recording session cycles. The demo frequently evolves into a completed product throughout time as finished elements are slowly layered on. In this kind of work flow, it's helpful if your template is set up with routing and audio printing channels to create your stems and a full mix in real time. Setting that up one time in your template will be substantially faster than doing it repeatedly for every piece of music you write for a project.

In the case of delivering audio for video games, the possibilities are so vast that it almost can't be addressed anywhere else but with your game audio director. The possible delivery formats range from a stereo

In video games sometimes they hire you for 60 or 100 minutes of music, but they need 300 minutes of music and they don't have enough money to have it all written originally. It's very common to deliver things in lots of different stems so that they can take your music and make different things out of it. They create different cues essentially. Sony is well known for that. When I worked for Sony I delivered every stem I created separately. Sometimes it's dozens and maybe as much as 30, 40, 50 stems. They're responsible for taking those and implementing them. Sometimes just one or three stems of a very complex cue can create a very interesting, sparse bit of music. If they're very familiar with the material and they get really into the weeds with it they can generate a lot of different, interesting cues.—**Garry Schyman**

mix for a mobile platform game to a mass of premixed surround splits that the game designer can use to create new cues. The needs of each game are different, as are those of the design teams and audio engines. Managing and editing the deliverables for a video game can be a large task, so it's important to know exactly what the end goal is before you begin.

4

TIME MANAGEMENT

GUARD YOUR CREATIVE ZONE

SINCE SCHEDULES are getting shorter and shorter, time management skills are an important part of creative productivity. Creative people usually have a particular context and mind-set in which they can be the most creative, but guerrilla composers have to handle a vast number of other tasks and responsibilities that pull them out of that space. Time is free but in limited supply. When the pressure is on you must take conscious and concrete steps to make sure that every minute is used well.

Our experience of time is very subjective, just like art is subjective, and every composer has a certain perception of time that helps put him into a creative zone. When you are in that zone you have the right feelings, energy, and state of mind to go about your artistic work in an effective manner. You almost certainly have a notion of what contexts allow you to be the most creative. A feeling of urgency is helpful for some and stressful for others. Some are early birds and others night owls. Seeing continuous evidence of productivity is important to some, while others want slow reflection. Some composers write in long blocks and others in short sprints. Before sitting down to write, one person needs quiet and another needs stimulus. Your mind-set can greatly affect the music that you write, and the ideal context will be different for everyone.

VIDEO: TIME MANAGEMENT. Pictured: Jack Wall. www.vimeo.com/
guerrillafilmscoring/timemanagementteaser

No matter how fast or slow the time seems to pass when you're in
your creative zone, in the end it's the rigid clock time that really matters.
Delivery deadlines are usually fixed with military precision. No matter
what your experience is like between now and then, you need to be
finished by a specific date and time. The key to success is to consciously
put yourself into your creative zone and guard that time fiercely. Give
yourself whatever you need to write effectively, whether it's twelve uninterrupted hours or regular breaks, time with a partner or time away,
external support or isolation, total immersion or total separation.

In the film world, composers do the majority of their work in the
last 5 percent of a film's production time line. A producer may work on
a film for two or three years, and a composer may get only four to eight

> I worked on a television show last year, and that was a really fun
> thing because I'd never done a television show before. It was fun
> keeping ahead of the steamroller, because the steamroller just
> keeps going no matter how fast or slow you're going. If you stop or
> get hung up on something it's going to go right on top of you, be-
> cause there's no way the show isn't going to air when it's scheduled.
> It's fun, I love that.—**Jack Wall**

From what I hear from my colleagues who do more mainstream work on tight deadlines, it's brutal. I know that I couldn't live in such a harsh reality. I just couldn't. It would kill me. I would just shrivel up.—**Miriam Cutler**

weeks to score it. By the time a film is 95 percent complete, many of the schedule slips that occurred earlier have put tremendous pressure on the people who are still working. As a result, film scoring work is often urgent. Television is even more time pressured because of the short production cycle. Advertising, for those energetic enough to do it, is in a constant state of frenzy. Video game composers, it seems, are the only composers who get a bit of a break when it comes to the schedule. Game composers usually begin to write early in the design process and are sometimes on a project for a lengthy period of time. That can be less stressful, but it is not necessarily a luxury. It can also be burdensome to be tied to a long-term project. As you spend more time on something, you are effectively making less money per hour. Every schedule has its own problems that need to be managed.

When the workload is daunting and the schedule is pressing down on you, remember that you have just as much time in the day as Oprah, the president of the United States, or any other influential figure you care to substitute. The workload you have doesn't compare to theirs, and it's completely possible for you to succeed in a way that makes you feel happy, healthy, and fulfilled. Oprah found ways to maximize her time and has done it continuously for years. That's why everyone knows who she is. She has probably always had an intuitive understanding of how to manage her time. Time management is just as important to success as passion, intelligence, and opportunity.

PLAN YOUR ATTACK

Your contract should include a deadline and a top level schedule. As soon as the contract has been signed, you should begin to detail your schedule. Knowing that you need to deliver a hard drive full of recordings in a couple of months isn't a precise enough goal to direct your daily work. It doesn't make much sense to dive in and start working

> Time deadlines tend to clarify the mind. When you're on a movie you have a certain amount of music to write in a fixed number of days. When you realize you need to write four or five minutes of music each day, then you make it happen. When you only have so many days to produce so many minutes of music you find a way to do it.—**Peter Golub**

until you know your short-term goals. Every composer does this in different ways, but there are some common threads in how the successful ones approach their schedules.

The most conventional approach is to schedule backward, because the most predictable time commitments are toward the end of the scoring process. With a little experience it's not hard to guess how much music you'll record in each session; how many sessions you'll need; and how much time you'll need for editing, mixing, mastering, and delivery prep. Once you've incorporated those elements into your schedule, look at the time that remains. That is your block of time for writing and planning.

When scheduling backward you need to know how and where you plan to record, because the time requirements are heavily dependent on your choices in that regard. You don't need to make definitive decisions about whom to hire or what studio to use at this early juncture, but you should have a good idea of how you want to produce the score so that you can predict and manage the time your production process will require. You need to be a project manager, allocating time and money resources where they are needed so that the work can be carried out as

> For schedules that are super tight, perhaps two or three weeks, my schedule is completely governed by the cue sheet. I'll try to take cues that have a similar vibe, maybe a love theme or an action theme, and group them together. When I do that it helps me move a little faster because I'm already in that mind-set. I'll write all those cues at once, and that becomes my schedule. On a longer schedule it becomes more of a complicated nuance.—**Nathan Furst**

In the trailer world, in the initial part of a job you usually need something written and produced in two days, maybe three days. That's generally the average. You work really hard, you pull an all-nighter, and you pull your team together to get the result you want to get. Then you hurry up and wait while they think about it. That is usually the course of action.—**Yoav Goren**

smoothly as possible. Do your best not to underestimate time requirements, because it is easy to do. Also be sure that you always leave a time buffer at the end. There are always surprises and schedule slips, and none of your schedule slips will excuse a late delivery. You will always be glad for the cushion.

MANAGE TIME TACTICALLY

Writing a film score can be a long march, so it's important to pace yourself. A core time management principle is that you need to assign times to things that have importance. Because composers are self-employed and often work from home, they can easily fall into a free-form routine of unstructured work, which often leads to doing the tasks that feel urgent rather than the ones that are actually more important. It also leads to losing focus and succumbing to distractions. Scheduling time in which you focus only on important things is crucial if you want to stay on target. The structure and support that is born from conscious scheduling is valuable to guerrilla composers and A-list composers alike.

Although it may seem like a good idea, writing a to-do list is not a time management solution. A composer's to-do list is about a million miles long, and writing a score is an endless pile of details. Some of them are creative and subjective, like the phrasing of an instrument, and some

Generally, if you're under the gun and have no budget for players or help, you're not going to have the time or resources it takes to pull off a complex, high-quality score, regardless of how talented you are.—**Bill Brown**

> It's important to not be worried about wasting time. I used to worry when I'd sit and play for a couple hours and nothing great happened, but I adapted my thinking to a different way where those two hours were not a waste. The whole process was a very valuable building block into something unknown in the future.—**Yoav Goren**

are dry and calculated, like determining the cost of paper for sheet music. To-do lists are nothing but a reminder of what is unfinished. They have nothing to do with time management and won't help you meet your goals in a more timely fashion.

A list that will help is a priority list, and that is very different. A priority list is a battle plan. Priorities define your most important tasks, but more importantly, they help you say no to the distractions that pull you away from those things. If your goal is to write six minutes of music every day and you know that you're going to crash and burn if you don't pull it off, you must focus on those six minutes before all else. Priorities are about focus, and when you set your sights on one thing, the others move to the periphery. Saying no is not an intuitive skill for most people and needs to be learned and practiced. Successful people say no to a lot of things. Highly successful people say no to almost everything.

The do-it-yourself nature of composing means that you have an endless stream of interruptions. It requires a conscious effort to remain on task because there are so many tasks to do and so many people to interact with. You should establish some practical conventions or filters for yourself that help you prioritize. That might mean not worrying about EQ until you've finished writing a certain stretch of music, turning off your phone and e-mail for a while, or asking your family to eat without you. Without focus you cannot do your best work. Thus, it is

> By staying organized and scheduling the process carefully, that helps alleviate one of the largest challenges of any project, which is pressure. I do all I can to remove as much pressure as possible, because when you're writing music you really don't want to be feeling those deadlines. You don't want to be feeling the pressure. You want to be feeling the music.—**Ryan Shore**

> I am someone who is mystified by procrastination. I don't even understand how that works. The process of procrastination seems like something so against human nature. To be able to watch television or stare out the window or do anything other than address the mission is incomprehensible to me. I get home from a spotting session and I have the thing half-written. I can't eat, breathe, drink, do anything until I'm on it, and that's where the obsession hits.—
> **Stewart Copeland**

key to establish tools and habits that enable you to follow your preset priorities.

Multitasking is a natural temptation when there are numerous tasks to be handled, but it's not a good idea. A study from the University of Chicago found that creative tasks require a large amount of working memory, or temporary brain storage, compared to more methodical tasks. It also found that multitasking requires the same temporary brain storage and clearly limits productivity in creative tasks. A study from the Massachusetts Institute of Technology measuring brain activity showed that when trying to multitask, only one or two areas of the brain work at any given time. Inside our brains we don't actually multitask, we switch rapidly between tasks. That rapid switching has measurable switching costs. A University of London study by the Institute of Psychiatry found that people distracted by incoming e-mail and phone calls saw a ten-point drop in their IQ. Several different studies have shown that multitasking can cause a reduction in productivity of as much as 40 percent. If you think you're an exception, a study from the University of Utah concluded that people who profess to be good at multitasking are measurably worse at it than those who do not. If you want to be productive you should not multitask, particularly when being creative.

> I am a big believer in front-loading work in the schedule. I work very hard early on instead of meandering in and then working hard at the end. That way I hopefully have decreasing workload pressures. I recommend that. I also recommend good nutrition and working at good emotional and mental health.—**Charles Bernstein**

> When I'm writing I like to do what I call ninety-minute composing modules. I'll come in for ninety minutes straight, I won't answer any phones or e-mails, and I just write for ninety minutes. I set a timer. Then I take fifteen-minute break, and I come back to do another one. I'll do four or five of those a day. If I have to do a minute and a half by lunch then I'll do that minute and a half, and at 12:00 I'm printing. It doesn't matter if it's done or not. Those are the things I do to make sure I'm on time. It's 99 percent perspiration and 1 percent inspiration. You just have to sit down and do the work. I find that if I have a lot to do, that's the quickest way for me to get it done.—**Jack Wall**

BALANCE YOUR LIFE

The curse of working from home is that you live at work, and it can sometimes be difficult to walk away from it. When you know how much music you need to get done each day to achieve your goals, you can comfortably stop working after you have made your day's quota. Having a good schedule and steady pace can bring you peace of mind.

The only way your writing schedule and daily pace are going to be successful, of course, is if you commit to that plan. If you don't, the music industry will chew you up and spit you out very quickly. You must be consistent. Musicians in other parts of the music industry are known for being flaky and unreliable, but not the ones in film, television, and video games. Successful composers are highly professional and have a diligent, if not obsessive, work ethic.

That certainly gives rise to the question of balance. Success in the music industry requires an enormous commitment of time and energy. Composers are not slaves, nor are they indentured servants or debtors.

> You can't stay balanced. Not in this business. I'm serious. It's different from a lot of careers. You have to think of it as if you're in a crowd of a million people and you're just trying to lift your chin above everybody else. In order to do that you have to work every day on standing on your toes a little more than everybody else.—**Yoav Goren**

You have to think about your life and what kind of life you want. This absorbs your entire life. I have years that I never really left this room and people just stopped inviting me to things, and it wreaks havoc on relationships and families. You better love it or you're going to wake up when you're fifty or sixty and go, "What did I do with my life?"—**Miriam Cutler**

When I began my career, I had very little balance between work and life. I worked and thought about work twenty-four hours a day. Perhaps that was necessary in the beginning. Due to there being so many people who want to work in this industry, I think in the beginning of a career it may actually be valuable to have a bit of an unhealthy balance, so that you can establish yourself and learn as much as possible.—**Ryan Shore**

They owe the music industry nothing, but it asks everything of them. Their personal lives are not sacred or even sheltered. Whatever their boundaries, whatever their limits of productivity or unemployment, whatever their priorities, all will be tested and challenged by the music industry. This threat to a healthy and balanced life is pervasive and affects everyone from aspiring graduates to career musicians.

Almost any lifestyle can be compatible with music. You can work as a composer from any city. You can do it part-time or full-time or 100 hours a week. It can be the number-one priority, or in the top five, or

I think creating a consistent balance is extremely difficult. We try to do that, but to a certain extent, we don't get to dictate our own schedules. Missing your deadline is not an option, but putting your loved ones on hold, unfortunately, is a possibility. You need to do that sometimes, and then you spend time to refill the well between deadlines. From a life standpoint you hope that you clock in even time, but month to month it's not going to look balanced.—**Nathan Furst**

> I look at the people who work here at Heavy Hitters Music who are also composers, and they gig. They work here for nine hours. They have to rehearse afterward or play a show, and then they write music all weekend. Monday morning they start the grind all over again. It's hard to balance business and creative and family life, and you can't forget your spiritual side either. Balance is a key essential ingredient to anyone's well-being and success.—**Cindy Badell-Slaughter**

> I don't recommend all-nighters. I don't recommend stressing or pushing yourself to the point of physical or emotional harm. I see a lot of that, and I've done a lot of that to myself. It's always counterproductive. I think good work habits mean you get a full night of sleep, and you eat well, and that you don't spend every waking hour working. You can't. Even if it's just small breaks, those are important.—**Charles Bernstein**

in the top twenty. This is an industry without rules. Everything goes, and anything can turn a profit if you're clever. When trying to create balance in your life you should first choose your ideal lifestyle and then select work that fits into that lifestyle. Those who have done it in that order are usually much more content with their lives and their careers. Consciously and proactively guide your life and work instead of reactively juggling whatever comes your way. In an industry as nebulous and undefined as music, you have the luxury and responsibility of creating your own destiny in a very real way every single day. Create your experience actively, not passively.

The last tenet of time management is to remember your love. Every composer starts out in this industry because he was attracted to and passionate about music. Guard that love, find the hot spot of that flame, and refuel it regularly. Use your time management skills to protect that flame. Without a love for music, composing is just another job, and as jobs go it's a tough one and probably a bad business decision. Make space in your life to pursue your passions and keep your sense of wonder alive. That is your voice, your joy, and your future in music.

PRODUCTION

5

WRITING

GET OVER YOURSELF

MOST PEOPLE begin with an idealistic concept of what it means to be a professional composer. That concept usually resembles some variation of an artist who gets paid to express himself in the way he thinks is the most profound. The fantasy is that composers can develop their artistic voice; put their art into the world; be discovered by successful people who are simpatico with their creativity; and ultimately be hired full-time to write in a consistent, productive, and profitable manner. That is the glossy impression history gives us of our classical composers and the glamorized image we have of our A-list composers today. It's an idealized concept of a connected, productive, and problem-free artistic career path.

If you are afflicted with the idea that a commercial working composer can also be a pure artist, the best thing you can do is get over yourself right away. In the music industry composers can be artists, but they are service providers first and artists second. They are serving a film, television show, game, or advertisement, and many of those products do not require music that is groundbreaking or thought provoking. Composers often need to write fairly simple functional music that does a job in a very specific way. At times there is a need for great artistry, but in other instances the right music for the job is not a work of art that makes the composer proud. There is no room for an artistic ego in

VIDEO: WRITING. Pictured: Ryan Shore. www.vimeo.com/
guerrillafilmscoring/writingteaser

the world of commercial composing because scoring is oftentimes more
like a craft than an art. If you want to sustain a career as a professional
composer you can't be precious about your music.

When working as a composer your job is to fulfill someone else's vision for the project, with the ultimate goal of selling a commercial product that includes music. If you're earning a living with your music, then
your music is also a commercial product, plain and simple. That does
not exclude artistry by any means, and just because there is a price tag
on it doesn't mean that the music can't be sophisticated. Monetizing art
isn't selling out. It's a business transaction that allows you to continue
as an artist. Nonetheless, you must always remember that you have a
supporting role and your music is a commodity.

As a practical craft-oriented composer there are many things you
can do to make your writing process more fluid, efficient, and cost effective. If you establish yourself correctly and focus on the right things
you can give yourself a head start, get your creativity flowing, and allow
yourself to enjoy the circumstances that lead to making great art when
the context allows it. As Thomas Edison famously said, genius is 99 percent perspiration and 1 percent inspiration. The pursuit of excellence is
the pursuit of focused and determined work. If you approach the work
intelligently you will get more accomplished and find your moments of
inspiration more easily.

CHOOSE YOUR FIRST TARGET

The beginning of the writing process is key because it sets the tone for everything that follows. It's important to know both where and how to begin, because both can make a big difference in how the project evolves. That is particularly true in situations where you don't have much time or the budget is small. In those situations you must immediately get yourself on the right track creatively to make sure you finish on time and stay within budget. Choosing what to write first is not the biggest choice in the compositional process by a long shot, but a well-chosen starting point can facilitate your writing and the collaborative process with your director.

Your director's insight is extremely useful in determining where to start and what type of music to pursue. Unlike a concert composer, who begins with a blank page, composers for media always have the external inputs of picture, sound, dialogue, and directors. They never have a truly blank palette because by the time a composer begins work on a project there are clear and well-developed directions in story, drama, style, and intent. Your director is your lifeline to all of those things. Directors join a production early on, and if they also wrote the script, they may have been living with the story and characters for many years.

Your first task as a composer is to become familiar with the director's experience and internalize his artistic vision. You need to get deeply into your director's head and learn to feel the drama the way the director does. If you do, you're much more likely to write music that is appropriate and on target. Regular, meaningful communication with your director is the best tool for getting your music started on the right foot and your best shortcut to success.

When you are beginning to write for a new project it's important to plan your method of attack and not start writing at random. You should choose your first battlefield tactically. You might choose tasks as widely varied as writing an abstract theme for a character, scoring an action scene, attacking a dramatic climax, or writing some simple underscore that isn't pivotal in the film or game. The important thing is not the task itself but why you choose it. Choosing a scene because it's an easy one isn't a great way to begin, because easy scenes have many possible solutions and they won't inform the rest of the film well. Choosing a scene because it's difficult isn't much better, because the scene might become

The musical direction for a project comes from the relationship and discussions between the composer and the filmmakers. Unless the filmmakers have very specific ideas for what the music should be, I like to focus the conversations about the emotions in the project. When I'm not certain of what I should be composing, I find that there are some basic questions I can always come back to in order to help find the music direction. Specifically: Why is there music in the film? What role will the music play? What is it that we want the music to say or what aspects of the story do we want the music to support? If core questions like these can be answered, that can help create musical direction. It's of paramount importance that the composer is on the same page with the filmmakers, so that everyone is working toward the same goals together.—**Ryan Shore**

a larger creative obstacle than it needs to be since the conventions of the score have yet to be developed.

When you are choosing where to begin your writing, the best solution is one based on what you will learn, not what you hope to accomplish. Writing, especially in the early phases, is all about exploring. The most valuable thing is not the productivity you achieve but the intuition and momentum you build. If you think of yourself as a student of the drama and a friend of the characters, your early writing will most likely be better focused than if you are a self-aware or self-absorbed composer.

The way to get moving quickly is to engage with the filmmaker as quickly as possible and find out if you're on the right path. There has to be really solid communication. I need to get into their heads as quickly as possible to make this financially feasible and also to deliver on time. I don't care how I get that information. If the director and I get together and drink a bottle of wine and get schnockered, I'll get to know that person and get to know their likes. Some people will bring in lots of music, we'll go through it all, and they'll explain everything they like and don't like. Sometimes I get very little information from the director, and I actually get more information from the editor.—**Miriam Cutler**

The place I begin changes according to the film. I prefer it when the film doesn't have any temp music, but what I don't mind at all is temp ideas. If I have a conversation with the director he might say he just listened to a band and he really likes their sound. That doesn't mean I'm going to go try to sound like them, but I try to ex-trapolate the magical experience for the director when he listened to that piece of music. The better you can read their mind the more on target you will be.—**Nathan Furst**

Choose a scene in the film or a level in the game that will unlock something seminal within the film for you. The scenes that are best to begin with are the ones that are the most unique to that project, the most deeply characteristic moments that set that project apart from others like it. They are the scenes that will most quickly show what works and what doesn't for the story, sometimes in a very unforgiving way that brings great clarity. At this stage, even writing the wrong music can be a good learning opportunity and not at all a waste of time. In the beginning, successful writing is learning what the film, characters, and director need and want.

CHOOSE YOUR INSTRUMENTATION

The first step of film scoring used to be determining which instruments you could afford to hire. Those budget limitations used to impose compositional limitations, but now there are so many great sample libraries available that money no longer creates strict limitations in instrumentation. You can synthesize any instrument virtually, and the results can be fantastic. On a project with a small budget you might choose to write for only a few instruments to keep everything live, but you could also choose to write for an eighty-piece MIDI orchestra and have those same few players record on top of it.

This provides incredible freedom for composers because the choice of instrumentation is now purely a creative one. The freedom to write for any size and type of ensemble and make high-quality finished recordings entirely without live players is unprecedented in the history of music. Artistic concepts now take precedence over financial means, so composers are liberated and free to realize all their ideas.

> The budget is definitely a creative constraint. It allows you to have boundaries, and you work within those boundaries to come up with great stuff no matter what the constraints are.—**Jack Wall**

The most important factor in determining what kind of instruments or sounds to write for is the genre or aesthetic you were hired to produce. Whether your budget is big or small, if you were hired for a particular type of sound that is what you must deliver. Regardless of budget, an action film probably wants a big-sounding score, and a children's video game probably calls for music that is substantially smaller in scope. If your project has specific stylistic needs, that will be the most influential factor in determining which instruments to write for.

Oftentimes, however, stylistic needs are not highly specific. You will usually have plenty of latitude in choosing your compositional approach, as well as in the creative and subjective process of choosing which live and MIDI instruments to write for. Some composers always write within the reasonable limitations of what their budgets allow so their finished products will sound primarily live. Others use MIDI for all the instruments they would like to include and hire only the players they can afford. As you might expect, there is no right or wrong way to go about this. The majority of the composers quoted in this book try to find a balance between the two extremes, but it is always context sensitive and up to you.

> The budget has never been a restricting factor for me. A lot of times a constriction, an obstacle, is a key to a great revelation. If I have a shot that doesn't work I need to do something. If I'm in G and I need to get to F minor, how am I going to do that? If you can't hire an orchestra, what can you do that's going to be sonorous and sinuous and does what an orchestra does? You solve that problem, and the solution to that problem is going to be revolutionary and really cool. You scratch your head and you come up with something, and that's called inspiration. So whatever the limitation is, limitations are often a good thing.—**Stewart Copeland**

There are really no limitations except the limitations you impose on yourself.—**Yoav Goren**

It used to be that if you had a low budget you started creatively changing your orchestration or your arrangement based on your budget. Now that's not necessarily what you do. If the director doesn't have a lot of money but he still wants it to sound like an eighty-piece orchestra then that's what you shoot for, to the best of your ability. You might do a full mock-up with an eighty-piece orchestra, bring one or two guys in at a time, and track them in such a way that it sounds like they're coming from far away. It's not perfect, but the connectivity of how they're playing will infect the MIDI orchestration a little bit, which is helpful.—**Nathan Furst**

It is most efficient to choose your instrumentation first. While you are exploring instruments and experimenting with sound sets, you may unintentionally be writing your first themes. Once you have an ensemble chosen you can set up a template that is premixed and sounds good so that you only have to do that work once. When your ensemble is fixed and your template built, the writing is much easier and faster. It will be much easier to begin to record and produce the music because there will be consistency from start to finish. The sooner you choose your instrumentation the more efficient your scoring process will be.

WRITE QUICKLY

If you are a composer of art music, you can set your own schedules and take as much time as you want to complete a piece. In the rest of the music industry, however, just like any other industry, you have to deliver results in a specified amount of time. Sometimes that period of time is very short, so if you want to survive as a guerrilla composer you have to develop the skill of writing very quickly without sacrificing the qualities that will get you rehired and keep you artistically satisfied.

The most common thing that slows composers down is self-censorship. If you are too self-conscious when writing and too self-critical then everything you write needs to be great. Of course, it won't all be great. When you are first starting a score it's important to get moving, not write something brilliant. You don't need to nail it perfectly the first time, and, in fact, you rarely will. If you find yourself listening back frequently or erasing notes as often as you write them, you might be too critical of your writing. Move forward assertively even if you haven't fallen in love with your work. If you don't allow yourself to move forward it's going to be difficult to find the brilliant music that lies ahead of you.

The greatest contributor to speed is the opposite of censorship—it's confidence in your skills and trust in your process. You need to believe that you are exactly the right person to compose exactly the right music for the project, and you have to trust that your creative process will lead you to that music in time for your deadline. Once you get moving the music will begin to uncover itself, but it will never have a chance to do so if you don't stay productive. Don't wallow in your successes or failures, just keep moving forward and let yourself sink into the process of writing. The more you do it the better the music will become.

These are the same qualities that make a good improviser, and a composition is really an improvisation that gets written down. Improvisation is pure fantasy. Composition puts that fantasy into a fixed form and refines it. When it's done well, improvisation is composition in real time. Most composers begin their writing process with some kind of improvisation, and little moments of improvisation happen from beginning to end. The more fluid you are as an improviser the faster you will be able to compose.

Many of the greatest composers in history were great improvisers. Bach, Mozart, Beethoven, Liszt, Paganini, Schubert, Chopin, Brahms, Rachmaninoff, Debussy, and many others were versatile improvisers. The same thing is true in the commercial world of scoring for media today. Composers who are successful and productive have different ways of accomplishing their goals, but somewhere in their process they experiment, improvise, and explore their ideas by physically making music with their hands. If you really want to achieve speed in composition, you should practice improvisation in many styles.

A good way to start writing quickly is to focus on the structure of the scene you're scoring and the dramatic hit points within it. The great

To write fast, grab the low-hanging fruit first and keep moving. Don't get hung up on anything. The thing about moving fast is that you're having more fun, and if you're having more fun the creative sparks are gonna fly. If you're stuck on a problem and you can't move forward, if you're beginning to experience self-doubt or get bored, move right past it. Stick to the fun stuff. Go for the low-hanging fruit and gather it all up, because that high-hanging fruit somehow gets closer. When you start solving those easy problems, other things that you thought were going to be a problem end up solved.—**Stewart Copeland**

thing about scoring for media is that you never have a blank page staring back at you. There is always a form, mood, and dramatic intention in place before you begin to write. When making any kind of art those three elements are probably the most difficult to create, so having them in place is a big advantage. The director is like a general telling you what the mission is, and as the guerrilla composer you simply need to execute it.

You should already know where music is supposed to start and stop. If you watch the scene with only a metronome a few times, you will quickly be able to discern the ideal tempo range. Once you have a tempo you can rough out the structure. Choose your hit points and adjust your tempo and meters so that the hit points land in musically convenient places. Every scene has a dramatic arc, so add some markers where the shifts in tone occur. This work is all fairly mechanical and doesn't require much musical intuition, but by the end of the process you have a musical form with a clear tempo, shape, and structure. Building your basic structure is typically quite simple when scoring to picture, and structure facilitates writing in a major way. Once your

I never worry when I start out about being efficient or getting the music exactly right. The point where everybody's pleased and everything works out is an end point, not a beginning. In the beginning, just write music. Just do your best. Just get the wheels turning and start moving.—**Charles Bernstein** instrumentation is chosen and your structure built your writing can progress efficiently.

A great way to test your structures and get your creative juices flowing is to write some simple foundational music from beginning to end of each cue. This is like a brainstorming session, so the only thing that matters when choosing which instruments to write for is that you follow your first instinct and that it is fairly easy to execute. This process shouldn't take too long. The intention is to fill each cue with a little bit of music so that you can react as a listener to your tempos and structures. You are also simultaneously brainstorming ideas for the score at large.

By the end of this process you will have an entire score with form, mood, intention, structure, hit points, and brainstormed ideas. Up to this point the writing you have completed will have felt more like busy work than true artistic creativity, and yet the big picture of your score is starting to emerge. You can go a long way in film scoring before you need to start looking for inspired ideas, and if you can manage to stay busy they will most likely appear on their own, no searching required.

You need time management skills to create space for your writing, and it is important to use the same skills to focus your time while actively writing. Since multitasking can reduce creative productivity by as much as 40 percent, you will achieve better results if you refrain from doing it. When you are at your writing station it is easy to get sucked into changing sounds, processing audio, mixing, and other nonwriting tasks. It's best to defer that fiddling for a later time because it interrupts the creative flow of your writing. Try to follow the work flow that was

I do a lot of television, and those schedules are always insane, always. You more often than not get called on a Friday night for a Monday delivery for some reason. Speed is always mandatory, and it comes from doing it over and over so that your turnaround time is next to immediate. I always create a sound palette, a concept for the score. When time is short I decide on using limited instrumentation, if it's appropriate for the project of course, but something that is going to be exactly the right thing to serve the film so I can also move quickly. This is an old Bernard Herrmann trick. When you're working with a tight schedule, limiting yourself to a small ensemble can yield incredible results.—**Timothy Andrew Edwards**

Especially if I'm doing television, I have to move quickly and I'll just start playing. I do free improvisation. I play what I feel. I just let it happen. You can tap into something that's not even you, really. You're swimming around in a pool of creative juice, and it's pretty magical.—**Jack Wall**

required in analog days, because you will be better focused and will probably get faster results. Write first, then choose sounds and instruments, then record, then mix, and then master. You could do all of those things simultaneously, but the writing, in particular, will benefit from uninterrupted focus.

Another good way to speed up your writing is to group similar tasks together. For example, if you set up structures for all of your cues at once you develop a rhythm and mind-set for the task, increasing efficiency. When you do one isolated task on many cues at once the work can sometimes feel repetitive and mundane, but it can also produce tangible and much-needed progress. You might write chordal structures for numerous cues at once or program percussion beds or refine the MIDI performances in specific instrument groups. When working on several cues simultaneously it will appear that you are making slower progress, but it often makes your work much more efficient.

Production value will come from having a good base, and having a good base is setting it up right. I suggest to people that they just slap some music on every scene. Decide where music starts, add a rhythm, something, anything, and move on. Without much thought, work your way down the movie from beginning to end and then go back to the top. Add more detail informed by what you did in other sections, and keep going back around in a circular work flow. This business of whizzing through it sounds like just a dodge, but, in fact, you're giving yourself a much better foundation because when you address 1m7, the scene where he meets the girl for the first time, you now know where everything's going to end up. You'll address that scene informed by the whole movie rather than just looking at that scene. The basis of what's going to be your production value is much more solidly founded.—**Stewart Copeland**

> I would say there's a pattern to almost every film I've ever done, and I've done a lot of them. First of all, none of them has ever been a piece of cake. They all have what I would call a healing crisis. There is always a low point somewhere. The very beginning is good, and then somewhere early on I confront a total crisis in which I think I'm not capable of doing the job. There's a total crisis where I feel completely lost and helpless, and then I climb out of that and it always has turned out well.—**Charles Bernstein**

You can also find time savings in grouping the cues by mood or theme. If, for instance, you work on all the scenes that will include a love theme you'll probably get through them more quickly. By doing them in a group you'll also approach them in similar ways, adding continuity to the film in the process. Writing your way through a film sequentially can work, but it is not necessarily the best way to approach it. Grouping cues by mood, theme, or function and then immersing yourself in one specific type of drama can spark creativity in valuable ways.

FORGET ABOUT WRITER'S BLOCK

If you get writer's block you must move past it right away, because writer's block has no place in the scoring world. In the same way that a mechanic goes to work and fixes engines, you need to go to work and write notes. The mechanic will lose his job if he scratches his head looking for inspiration before he makes a repair, and similarly you will not get many gigs if you are unable to write on command. You cannot allow yourself to indulge in writer's block.

None of the composers interviewed for this book have had issues with writer's block, and that's because no one who is a prolific and successful writer in a schedule-driven industry has the luxury of allowing time for it. Writer's block is learned and can be unlearned. In that way it's a lot like stuttering. People with severe problems stuttering can often still sing a song without trouble because music always moves forward and doesn't allow time for stuttering. In song, there is no time to form the habit of stuttering. Writer's block is similar. If you simply don't allow it or put yourself in situations that don't allow it, it will go away.

The truth is that nothing is blocked. The core of writer's block is a lack of confidence. It is an internal insecurity with which people paralyze themselves. It can also come from a misguided belief that inspiration is required to write, or that a desire for a specific combination of mental and emotional states before anything can flow. It is waiting for divine inspiration and perfection before starting. That should be the end goal, not the beginning. Writer's block is simply a fear of failure. Once you realize that failure is part of success you can move forward.

Music is a language, and you cannot fluently write in any language unless you practice. When you first start composing, your music won't be very refined, but the more you write the better you get at it. If you struggle with writer's block, you must consciously stop struggling. Accept the fact that your ideas aren't great at that moment and write anyway. It may sound dismissive, but the best way to get rid of writer's block is to stop worrying about it, get over yourself, and simply keep writing.

The key to creative productivity is productivity itself. Although it is widely understood that instrumentalists need to sit and practice their instruments, people don't often think about composers sitting down to practice composition. When players are practicing they focus on the difficult parts, the things they can't do yet. The practice is often dull, repetitive, or ugly to listen to, but that diligent, uninspired time spent is the key to becoming an inspired player. The same is true for composers. If you want to become a great composer, you need to do it a lot. Most of the time you spend writing will be uninspired and require a lot of diligence, just like when you're in a practice room. Don't worry if you don't love what you're writing, just write. Productivity breeds more productivity.

> If you hone your craft enough, and that means spending a lot of time doing it, well past any reasonable amount of time that you really should be doing it, then inspiration is what emerges at the end. Inspiration is the result of all that time spent, all that banging your head against the wall, or laughing it up because you found something just incredible. You can't buy that. You can't manufacture it. That time spent results in a true, passionate core that comes out.—**Yoav Goren**

> I don't believe in writer's block. I think it's a misnomer. Nothing is blocked when you have what people call writer's block. Block implies an impediment that stops your forward progress. I always call it a lack of being pregnant. It's as if you're not pregnant and you're thinking, "I've got to give birth." The problem happened before that moment! You have to be impregnated. You have to be inspired. There's something that precedes the moment of creativity that if you don't do that, then the moment of creativity won't follow. It's a natural process. Curing writer's block is about fertility. It's about feeding your creativity so that when birth is required you have gestation preceding it.—**Charles Bernstein**

It could be that rather than suffering from writer's block you are having difficulty finding a solution to a particular problem that has presented itself during the course of your work. When this circumstance presents itself, one great thing to do is write several different solutions to the problem, essentially throwing darts and hoping for a bull's-eye. Another option is skipping over it, because something you write elsewhere may give you the idea you need. You can try putting different temp music in to see if it inspires you, and if it does you can take an idea and make it your own. Of course you can talk to your director, because outside input is often most helpful. The common thread here is that you are proactively moving forward and not waiting for your muse to appear. Don't spend too much time scratching your head or thinking about the problem while sipping coffee. There is always plenty of work that needs to be done on a score, so stay busy and keep your creative wheels moving.

> I think we all have to remember to listen to a lot of music because it often acts as a spark for creativity. You need to listen to music within your industry. Listen to what your competitors or colleagues are putting out. Trends change very quickly, especially in trailers. If you want to get into trailers you have to listen to trailers all the time. I know guys who do that a couple hours a day. You really have to home in and clearly see what you're shooting for.—**Yoav Goren**

Sometimes you get a phone call and suddenly you have three weeks to write a score. In that situation you don't have time to have writer's block. In that case fear is incredibly helpful. It's one of the best motivators you can have. But I do get writer's block sometimes. What I do to push through it is just keep writing bad music. Terrible, horrible music. Just keep writing it. The worst stuff, the stuff that makes you want to quit the business by early afternoon. Just keep doing that. The uninspired writing is always a very useful process, because along the way you'll learn some things. It's all helpful, and eventually you'll have the opportunity to throw it out.—**Nathan Furst**

FIND YOUR VOICE

When composers feel as though they haven't yet found their voice as an artist, or they don't know what they want to say musically, it can slow them down and be a cause of writer's block. Some people experience this as a very conscious struggle, and the luckiest of composers never really think about it. It's difficult for artists to put themselves into a box and put a simple label on the art they make, and many people have such broad interests in music that they feel unable to describe themselves succinctly. If you worry about finding your voice, rest assured it is there, whether you have found it or are still searching. An artist's unique voice is much easier to identify from the outside, and the artist may not recognize it for many years. If you look at the catalog of productive artists in any medium you will see their unique essence in their earliest works. It's quite likely that they struggled with finding their voice for years or decades, but in hindsight it was always there.

Your voice as an artist is the sum of your perspectives, situations, aesthetic tendencies, technical abilities, interests, education, problems, desires, hopes, and dreams. It comes not from what you do but who you are. It is revealed by expressing many different things via art throughout time and then finding a common thread. The good news, then, is that you don't need to identify your voice to make great art. Perhaps you will never identify what your strongest voice is, and that's okay too. As a composer, all that matters is the one piece of music you are currently working on and the drama you intend to communicate through it.

> Of the varied challenges a composer faces, the biggest challenge is the actual writing. You can't repeat yourself because, especially in trailers, where I mostly work, the trends and styles change very quickly. It's a mind-boggling whirlwind, and you have to stay on top of the trends.—**Yoav Goren**

If you have not identified your composer's voice, trust that it is already there and just write.

An apprentice piano tuner needs to tune about 200 pianos before one is fully in tune. Only after that can the tuner begin to explore the subtle art of equal temperament. Similarly, the key to becoming a successful, prolific, insightful, and self-aware composer is nothing more than doing a significant amount of writing. Practice regularly, refine your skills, explore your emotional landscape, educate yourself, don't let

> I try not to spend a lot of time consciously thinking about how a new composition might relate contextually to other music I've written for other films; therefore, I'm rarely consciously thinking about what my overall voice or sound may be. I only focus on the film I'm working on in that moment, and I think about what I feel would be my best musical contribution for it.—**Ryan Shore**

> Purely on the compositional level, our voice is about our personal taste, but unfortunately it's not always up to us. We have to be really good composers, but we're not just pleasing ourselves. I sometimes think about the difference between our voice and the voice of the movie. Sometimes we can let our voice come through, but other times we really want to submerge our voice in the message of the movie. When we're writing music we can be a personality or a chameleon or somewhere in between. Sometimes a movie allows us to be the self that we're longing to be and gives us a chance to use the voice that we most enjoy using. Other times we're completely at the mercy of a style that we just have to do.—**Charles Bernstein**

If you learn about yourself as a composer long enough, you'll be very self-aware in my opinion. You'll know where you tend to lean, and your personal taste is what you can rely on. If you don't have any good ideas, then you rely on who you are as a composer and what you always like to do. When you start doing that thing I can almost promise you that you'll find your way.—**Nathan Furst**

You have to write outside of yourself while maintaining your identity. It's always a challenge not to fall back on what you rely on normally or what you relied on three years ago or five or ten years ago. You have to go into new directions on every project. It's challenging every time to write well, to not repeat yourself, to push the envelope a little bit, and to get the production value A++. It's challenging even though I've been doing it for twenty years.—**Yoav Goren**

yourself stand still, and, most importantly, write without ceasing. The best cure for your writing problems is to simply write more.

When people are thinking about their voice as a composer they are almost unanimously thinking about the notes they write. It is important to realize that your voice consists of much more than that. The way the music is brought to the listener's ear is just as important as the music itself. Production techniques and values are very much part of a composer's voice. The tone of guitar, bass, and drums defines genres just as much as the parts they play. The tools and methods you use to produce your music are very much part of your voice. If you have cheap equipment, bad techniques, and old samples your composer's voice will sound amateurish. If you are an amateur but have fantastic production values, your voice will sound more mature. Sonic qualities leave just as much impression on the listener as pitch content, so spend time cultivating your voice as a producer.

6

DEMOS

PRODUCE AMAZING DEMOS

WHEN YOU are writing a score, the importance of high-quality demos can't be overstated. Extremely detailed demos aren't only expected, they're mandatory. If you are working on a film or video game, your demo will be listened to by directors and producers who want to hear exactly what their project will sound like with music. If it doesn't sound amazing it won't be approved, period. In the context of television, advertising, trailers, and music libraries the demo stage is often skipped, and it's likely that the track you submit will either be used as is or rejected completely. In each case, your music needs to have as much impact as possible because the marketplace is saturated with music, and there is only one first impression.

The situation is even more extreme when the tracks are not work process demos but show reel pieces that are supposed to get you work. In those cases, the quality of your recordings should be better than soundtrack quality and absolutely A++ production value, even if you're a bedroom guerrilla composer. Show reel demos usually get a few seconds of listening at the beginning and a few seconds in the middle at best. You have to present a finished product. There are no second chances, and tracks that sound like demos are no longer good enough.

You and your recordings must stand out from the crowd in every way possible. The reason that most directors search for new collabora-

VIDEO: DEMOS. Pictured: Craig Stuart Garfinkle. www.vimeo.com/
guerrillafilmscoring/demosteaser

tors through word of mouth is because a search from scratch is a huge
amount of work. Any director or game designer who begins a broad
search for composers will quickly find that he has hundreds of composers to choose from, all of whom probably fit his fundamental needs
of genre and experience. If he only allows fifteen seconds of listening
per composer, a director with that many choices could still spend hours
listening and taking notes.

If the average amount of competition for a project is 200 composers (a realistic number), statistics would say that you have about a 0.5
percent chance of getting each gig for which you submit demos. The
reality is actually worse. Directors don't like listening to hundreds of
demos before every project, no matter how good they sound. They will
disregard as many of them as possible as quickly as possible to speed
the process along. An inadequate demo will disqualify you immediately.
At the end of the day, it often comes back to a core group of compos-

Music is very subjective, and everyone hears it differently. Particularly, the way that nonmusicians hear music is very different from
the way musicians hear it.—**Ryan Shore**

You can have the most amazing piece of music that's ever been written on the face of the earth, but if it sounds like it's coming out of a 1990s synth, no one's going to care. All they'll say is, "God that sounds like a bad video game from decades ago." They don't listen to only the notes, they hear the whole production. One note that sounds amazing is more valuable than a Rachmaninov score with bad MIDI.—**Nathan Furst**

ers who tend to get most of the good work. This may be because they know people or have name recognition, but a big part of it is that they know how to put together demos. They know what is needed. They have appropriate material from previous projects. Their demos sound great, and they know how to package and present them in a way that immediately gives the director reasons to trust them.

No one wants surprises during the production process, and with the current state of the music industry, it is no longer necessary to tolerate them. We live in a high-fidelity world where great production value is readily available, raising the bar and turning possibility into obligation. The days of mediocre MIDI mock-ups are long gone. It requires exactly the same effort to play an idea on a dated virtual instrument as it does to use a state-of-the-art one, so there can be no excuses. There is minimal room left in the scoring industry for things that sound like sketches. You are only safe to send out a sketch of an idea if you already have the gig, if the person to whom you are sending it already trusts your artistry, and if you have established some history in the working relationship. Established collaborative relationships are the only ones that can survive rough demos.

I often record live for demos to make them sound as realistic as possible, because nothing is ever wasted. You'll use it somewhere, sometime, someplace. Recording audio locks things in a little bit. If I have to make a change, I either abandon it or I'll use it somewhere else. If I make less money, that's life. I have a musical morality, and I won't avoid live performances.—**Laura Karpman**

It's always scary the first time you show a mock-up. You don't know what they're going to react to and whether they're going to hear past the MIDI. I give them my disclaimers, and I say these are the ideas, these are the concepts. We can discuss the sounds, but understand this is about the composition and the tone and the music and how it plays for that scene. Don't worry about it being beautiful. When musicians play it, it will be beautiful.—**Miriam Cutler**

Compared to the analog days, the music production process has become elongated. Recording used to happen only at the end, after everything was written; however, production is now spread out from the time the first notes are written to the final mix. You must produce demos throughout the duration of the writing process, which means you need to make mixing and producing decisions along the way. Mixing is integrated into composing, and most composers move fluidly from one to the other because of the need for high-quality demos.

Your demos might be used in test screenings or early previews of the movie, and they may be used adjacent to fully mixed temp music from commercial soundtracks. For projects that have lower budgets and smaller recording sessions, your demos may already include many of the final elements. It takes a bit more time to make great mixes of your demos when you're done writing but, surprisingly, not that much more time. If you send a sketch or rough demo, nine times out of ten the listener will say it doesn't sound finished. Directors want to know exactly what your music will sound like. If they aren't sold on the demo it's not their fault, and you would be unwise to sell them something they don't want to buy.

My philosophy is no excuses, no explanations. I don't want to be doing caveats. I just say, "Here, check it out." You might have options, that's another way to go. Options are a good thing to have when the director says, "I don't like it" and he's trying not to make eye contact with his producer yet. If you give them a couple great demos then you have a conversation going rather than a rejection.—**Stewart Copeland**

BUILD GREAT TEMPLATES

Setting yourself up with a state-of-the-art writing rig that's capable of creating extremely high-quality demos can be expensive. This is one area where it is not really possible to get fast, good, and cheap all at once no matter how savvy a guerrilla you are. There are obvious trade-offs, mostly between the good and the cheap, and there probably always will be. If you have not invested in good tools your quality will be lower, and your speed of demo production will likely be lower as well. The equipment, computers, and software get better and cheaper all the time, but there are real and substantial costs to building and maintaining a writing setup.

If you want to compete at a high level as a composer, you need to invest in the most current and high-end gear you can afford and continuously update and improve it. There are limits, however. Collections of gear and software can easily become a money pit, so there has to be a balance between staying current and buying so much that your profession turns into a hobby. The tools should pay for themselves, but the bottom line is that the more high-quality tools you have, the faster you'll be able to work and the better a composer people will believe you to be.

Whatever your tool set is, there are some common ways in which you can set yourself up to get the most speed and quality when making demos. The most important is that you have a writing setup that is working well and ready to go at a moment's notice, which can be a challenge in the ever-evolving world of music software. You should have your studio wired and your DAW templates built so that you can attack a wide variety of projects instantly. When it's time to sit down and write, you shouldn't be wasting your time trying to find an oboe or a gritty bass sound. Like a soldier who keeps his weapons ready, you should keep your writing setup well prepared so that you are able to attack a new project at any time.

Many composers accomplish this by building massive templates that have every sample library they own loaded and ready to record. There is enormous breadth in the types of instruments and sounds that may be necessary to write a score, and the possibilities of genre hybridization are endless. Most composers naturally want to have a diverse palette of sounds at their disposal, and they want the highest-quality sounds possible. By having plenty of available horsepower and a massive MIDI template, it's possible to have your entire arsenal available in every cue.

Many people like this approach because time is never wasted finding and setting up sounds.

Nonetheless, loading all your sounds at once isn't always a practical solution, nor is it always possible if you have an extensive collection of libraries. Having a massive template that's filled with every possibility can also make your work process cumbersome at times. A common alternative is to have a smaller writing template that contains the sounds you use most frequently, something akin to a sophisticated sketch pad. As your writing develops, you can begin to add additional sounds to that basic template. This approach keeps your template limited to a more manageable size and demands less of your computer, and it still enables you to sit down and start writing immediately after getting a phone call.

Another option is to have specialized templates built for groups of sounds that you can import as needed. For example, your orchestra could be split into winds, brass, percussion, and strings, and you could have additional templates for synths, band-related instruments, world instruments, and so forth. If you are writing in a nonorchestral genre and decide that you want to add strings, you can simply import your string template and keep writing. It's a good middle ground between the exhaustive template and the sketch pad template because it allows you to build exhaustive templates while adapting your template size and computer processing requirements to meet your immediate needs.

After building your MIDI templates you should build your audio processing templates since mixing and mastering is an integrated part of composing. Set this up at the beginning rather than for each individual cue. Your template should be prepared to record your MIDI as audio, route and bus that audio, and print mixes and clicks. If required, you should be prepared to print stem mixes, as well as a summed mix. If you're working in surround you should also be printing a stereo fold down. Your audio routing should ideally be set up so that you can print everything you need in one pass while you listen. Some composers also

My equipment setup is highly tweaked, and I've premixed my palette so reverbs and panning are already in place. This way, when I get a call to compose something, I'm ready to go, and I can deliver music as quickly as possible. Building solid sample templates is a very effective way to save time.—**Ryan Shore**

I have all of the latest sample libraries; create my own custom samples; and record, mix, and prepare custom ambiences and loops for each project regardless of the budget. I also keep the full orchestra with all its articulations up and running on a separate system, connected to the main sequencing system via Ethernet, so any ideas that come to mind can be implemented quickly and efficiently. I'm always updating that orchestra system and my template.—**Bill Brown**

set themselves up so that their printing happens inside a Pro Tools rig regardless of which sequencer they use. Doing so means that their prep for recording and mix sessions is already completed by the time they are done writing a cue.

Your template should be premixed so that you can open it up and quickly generate something that sounds finished. It is worthwhile to spend time EQing your MIDI, adding reverbs, panning, moving instruments toward and away from the listener, preparing common effects, setting up compressors where you are likely to want them, and so on. You should also set up your mastering chain. Even if someone else will master the final product, your demos will be better received if they sound mastered. Premixing your template can save a substantial amount of time.

Being properly set up is crucial for efficiency and quality in your writing and demo process. The way you are set up determines the quality of the sounds you produce, and your production values are as much a part of your composer persona as the notes you write. Every hour spent setting up and improving your writing studio is time well spent. Since you will be exploring sounds and production techniques, it's likely that you will write some good music in the process. Whether you have simple or sophisticated tools, spend time with them and organize them thoroughly so that when it comes time to use them you are prepared to do great writing in the fastest and most uninhibited manner possible.

MASTER YOUR MIDI

Virtual instruments (VI) will always be limited, but the limitations get smaller and smaller all the time. There are numerous instruments that still do not play well when sampled, but there are just as many VIs that are indistinguishable from legit high-quality recordings. One of the keys to choosing an instrumentation that will suit your budget and allow the MIDI to sound convincing is to have a good understanding of what types of things sample well. That knowledge will help you squeeze the most quality out of your libraries and help you focus your live players on the areas where MIDI won't serve you as well.

Short articulations have fewer variations than longer notes. Hence, since the invention of samplers, instruments with short articulations have sounded more convincing than sustained, legato, or expressive sounds. If your writing is subtle or uses sophisticated techniques, live players are always better. If you are using the sounds in a conventional way you can get away with samples quite easily. In many libraries, the short articulations sound so good that they are just as effective as live recordings.

To use a common example, think about bringing a set of timpani into your home studio to record. The timpani that everyone wants to hear is in a large concert hall far away. If you record them with close mics in your personal studio, you will need to go to considerable lengths to make it sound like they are far away from the listening position in your final recording. Unless you have access to a large recording space you are probably better off using timpani samples. The exception to this would be if you are writing music that is truly idiomatic to the timpani and does more than just strike four inches from the edge with a mallet. If it's a part that requires a true timpanist it may be advantageous to record live despite a small recording space.

The longer a note is, the more opportunity a live player has to be expressive with it, which is, of course, context sensitive. The players who recorded the sample libraries were obviously not working in your musical context, so there will always be a slight disconnect between the samples and your music on longer notes. The sample libraries have been working hard for decades to alleviate this problem, however, and there are many sounds that can work well. Sustained strings, brass pads, harp, and piano are convincing with samples. Once again, it depends on the musicality required in the part, but if the writing is not too sophisticated, samples can be extremely believable.

It is almost always good to use MIDI for special effects. There are a lot of strange or ugly noises that instruments can make, and they have been sampled extensively. They tend to require less subtlety than other

> If it's not possible to record with live musicians, the production quality and emotional effectiveness will come from spending time programming the MIDI to make the music sound as real as possible.—**Ryan Shore**

aspects of music, and the libraries have already carefully produced the sounds to be very effective. If you are using *col legno* strings, low brass blats, wind clusters, prepared piano, or any other sound effect that comes from orchestral instruments the samples are great. They may not blend perfectly with the rest of your audio, but those sounds are not ones people identify with as closely, making the weaknesses in the samples less noticeable. If you need a tense aleatoric rising string gliss, there are plenty of those in the libraries, and you don't usually need to record a new one.

The tasks in which MIDI falls short are the ones that require the most humanity. A solo instrument is going to be less convincing than a section sound. Music that needs a true ensemble feel or groove is going to be tough to do alone. Lines with breath in them can be difficult at times, particularly in the brass, which has a wide range of dynamics and timbres. If an instrument is featured, given a solo, or particularly expressive you probably shouldn't do it with MIDI. When your featured instruments are live they communicate much more strongly, and the rest of the MIDI ensemble will be much more believable as a result.

The ideal way to learn what works effectively in MIDI is to learn how to use the instruments in real life. When bankers are being trained to identify counterfeit money, they spend most of their time studying real money. A deep knowledge of the real thing gives context and clarity

> In the MIDI world there are a lot of shortcuts for programming and editing, so I don't get lost down the MIDI programming rabbit hole often. It's usually easy to get good results quickly. In certain instruments the character of the sound changes substantially with little micro changes in the MIDI, and that will bring me down a rabbit hole right away. Sometimes there's no way around it because you have to get it right.—**Charles Bernstein**

I'm very frustrated by programming MIDI. If I'm going to spend that much time on something, I want it to be real music from a real instrument. It's much easier to have somebody play something than to get a MIDI thing to sound right. I try to avoid spending too much time programming because I think it's just a big waste of time.—**Miriam Cutler**

when evaluating the fakes. The same thing is true when working with MIDI. If you have a deep understanding of how to write for live acoustic instruments, you will be much better at programming your MIDI effectively. That knowledge can inform your writing goals, help you decide what your instrumentation should be, and assist in getting the most out of your budget.

Live musicians need excellent technique and complete control of their instruments to achieve the best possible sound, and the same is true when programming MIDI. Whether your MIDI is for string orchestra or drum and bass club music, if you want to get the highest quality you must have complete control. If there is a parameter that you can control you must control it. Even if you are in a hurry, do not take shortcuts with MIDI performance details. The performance is everything, so save time in some other way. You need to understand how you can tweak your virtual instruments, and you should make a habit of tailoring your sounds to the musical goals at hand. If you just call up a patch and use it, you will sound like everyone else. The deeper you get into your sound libraries the more convincing and unique your demos will be—and with no additional cost.

GET THE GREEN LIGHT

Once you write your demos and they sound like finished master recordings, you need to get them approved. There will be times when the concept for a cue is fantastic but the demo doesn't quite do it justice. In those situations it requires the director to trust the composer. The composers quoted in this book have a unanimous opinion about this scenario. If the director trusts you, you're in luck. If the director's not sold on the demo, you should not try to convince him. If he's not sold,

Sometimes the demos don't convince them, but I learned a long time ago to never argue with the director. You might win that argument and get the cue you want, but then for the next 1,000 times they watch that film in festivals they're going to hate your guts because they're never going to like it. Every once in a while they may decide, "Oh, she was right." Most of the time, because we're all working off our gut instincts, if their gut instinct is saying no, I'd rather just go with that.—**Miriam Cutler**

you have to make a better demo or write something better. There should be no negotiating or convincing because it's the director's film, and you want him to be completely happy with the music.

When working on difficult scenes, a common approach to avoiding flat-out rejection is providing several options. Presenting options can also be particularly helpful in the beginning of the process, when the artistic direction and conventions of the score have yet to be established. If there are several different options for a scene it's easy to compare them and start a conversation about what's good, what's bad, and what would be perfect. With only one option the most natural conversation is a simple yes or no.

Even if you present options, always be prepared for rejection. You will have cues rejected on every project your entire career. Get used to it, and learn to deal with it. You should not only deal with it, but plan for it. Music for media never stands on its own; it's part of a much larger project with many moving parts. Remember that when music is rejected it's usually about the fit, not the quality. Don't take rejection personally, and don't let your ego get in the way of your progress. When music is rejected you have not failed, you have simply discovered something

I'm not there to sell them something they're not buying. If they're not behind what I've done 100 percent, I'm not going to spend any time convincing them. I'd rather rewrite the cue. I want them to think there's literally no other composer that could have written their score and no other notes that could have gone in that frame. Only when I get to that point am I personally happy.—**Nathan Furst**

I like to start over, especially in the beginning, I like to give options while I'm still finding my way. The first idea came on one particular day after one particular lunch. It's good to try something else. If you just do one option and your director doesn't love it right away, then you have to wait for the next meeting, when you'll have another shot at that scene. It can really slow things down. If you present two options it will give you more information and can cut out an extra meeting because you have something to compare the first one to.—**Peter Golub**

You have to be an endless fountain of ideas, and the best way to be an endless fountain of ideas is to learn to let go of things very quickly. You can't be attached. You have to believe you're going to have more ideas. If you think the rejected piece of music is great, then put it aside and use it for something else. Throw it in a bin and let go of it.—**Miriam Cutler**

that doesn't work. By asking your director why it doesn't work, you can learn a great deal about the director's intent and the music that the film requires. After each new idea you will be closer to being on the right track, until you discover something that both fulfills the needs of the director and satisfies you artistically. Rejection is not failure, it's a signpost to success.

At the end of the day, your demos have to speak entirely on their own, and they need to communicate exactly what the director is hoping for. There is little room for raw concepts or half-finished ideas unless your creative relationship is already secure. As a rule, your demos should represent the best of your abilities, both as a composer and producer, and they should sound like a finished product that's ready for release. That's how you develop a director's trust and a reputation for quality.

7

SCORE PREPARATION

MAKE HIGH-QUALITY SHEET MUSIC

NOT EVERY SCORE will need to be written down as sheet music before it's recorded, but the vast majority have at least a few live players, and those players almost always need something to look at. Because scoring for any kind of media is highly specific in terms of drama and timing, the parts for live players are typically written out note for note. Composers vary in their need and ability to notate their ideas, but the larger the project and the more live musicians, the more important sheet music becomes.

No matter how big or small your budget, out of the entire scoring time line the most expensive days are the recording days. Postproduction usually costs less, and preproduction can be quite inexpensive if you overlook the investment you already made into your writing studio. At each budget level, it's common for half or more of the music budget to be used within just a few days of recording. Every effort must be made to achieve speed and quality in the studio to keep costs down.

One of the most important keys to efficient recording sessions is excellent sheet music that is well thought out, well orchestrated, well notated, and well organized. Sheet music is a written language that allows the abstract concepts and emotionality of music to be written down, much like written words can express the abstract nature of thoughts and feelings. If your sheet music is fluently and eloquently written your

> Sheet music requirements depend on the genre and context. If it's an orchestral date, every nuance is on paper. If it's just myself with a musician or two in the studio, we have more space to improvise and invent as we go.—**Bill Brown**

communication in the studio will be substantially more effective, leading to a better end product. Whether you use an orchestrator and music copyist or prepare it yourself, high-quality sheet music is essential.

Another reason sheet music is essential is the impression it leaves. The music industry is a relationship-based industry, and the way people feel about you has a huge impact on the amount of work you get. If you provide sheet music that is unclear, doesn't follow conventions, is not laid out nicely, and doesn't help the eye to flow easily on the page you will be judged as an amateur before a single note is heard. If your sheet music begins to cause problems during the recording session, even those who don't read music will get a negative impression of you. Being perceived as underqualified is bad for business.

On the other hand, if your sheet music looks flawless it can leave a positive impression. It will help you appear competent, organized, professional, and educated before even a single note is heard. The real benefit to excellent scores, however, is that recording sessions become substantially easier. When your ideas have been expertly communicated

> Obviously, with an orchestra you can't leave anything up to chance. It all has to be there. When individual people come in then it varies, but if there's a melody line or they're supposed to fit in with the score in a very precise way I write it all out. With orchestral instruments, even solo, I write out every single note and articulation and give it to the player instead of putting them on the spot. When you have great players you often want to leave a little bit of room, because they might do something really interesting and you want to be able to capture that. Especially with world instruments, guitars, or other instruments where improvisation is indigenous, it's good to have the idea written down, but not so precisely that you contain them.—**Nathan Furst**

> I prefer to offer a fair amount of detail in my scores, but I've been in situations where players came in and blew my expectations out of the water. It's wonderful when that happens. I'm open to their ideas, but I want to give people as much information as possible to work from so their job is easy and the final product is satisfying.
> —**Timothy Andrew Edwards**

on the page in a way that's easy to read, there is little for the musicians to do other than learn the part and execute it.

PURSUE MUSICAL LITERACY

There are plenty of successful musicians who do not know how to read music, and there are plenty of celebrity film composers who entered the industry without knowing how to notate their own scores. This is a perfectly viable approach to take because there are many orchestrators and music copyists available to help you, but working without that knowledge costs time and money. In recording sessions, your communication with musicians may be slower and less efficient because you will be missing some vocabulary and comprehension; however, hiring copyists and orchestrators for their specialized expertise can be a great way to learn about notation, because you learn to read and write from your own music.

If you don't read and write music, keep in mind that at some point it becomes hard work to stay on that path, and it's actually easier to become literate. Contrary to what is often said, learning to read music is quite easy—much easier than any other written language. If you learn where the notes are and understand the most basic rhythms, articulations, and other markings, you can achieve a good working knowledge fairly quickly. Total fluency takes time and practice, of course, but music notation is systematic, and it's basically unchanging throughout the world. Music notation and numbers are the only forms of writing that transcend language barriers, and they are universal because of their simplicity. Musical literacy is very accessible.

Composers in Hollywood and elsewhere generally do not hire orchestrators and copyists because they are musically illiterate. Orchestrators

> Since I'm almost always working with a few instruments at a time I can easily do my own score prep. On those occasions where I have to go into Capitol or go into a studio and conduct, even if I have only a small orchestra, the music prep is a problem. I can't do prep on that level. I can do it on the level which I mostly work, but whenever I have larger sessions I farm out the music copyist work.—**Charles Bernstein**

and music copyists are usually hired by composers who could do the work but either don't have the time or would prefer to focus on other things. Orchestration is subjective and creative, but many orchestration intentions can be made clear through MIDI and well-programmed demos. Copyist work is a specific type of editing and publishing, and although it requires a well-trained musician, it is a craft-oriented process and not a creative one. As a result, it is common for fully literate composers to pass off the sheet music preparation work to other people.

If you do have the time, preparing your own sheet music can save a lot of money. Score preparation is a fixed, hard cost of production, meaning it's an unavoidable part of doing business as a composer. In the typical package-deal scenario, if you can't do it yourself you reduce your income by paying for it. If you have the time and experience to do it, the savings can be substantial. Some aspects of music notation are process- and craft-oriented, but making your own sheet music is also a chance to look at your music in a new light. It can be very clarifying to see your music the way the musicians will see it. A copyist doesn't usually have any authority to change the music, but when you create your own sheet music you get one last opportunity for creativity before your

> When trying to contain a budget, I'd say my biggest problem is always music prep. It's expensive to get really good music prep with experienced people. That has always been the part of my process that's the most difficult to control because it's hard if you have sixty-seven minutes of music and only a week or two to get it together. It's really difficult to get all the information you need onto the page perfectly.—**Miriam Cutler**

sessions begin. It can be time consuming and schedules often do not permit that extra time, but score preparation can be a valuable process both monetarily and creatively.

CLEAN UP YOUR MIDI

If you're going to prepare your own sheet music, the first thing you have to know is that no matter how good software gets, it will not do everything for you. Once you choose a notation platform, you need to know it inside and out. When it's time for score preparation you usually won't have a lot of time. That means you can't be digging through manuals or menus trying to figure out how to make the tool work. The tools for score prep get better all the time, but like anything else, the final product is only as good as the person using it.

The major DAW platforms integrate some form of notation so that you can see your MIDI represented as sheet music, but to date none of them are viable solutions for anything but the simplest of projects. If you are working on music that isn't too sophisticated, and especially if your players are coming to your studio one at a time, printing your scores from inside your DAW might be a viable option. It can be advantageous when your scores and your MIDI are connected dynamically. The sheet music won't look as nice as it would if it were prepared in Sibelius or Finale, but you are able to skip an entire step of the production process, which can be quite helpful. For the most part, however, printing from inside your DAW is only a quick and dirty solution. You are better off moving your MIDI into a proper music notation platform as soon as you begin to care about the aesthetics of your score or as soon as your recording sessions get expensive enough that you don't want them unnecessarily interrupted.

There are about six common music notation platforms, only two of which are frequently used for publishing or professional work. There is an art to preparing music in a way that it is visually graceful and musically functional, and the software still can't produce publication-quality results directly from MIDI files. Despite the simplicity of the individual elements of music notation, there are too many variables in music for that to be possible. Part of this comes from the MIDI standard itself, which is quite limited, and part from the fact that the MIDI file has no knowledge of what kind of sound is being triggered by each note.

There is also a big difference between performance MIDI and notation MIDI. The way we perform notes is not the same as the way we like to see notes on the page. There are a great many ways in which the MIDI from a well-programmed demo needs to change for sheet music. For instance, if we play staccato eighth notes, the MIDI will most likely write alternating sixteenth notes and rests. We may intend for them to be even eights, but if our rhythm is loose, they can come out overlapping or as more complicated rhythms. We may sustain a note with the pedal, but the MIDI sees only a short note. A timpani patch may have left-hand and right-hand samples spanning the keyboard, so the MIDI will notate the right hand on a second staff in treble clef. Many sample libraries use key switches that are represented as MIDI notes, but they never belong on paper. The number of MIDI tracks is almost always different from the number of score staves too, so the MIDI needs to be expanded or collapsed on almost every cue. When converting a sequenced demo into sheet music, the MIDI always requires substantial changes.

When converting MIDI to notation, you need to examine each note and think about how you want it to look on the page. Notes should be quantized to the exact durations you want to see on paper, meaning you quantize both the attacks and releases. Before exporting your MIDI you should go through each cue track by track and note by note. Note overlaps that create a legato feel in the demo should be removed. Tracks that use the sustain pedal should have the notes extended to their full duration. Since they are almost always either too short or extremely long, percussion note durations usually need to be changed. Each MIDI note needs to be examined through the filter of how it will translate to written notation and quantized so that it will look as it should. You should always include key signatures and time signatures in your MIDI files because it makes the MIDI import much more playable and readable. It is much cleaner to change time signatures in your DAW, so make sure they are correct before you export.

Your notation will be much cleaner if you split your MIDI out to the number of staves that you'll use on paper. Splitting one MIDI track into many is usually best done in the DAW. Instruments that use the grand staff, for example, piano and harp, will need the hands separated to two different staves. Other instruments that need separation should also be split out to the staves that you intend to use. Common instances would be a single MIDI track for four horns or a full string ensemble. When too much information is on one MIDI track, the notation gets messy.

Other types of MIDI tracks typically need to be collapsed down, but this is usually best done in the notation program instead of in the DAW. For example, you may have ten different tracks for violins all using different articulations. The distinction between articulations can be lost if the collapse takes place inside your sequencer. It's best to add the appropriate dynamics and articulations inside the notation program first to preserve detail and only then collapse the MIDI tracks to one staff.

DETAIL YOUR SCORES

In the same way that having good templates is important for demo production, it's important to have good templates for your scores as well. You'll need to build a new one for each project, but by consistently refining your engraving rules, shortcut keys, font choices, staff sizes, default placements, and so forth, this task will become easier. You can build a new template based on older files and carry those choices from project to project. Choose a staff size for your score that barely allows all the instruments to play at once. This approach will usually give you only a couple of cramped pages. Otherwise it produces the most clarity possible. With sheet music, the adage "less is more" usually doesn't fit. More is more, bigger is better.

When building your templates do not use uncommon fonts, especially alternative music notation fonts, unless you don't anticipate sharing your notation files with anyone. When a score is opened and fonts are missing, other fonts are automatically substituted. Be aware of that and send fonts along with your score files when necessary. Your template should include each instrument that will be used in the score, and you should not delete unused staves. You can hide them in the score, but keep the staff so that you can print out a tacet sheet to answer the inevitable question of whether a player should have a part. Recording sessions use nontransposed scores because the music is often changed on the fly, and the score is easier to read that way.

There are important differences between scores that are published and scores made for recording sessions or live concerts. In live scenarios functionality tends to be more important than elegance, although both are always important. Even though it clutters the page, numbering each measure is common, and doing so facilitates conversations in the studio. Large time signatures are common on conductor scores if the ensemble is large. Double bar lines are used much more frequently than in concert works to mark any tempo, texture, or structural changes of note.

The first step is to get the music onto legal score staves. Depending on how you programmed your MIDI, this might be a simple or nightmarish task. This is where your orchestration choices begin. A trombone section patch would be split to the appropriate number of staves. If you have a three-note chord and four live trombones, the note you assign to the fourth trombone makes a big difference in the tone. If there are a variety of MIDI tracks that correspond to short, long, fx, and other trombone sounds, they may need to be collapsed to one staff. These kinds of minor choices compound continuously, so as you wrangle your MIDI, you are actively sculpting your music.

Once the MIDI is imported and on the correct score staves, the orchestration work can begin in earnest. Many people incorrectly define orchestration as the assignment of notes to instruments, which, by this time, is already complete and in the MIDI file. This is more correctly called instrumentation. Even many published orchestration books are actually only about instrumentation. Orchestration includes instrumentation, but it is much broader and includes arranging, voicing, dynamics, expressive markings, articulations, phrasing, breaths, bowings, colors, the balance of acoustic mass, conductor markings, and any other aspect of music notation that you can think of. Orchestration is the art of managing groups of instruments and explicitly notating the subtleties of the music to help the music to speak with maximum eloquence. Orchestration is just as important as the instrumentation, and an orchestrator with experience and good technique can substantially elevate the quality of the music.

Sight-reading music is difficult enough as it is, so you want to give your players as much help as possible during the recording sessions. The more detail and subtlety you can notate the more likely you are to get the desired performance. When preparing sheet music for recording sessions, don't be afraid of overnotating. Dynamics should be reiterated after long rests. Each articulation should be clarified and each phrase marked. When necessary, give indications about the click and tempo. If the music notation seems like it's still not specific enough use language to clarify. Try to anticipate the questions the musicians might have and mistakes they might make, and give them the information they need to capture your vision.

Since many foreign orchestras provide more competitive pricing and contract terms, it is commonplace to record in other countries. Remote sessions are quite common, and you can use orchestras from throughout the world from your bedroom. If you are planning to record overseas do not use English in your scores. Use the traditional Italian terms for everything. An orchestra in Prague may not understand "a little more quickly," but they will understand "poco più mosso." The Italian terms have transcended the language and become a part of music that all trained musicians understand.

MAKE YOUR SCORES BEAUTIFUL

Once your orchestration is finished, it's time to begin cleaning up the score. This is where sheet music preparation turns into a publishing venture and not a musical one. The dynamics, articulations, slurs, and other music elements have default placements but often need to be improved to achieve a truly professional look. Some notation programs automatically avoid collisions between notation elements; however, this is not always the case, and none of them get it right 100 percent of the time. At the very least you need to ensure that your music is clear, readable, and not colliding with anything else on the page. Also be sure that everything is attached to the correct staff and beat. If an element's attachment is incorrect in the score it may end up in the wrong instrumental part.

The layout of your sheet music makes a big difference in how it will be perceived. Always use portrait orientation, and make sure the scores and parts end with a full page. Pay close attention to the horizontal and vertical spacing, looking at both the notation and the white space on the page. The balancing of white space is a crucial aspect of any form of publishing, and music is no exception. You should adjust your layout so that the density of notation is similar from page to page, the pages are balanced within themselves, and adjacent pages are similarly weighted with music. This aspect of score preparation is a subtle art, and the automatic layout and spacing options in the programs serve only as a starting point. For scores with a truly professional appearance, you should control every aspect of your music spacing.

The preparation of the instrumental parts is an iterative process, and once you have a system in place it's easy to do quickly. Like the score, you should have bar numbers on each bar. The staff size should be as large as possible to make sight-reading in dim studios as easy as possible. Your margins can be small to help compensate for this. Whenever possible put a rest or an empty measure on the last measure of a page, allowing time for the eye to travel up to the next page or for a page turn. Your parts will inherit the relative placements of the score, which should look good if you have a well-prepared score. Regardless, you will need to spend time making good layouts and cleaning up positioning to make sure that everything is as clean and clear as possible. Always bind or tape your parts, because loose pages can easily cause wasted studio time.

It's wise to notate one cue in its entirety so that the score and the instrumental parts are complete and ready to print before you continue notating the rest of your score. Doing this will establish the notation conventions required for that particular score, and using that file as the basis for your template will help you avoid duplication of work as you move through the rest of the music.

Score preparation is a detailed craft that takes years to perfect, and it is best learned as an apprentice under a master music engraver. These suggestions will only get you started, and a serious study of music notation and music engraving standards is required if you want your scores to look truly professional. If you plan to do your own score prep, your scores don't need to be the same quality as a published master engraving, but they need to be good and clear. If you choose not to embark on a serious study of music notation have some references handy, as there are centuries of tradition that inform the best practices.

COPYISTS CAN HELP

Good music preparation requires a great deal of time, copious musical knowledge, and ample publishing expertise. If you're lacking in any of these departments you may decide to bring a music copyist into your project. A music copyist's craft is specialized, much like mixing and mastering, and score prep is something many composers choose to outsource if they're able to afford it. Rates vary widely, but it's safe to assume that you get what you pay for. The lines between orchestration and music copying are blurry, and the tasks overlap extensively. Orchestrators will often make their scores print ready, and copyists are often required to make some orchestration decisions. Most people that do one job can do the other, and it's becoming increasingly common for the two to be bundled together.

The people that specialize in orchestration and score prep can usually work in any way you need them to. You can take your music as far down the line as you like or let go of it as soon as you'd like, and they can pick it up and carry it from there to the music stands, with or without your help. Every composer has different abilities, levels of involvement, and amounts of available time, and copyists are accustomed to this. For other parts of the production process there are established conventions for the status and form of the music when it is handed off to the next team member, but not with orchestrators and copyists. When your knowledge or time runs out, you can simply stop and hand your work to them. They will make your music look and sound great, as well as take care of the details and make you look good in the studio. They can be an amazing resource, fill in the gaps in your experience, and reduce your workload.

8

PREPARING FOR SESSIONS

GET IN SYNC

MOST COMPOSERS choose their method of synchronization at the beginning of the writing process, but you can freely change the way you accomplish sync until you begin to record your first audio tracks, at which point you need to commit to a method. The predominant method is to use a click because it's the simplest, fastest, and easiest way to line things up. If you are not recording your music completely live on a single recording date the use of clicks is almost mandatory because it's difficult to stay perfectly in sync with prerecords without them.

Not all music has a rigid tempo, however, and so a fixed click and meter is not always the right solution. To preserve the efficiency of the click it's common practice to build a variable click, one that lets the tempo float in a controlled way instead of rigidly enforcing a certain tempo. Variable clicks may have rubatos and accelerandos in them, but they may not. The variation could be as simple as a sudden unprepared tempo change to match a change in drama. It's somewhat slower to record with variable clicks because players have to learn the contours of the tempo, but it can elicit natural-sounding performances full of breath and expression.

The time it takes musicians to learn a variable click is frequently unavailable because of the schedule pressures of recording sessions. In cases like these, a highly rubato click is problematic, so meter changes are often used instead. By adding extra beats in measures you can create the feeling of rubato even when the click is running at its fixed robotic tempo. The music can be perfectly replicated and synchronized each time, and there is no learning curve for the musicians. Using meter changes to create a written-out rubato such as this affects the listener much like a true rubato would. For the sake of efficiency, meter changes are a good middle ground between rigid clicks and a free tempo. However you use them, clicks will be your easiest and most reliable solution for synchronization.

When recording with a click, be sure to use one that will not bleed from the headphones into your mics. The industry standard is the Urei click sound, which is a clean and precise snap without any tonality. Using sounds like cowbells and wood blocks might be tempting, but they will bleed into your mics much more easily. You should always pick something without tonality, for instance, a bass drum or Urei click, when recording. Another alternative is to use closed-ear headphones, which have far less leakage then normal headphones and will allow you to have louder and more tonal clicks.

The old style of synchronization was not with clicks, but rather with punches and streamers. This method is almost obsolete today, but some DAWs allow you to use it. They overlay visual cues on the video, letting you conduct not to a click, but to visual cues. This allows for a much freer interpretation of tempo, making the music more fluid. There are certain advantages to working this way, but using punches and streamers demands a skilled conductor who is well practiced in conducting to picture without clicks. Although this method can greatly enhance the ensemble feel of the music, it is a disappearing skill. The use of punches and streamers can be more difficult if you already have prerecorded audio during your sessions, although it's not impossible by any means. If you are have both prerecords and visual cues, be sure that you or your conductor is prepared to guide the musicians through the session.

You also need to be in sync with your director. Before you start to record, ensure that your director has heard all of your demos and fallen in love with each one. Your demos represent the sound that his film will have, so they should be extremely detailed, and you need to confirm that everything is approved. Many directors have asked for changes during recording sessions. Although it's possible it's something you want to avoid, as it's inefficient and can put pressure on the recording schedule.

If you have the time, it's wise to have one last meeting with the director during which you watch the scenes and get a final approval. No matter how you go about it, make sure you have the green light before you enter production.

MAKE YOUR PRERECORDS PERFECT

The production value of your final product begins to take shape with your first prerecords. Whether they're synth sounds or acoustic instruments, your prerecord tracks are like the first brushstrokes on a canvas and have a big influence on what will follow. Some prerecords are merely placeholders for things that will be replaced later, but many of them will make it to the final mixes. The sonic quality of your prerecords becomes very important. Errors and weaknesses can compound, as can excellence and quality. Make each element of your prerecords sound as amazing as possible so that your sessions have the best chance for success.

When beginning to prep for recording sessions, one of the first things you should do is print your MIDI tracks to audio. This used to be an essential step in conserving computer processing power. Thankfully this is not always the case today, but MIDI setups change constantly and you will want to be able to open your files years from now and play everything back. It's also required if you are going to record in a studio other than your own. For one reason or another you always need to print your MIDI, so it's best to do it before you start recording to reduce the chances of errors or oddities by removing the dynamically created synthesis and putting the music into fixed form. It also lessens the load time when switching between cues, which can be crucial during time-pressured recording sessions or for projects with large templates.

It's at this stage that you commit to a MIDI performance, so make sure that your MIDI is programmed to be as expressive and musical as possible. Unless effects are an inherent part of the sound, you should print your MIDI dry. Apply effects to the audio and not the MIDI instruments before they're recorded to avoid limiting your choices in the mix. Printing MIDI is a noncreative process and a good one to outsource to an assistant if you have one.

The picture is never truly locked, and because music is dependent on time, picture changes always create problems. If your writing is still entirely in MIDI it is highly flexible and can be quickly molded to fit new edits of the scene. If you have already begun your prerecords a new picture edit could create a substantial amount of work and possibly could require that you discard your prerecords and start over. Be prepared to redo your prerecords from time to time. While recording, keep detailed notes about your recording setup, signal path, and settings so that you are able to duplicate them exactly and seamlessly integrate the patches if necessary.

Recording final audio elements throughout the composition process is an efficient way to work for several reasons. Since the music evolves into finished form little by little, it gives the director a clear idea of how the finished product will sound. When appropriate, this slow building of finished layers is better than relying on MIDI mock-ups until they are replaced in your recording sessions. Recording throughout your writing process also puts some recording tasks behind you, which makes the production workload much lighter toward the end of the process. It also saves money because you will generally be recording on your own time and with your own equipment.

A frequently used technique for saving more money is recording with only one player at a time. It consumes more of your time, but the musicians are free to move at their own pace without hindering anyone else. Their time is often more productive as a result. Since you are paying for your musicians' time and not your own, this approach makes sense if your schedule can accommodate it. You end up with more editing work to do and spend more time tracking, but since budgets tend to be small, entire productions are often done this way.

In the context of recording one musician at a time, it is important for everyone at each stage of the process to have a clear picture of what the end goal and finished product will be. High-quality prerecords and

A lot of what I record I do overdubbing one player at a time in my studio, but it takes a lot more time that way. I've always been willing to invest myself into the process, and that's the only corner I can really cut. I would never cheap out on the musicians. I have to pay my music prep people fairly. I have a really good mixing engineer that I work with. The only place I can really cut corners is myself, so I invest the time and hope that I'm making an investment in something worthwhile.—**Miriam Cutler**

In my experience great-sounding prerecords (be they synth, virtual, samples, or something that the composer has actually recorded themselves) tend to be born from a creative approach. If the composer takes the time to create and program unique, ear-catching, and suitable prerecords, the final music mix of that cue will turn out better. I always recommend that composers not "bake in" reverb into their prerecorded audio tracks, as this can create sonic problems later.—**John Rodd**

well-developed demos will help your musicians see the big picture, something they need to understand the vision that you and the director have agreed upon for the scene. Without the highest-quality demos, your players will have a harder time fully immersing themselves in your music. If some elements of what your players are listening to are mediocre their connection to the emotional aspects of the music will also be mediocre, yielding a mediocre performance. Each player who becomes involved in the project after them will feel that mediocrity, and it will compound. Each track you create should be as impressive as possible. If your prerecords can paint a clear picture of the tone, vibe, groove, and attitude you're trying to achieve, your players will give markedly better performances.

You should be prepared for flexible headphone mixing. Depending on the instrument and musical context, your players will need to hear different things. There may be elements of your demos that are distracting to the musicians or other elements that they need to hear more clearly. This is less of an issue when recording one player at a time because there is only one headphone mix to worry about. If you have multiple players coming in, be prepared to give them individual mixes. Personalized headphone mixes make the musicians more comfortable and solicit a better performance, so it is always worth the effort.

PREPARE THOROUGHLY FOR SESSIONS

To be quick and cost efficient, and get good results in the studio, you need to be thoroughly prepared. Between the technical studio setup, sheet music, engineering, players, schedule, documentation of progress, and performances there are a lot of details that need to perfectly align. When composers go into production it can be just as complicated as it is for filmmakers; however, unlike a film director, composers typically do not have producers and other support staff. When preparing for recording sessions you must take off your artist hat and become an event planner, because only through thorough preparation will you be free to be an artist during the recording session. Book your musicians as early as possible, and don't underestimate the time it will take to record. It's difficult to do inspired work when you're rushed, and if there is extra studio time available you will always find a way to use it.

When you have several sessions in a row, allocate time between them to edit your takes. When you prepare the finished edits of one session it will increase the quality of the next one. It's important to do this because production value and performance quality have a distinct compounding effect when you are recording in layers. When you give your players the best possible representation of what came before them, you will elevate their performances. It's most efficient to choose the final takes shortly after a session, while your memory is still fresh.

The next step is to triple-check your scores, because the accuracy and visual clarity of your sheet music is tantamount to smooth sessions. You don't want to be examining your sheet music for errors or fixing mistakes that you could have caught on your own time while you are paying for musicians and studio time. If the schedule permits it, get the sheet music to your musicians in advance. You should know your recording order and what you hope to accomplish each hour. The scores should be organized according to that order and sitting on the music stands when the players arrive. There is no reason to pay for a musician's time as he shuffles through a pile of papers looking for a cue. Furthermore, provide pencils on each stand so players can make notes.

The technical studio setup is important and always seems to take longer than anticipated. Set up and test the studio early so that you have plenty of time to troubleshoot problems that surface. It's best if you test each piece of gear and signal path that will be used in advance. When the musicians arrive the studio should be ready and waiting for you to hit record, with levels set at good approximate volumes and mics in either good or final positions. Technical problems and troubleshooting are not a good reason to keep your musicians waiting and your budget bleeding.

When a composer does not have the resources to hire an expert to prepare their Pro Tools sessions, a huge responsibility falls on their shoulders. The most common mistakes I see are surrounding frame rates, Quicktime movie frame rates, bars and beats, temp music, sample rates, bit rates, tempo changes, and sync.—**John Rodd**

Your DAW should also be ready to go. You should have your sessions prepped, inputs routed, and tracks armed so that you can simply open a session and hit record. The flow of a recording session is key, and regular interruptions for computer setup can disturb the vibe. Keep your players immersed in your music by having your sessions thoroughly prepared and ready to go so that you can almost forget about the gear when you begin to make music. There are many technical details involved in setting up DAW sessions for recording sessions, and they need to be perfect.

You should also think about the musicians' experience during your session and what vibe you want the session to have. Particularly in Hollywood, where musicians make few mistakes, it's easy to think about the people as if they are the instrument they play. It may sound obvious, but it's not a brilliant violin-playing machine, it's a person. The larger the group gets the easier this is to overlook, particularly when working through a music contractor who brings players to your sessions who you may not know.

You should create an environment that the musicians want to be in. Make them feel appreciated and happy to be working with you. You should also think about the emotional needs of the film to some degree and try to guide the studio interactions toward that emotional state. If

The key to efficiency in the studio is prep, prep, prep. A recording session is like a chain that is only as strong as its weakest link. You have to write good music, your Pro Tools sessions have to be ready, the sheet music has to be properly spaced and properly prepared, the engineer has to have things under control, and then of course you need great players. All of those elements need to be present for every session.—**Garry Schyman**

My writing template helps me prep for recording sessions. I mix into Pro Tools, and my template is built so that I can simply take that session to a scoring stage. It has my stem session, my tempo map, and the click track printed. I just take a drive with me and we're done. My session prep is finished by the time I mix the first demo.—**Jack Wall**

you're working on a comedy you can have a lot of fun. If you're working on a serious piece a more somber tone will produce better results. During the sessions, you are a director extracting specific emotions from your musicians. Make sure you take care of your players and also create an environment that is conducive to the task at hand.

You should be doing this habitually anyway, but before your recording sessions begin, make complete backups of your files. Make duplicate copies of your work on a separate drive, because every hard drive can fail and all kinds of things can happen to your files while you are working with them. To ensure that you never lose anything, run backups between each session, as well as after the last one. It's painful to lose your work, and it is doubly painful when that work was from a recording session because that time is the most expensive per minute of the entire scoring process.

The last thing to do before a recording session is prepare yourself mentally. Your ability to be effective will be diminished if you are stressed out, tired, busy, nervous, worried, frustrated, or dealing with any other state of mind that pulls you out of your music. You must be an inspirational leader and lead by example by being more emotionally invested in the subtleties of the music than anyone else. You need every ounce of your brain power and charisma for the producing, directing, listening, and decision making of recording. Anything that is on your

I learned throughout the years to make time between sessions to prepare for my next one. I don't like surprises at my sessions. It's not for the meek, I have to tell you. Half my music budget is in the studio that day, so that's it. If it fails then I fail. That's the scariest part.—**Miriam Cutler**

I'm a big believer in giving players their music early whenever possible. They may look at their music in advance. They may not look at it. They may not need to look at it. But I would like them to have it so they can spend time with it if they choose to do so.—**Timothy Andrew Edwards**

When I'm preparing for a session, I actually try to meditate a little bit. When somebody comes in, they're only here for a few hours and they don't necessarily know me or the project. I don't want to bring my problems to the table or create a stressful environment. I want it to be a very comfortable atmosphere so that all they're thinking is, "Wow, it's really nice to just sit here and play." You can't necessarily do that with money anymore, and even if you can it doesn't guarantee you'll get the best performance. You get the best performance when you cultivate them as people and engage them.—**Nathan Furst**

mind and could pull you away from these duties needs to be set aside, as great music cannot be made without one becoming truly lost in the moment. Time is often hard to come by prior to a recording session. Make an effort to be well rested and properly nourished. Whatever it takes, prepare your body and mind so that you can be a pure creative during your sessions.

THE STUDIO

CREATE YOUR ENVIRONMENT

WHEN YOUR SCORE enters the production phase, the recording studio you use will have a huge impact on the final production value. In most cases that recording studio is your own. Even if you go elsewhere to record a portion of your music, there is always some production that happens in your studio. Production values matter even more in the final product than in demos, and the sonic qualities of your music have just as much impact on its effectiveness as the composition itself.

Your studio is your cave, and when deadlines are looming you will need to hide in your cave for extended periods of time. It is the nest in which your art is hatched, so spend some time nesting to make it as close to your ideal environment as possible. Your work space should be comfortable, stimulating, and technically sophisticated—able to put you in the mind-set you need to be in to be creative. You should take the design of your studio very seriously and do everything you can to get a million-dollar sound out of it.

There have been many studies conducted about work environments and how they relate to productivity and job satisfaction. There is a broad consensus that light levels, the presence of natural light, noise levels, color, temperature, privacy, and ergonomics affect worker contentment and productivity throughout time. These elements have minimal impact on performance in short-term scenarios, but with prolonged exposure they begin to have a measurable effect. Just as important is a worker's ability to customize his work space, which appears to have the same weight as all of those other things combined. When people are able to make a work space their own, they feel better about it and work better in it.

The way your studio appears to others also matters. The impressions your work space leaves on your clients will have an effect on their impression of you, your professionalism, and your success. Clients will often come to your studio for the presentation of demos, which is often the first time directors see their product in a form that is near completion.

When designing your studio environment do not forget to take the client's experience into account, even if you have only a small space to work with. Directors are often accustomed to seeing their film on computer screens and in small editing rooms. In almost every scenario, the sound quality of playback is lacking. If a director is impressed with the look and feel of your studio, sits in a comfortable spot, and watches his movie on a big screen with good sound his experience will already be better than average, and he will be naturally biased in your favor.

There is a lot to be said for a space that looks and feels like a high-end professional studio. A nice design aesthetic will show that you are doing something important and take pride in both yourself and your work. If you actively enjoy the space you are in, you will be much more relaxed and content when working there, which will be reflected in your work. There are many potential benefits that can come from having a professional and purposeful work environment, so give it some thought and design your studio to represent the type of career that you want to have.

FIND YOUR ROOM'S WEAKNESSES

One of the most important tools in the recording process is the room itself, so you need to find the sonic weaknesses in your room and compensate for them. There is good reason why certain recording studios and concert hall venues achieve favorable reputations for their rooms. Rooms for making music leave a sonic footprint, and that includes the rooms in which you mix and master your music. That's true even if you're doing an all-MIDI score and mixing completely inside your com-

> The better one can hear how they are shaping the sound of a mix, the better mix decisions they will make and the better that mix will translate to all other playback systems. A good listening environment that has been well treated with bass traps will help with this, as will good-quality speakers. The acoustic properties of the listening environment are of key importance.—**John Rodd**

puter because the quality of the listening environment will affect your mixes. Since every creative space leaves a mark on your art, you should give your studio the best sound possible.

Most composers do not design and build their studios from the ground up because it's cheaper and easier to adapt an existing space. The vast majority of home studios are rooms or garages that have been repurposed for music. Since they were not built for that purpose, there are always flaws and obstacles. When you convert an existing space into a studio there's obviously nothing you can do about the size of the room; however, by addressing the most common problems you can make it much more conducive for music making.

The most common problems that home studios face are outside noise, low ceilings, parallel walls, uneven frequency response, bass buildup, early reflections, and lack of room ambience. These problems are so commonplace that it's likely your studio suffers from all of them, but try to determine which are most problematic. If you are using the same space for both recording and mixing, you have the added complication of needing a dual function room that is neutral enough to allow both activities. The acoustic design of studios is a deep and complicated subject, but there are numerous things you can do to address the most frequently encountered challenges. Creating a perfectly controlled sonic environment is always going to be costly and technical, but you don't have to spend a lot of time and money to substantially improve the sound of a space.

ADD SOUNDPROOFING

Outside noise is probably the biggest and most irritating problem a studio space can have, and it's a difficult one to solve. The noise might come from traffic, voices, plumbing, footsteps, airplanes, gardeners, or anything else you can imagine, and it is never welcome. Unfortunately, this problem is particularly challenging when repurposing an existing space. The vast majority of composers don't want to build a new ceiling, floor, and walls to make a properly soundproofed space, so some compromises are necessary.

There are only two things that can stop sound: mass and dead air space. This is why studios that are built from the ground up have double-studded walls that don't touch with insulated air space between them. They also typically have floating floors and ceilings for the same reasons. You can't truly soundproof a room without getting into serious construction efforts, but there are some simple things you can do to address the most nagging problems. The weakest links in your soundproofing are always going to be your doors and windows.

Since windows have little mass they are bad at stopping sound. Even if they are weatherproof or double paned they usually have small air leaks, which provides a direct path for sound to travel. The last 1 percent, or perhaps 0.5 percent, of the air gaps account for a disproportionately large percentage of the sound transmission, so all air gaps should be sealed. Most windows are already sealed to the window frame, but many have small air gaps between the window and the structure. To seal these, you can put a bead of caulking around the edges of the window where it meets the frame. Sound can also sneak past window trim and through the window frame, so you may want to caulk the edges of your trim as well. The most problematic air gaps are those around the edges of windows that move. Although it's an imperfect fix, the best way to address this problem is to use weatherproofing solutions. Get weatherproofing materials with the highest density available and seal up your windows as best you can.

A fairly painless solution is to add a second window to the inside of the windowsill, making a double-paned window with an air gap of several inches. If the two windows are not the sliding type, they will obviously need to open in opposite directions. If the new window is a double-paned weatherproof window, it will serve you better. If it's a soundproof window it will serve you even better yet. Windows are only held in place with a few screws, so adding a second window in the frame is not as tedious as it may sound. Once you have two windows with all edges sealed, open the inner one and run heavy insulation around the edges between the two. This will absorb some of the outside sound before it has a chance to resonate through the inner window. By using a second window you'll have a functional window that still lets light in and is far more effective at stopping sound than before.

If the building is not yours or you want a more reversible solution, you can mount a piece of clear Plexiglas—the thicker the better—on the inside edge of the window frame. Plexiglas is less dense than glass and less effective at stopping sound as a result, but it's affordable. The only impact on the building is a few screw holes that can easily be patched. It's best to seal the edges with some kind of caulking, but if you don't want to leave marks on the walls you can squeeze foam weather stripping between the Plexiglas and the wall instead. If you still want to be able to open the window you can mount the Plexiglas on hinges and add a few latches to hold it firmly in place when the window is closed.

Doors are another major source of outside noise, and the causes and solutions are essentially the same as those for windows. Doors are a single membrane with no dead air space so they can readily pass frequencies, especially low ones. With a fairly small investment you can add a second door that opens in the other direction. It may sound like a sizable project, but it is, in fact, reversible. The impact on the building is the installation of a mere two or three hinges and a latch. A second door is a relatively minor addition that can render big results.

The new door should be a heavy, solid core door. When installing double doors you must be sure to seal air gaps, just as with windows. Each door has jambs on the sides and top, and it is simple to install weather stripping that will be tightly compressed when the doors are latched. The most troublesome air gap with doors is the one at the bottom, which can be quite large. There is no reliable solution other than adding a jamb to the bottom of the door as well so that the bottom has something firm to press against when closed. This extra piece of doorjamb, which will cost you only a few dollars at a hardware store, will make your double doors worth every penny. Once the air gaps are sealed and the dead air between your two doors can no longer escape into your studio you will see substantial improvements in your room's soundproofing.

COMPENSATE FOR ROOM DIMENSIONS

Low ceilings are a problem because they box in the sound. Even if you have a fairly large room, a standard eight-foot ceiling will make your space sound small. Sounds will be able to bounce freely between the floor and ceiling until they decay, and these reflections happen so rapidly that it is only slightly better than recording in a little bathroom. Carpet only absorbs high frequencies, so the midrange and bass will still suffer. Even if your ceilings are a bit higher than normal, the distance between the floor and ceiling is usually the shortest dimension in a room. Thus, that dimension is the most detrimental to the sound. The most highly respected concert halls and scoring stages in the world have extremely high ceilings. To make your studio sound better you simply need to remove your ceiling.

You can't create the large vibrating air space of a concert hall, but there are guerrilla tricks for removing your ceiling. All that matters in studio design is the perspective of your ears and the microphones, so it's possible to have a low ceiling that keeps you dry and warm and yet is sonically not present and doesn't reflect sound in undesirable ways. The solution is colloquially called a cloud, but instead of holding rainfall or data this cloud holds sound. If you add absorbent materials to your ceiling that are effective enough, your shortest room dimension will seem to go away. If it doesn't go away completely, the effects can at least be diminished.

When treating your ceiling it is not necessary to treat it all. The only portions that matter are those directly between your mixing position and your speakers, and the parts that could potentially be directly above a microphone. This is where you want to hang your clouds. The rest of your ceiling doesn't matter, because parallel reflections in other places are not going to reach your ears or the microphones. The smallest dimension in your room will suddenly be invisible to your ears and the mics, and your studio will sound better.

Parallel walls are another big problem. Parallel walls allow sound to bounce back and forth in a linear fashion, which is what makes a room sound small, boxy, and undesirable. A beautiful-sounding concert hall sounds that way because the reflections reach our ears at a variety of times spanning several seconds. When parallel walls are present the early reflections are sent back almost immediately, meaning the reflected sound and the source sound hit the ear almost simultaneously. This meeting of sound waves can sometimes cause phasing issues in the recording. The sound that parallel walls produce does not improve until the room is quite large. Even so, most large concert spaces and recording studios are designed with nonparallel walls because even on a grand scale it's nicer to avoid them. If you want to make your studio sound more like the great concert halls of the world you need to move your walls.

Thankfully there are cheap ways to do this as well because, once again, the only perspective that matters is that of the mics and your ears. To move your parallel walls you need diffusion. Diffusion makes sound bounce off a surface in a variety of directions, avoiding the immediate reflections caused by parallel walls. Efficient diffusion is valuable, and you should experiment with it before you begin to deaden your space with sound absorption. It's better to control the sound than remove it. The end result of diffusion is that the randomly reflected sound reaches your ears or the mic later, and while it's not the same as being in a concert hall it's much better than the sound of a small box.

In trying to achieve properly designed diffusion you must take into consideration sound frequencies and how they interact with the physical dimensions of your room, but this requires careful measurement and construction. If the shapes in your diffusion are varied enough you will get sufficient results. Diffusion can come from anything, and it doesn't need to be an official product from a company selling sound treatments. Although imperfect, book shelves filled with a random assortment of items are a low-cost and functional source of diffusion. You can also create diffusion from random wood shapes, art, deeply textured walls, furniture, or anything else you can imagine. The important thing is that the shapes of the surfaces are random in both size and angle so that a wide frequency range is affected.

When setting up your studio the room dimensions are crucial, and there are three things that are equally a top priority. Fire the speakers the long way down the room; put as many good, nonfoam bass traps as possible in the corners; and avoid listening from the middle of the room. The mixing position should be one-third of the way in, and the client should be two-thirds of the way in.—**John Rodd**

For your diffusion to have any noticeable effect you need to treat at least 25 percent of your parallel wall space, preferably more. Just as with your ceiling treatments, you should choose the locations for your diffusion based on likely microphone positions and your listening position when mixing. The back and side walls are common choices. If you don't trust the efficacy of your chosen diffusion add a bit more.

IMPROVE FREQUENCY RESPONSE

Uneven frequency response is a tricky and pervasive problem. Even if you were to record or mix in a completely anechoic space with no sound reflections, your mics or speakers would still have certain peaks and dips in their frequency responses. Uneven frequency response is completely unavoidable, and there is no way to achieve a clinically flat frequency response. The good news is that we don't need scientifically perfect conditions to do great work, and the most common source of uneven frequency response is not from the mics or speakers. The room is usually the culprit, and room treatments are much cheaper than new monitors or a new mic locker.

Every room has unique resonant frequencies that result from the dimensions and contents of the room, much like every half-filled bottle sings its own unique note. These resonances are usually much more prominent than those in good mics or speakers. The uneven response is usually from sympathetic resonances that allow certain specific frequencies to decay more slowly than the rest of the spectrum. The tricky part is that those resonant frequencies vary depending on where you stand in a space, and in a small space they can vary wildly. The solution is to analyze those frequencies and locations and add room treatments that address those specific frequencies in those exact listening positions.

Few people have the time or money to spend on such precise analysis because finding and targeting specific problem frequencies is difficult and technical. Broadband absorption with sound panels is the most common way to deal with room resonances. This is a much more accessible option than specific room analysis, and it can be pretty cheap. As always, mass is important, so get dense, thick sound panels and avoid buying lightweight foam products. The thicker the panel, the more sound will be absorbed. The goal is to reduce the room resonance enough that the spikes and dips in the frequency response become insignificant compared to the volume of the performance or the speaker volume. It doesn't cost a lot to significantly improve the flatness of your room's frequency response. A few high-quality sound absorption panels on the walls can address the issue of resonance quite effectively. If you add too many, the room will start to sound dead, and the silence will begin to cling to your ears. Just as with everything else in music, use your best judgment and taste.

When recording or mixing you should be listening to the sound sources and not the resonant frequencies of your room. Of all the room frequencies that can disturb you, bass frequencies are the most likely culprits. Bass response is particularly challenging because it's difficult to control, and the bass response of rooms and studio monitors is inconsistent as a result. As frequencies rise the response curves tend to smooth out, but low-frequency responses are all over the map for both physical spaces and speakers. Because bass response is such a common weakness in both rooms and speakers, it is highly advantageous that you control your bass in every way possible. Almost every small to medium room will have issues with its bass response, so it's a pretty safe bet that every home studio could benefit from bass traps.

Sound waves in the bass frequencies are longer and have more energy, so they require special consideration when treating your room. Bass has a tendency to build up in the corners of rooms and resonate outward. Hence, most commercial bass traps are designed to sit in corners. Once again, mass and dead air space are your friends, and when treating bass they're more important than ever. If you put the heaviest of your sound panels diagonally in the corners of your studio you will accomplish several things. The mass of the panels will absorb as much bass as possible, and the dead air in the corners will help the bass decay before it tries to pass through the insulation again. Light foam products will not help with bass management in any significant way. If you fill

Bass traps in the listening environment are of key importance. Many rooms that have been put to use as a listening environment will have significant issues, especially in the bottom end, and bass traps in the corners of the room will generally help the acoustics.—**John Rodd** your corners with heavy insulation your bass response will become more accurate and your mixes better balanced.

The sounds that we all like to hear on recordings are from large recording studios and concert halls, and those are the ones most reverbs emulate. It's unlikely that the room ambience of your studio is one that you adore and want to use as the primary ambience of your finished recordings. In excellent recording spaces room mics can replace reverbs, but few composers have the luxury of using such an approach in their home studios. Sadly, there is no perfect alternative to a large physical recording space. Listeners will not be fooled by an ugly bedroom recording with reverb. The goal in designing a home studio is to create a sound that is balanced and acceptable enough that it can blend seamlessly with a high-quality reverb. There are myriad reverbs to choose from, and if the raw audio is great it will accept reverb in convincing ways.

With careful consideration of the most common problems of outside noise, low ceilings, parallel walls, uneven frequency response, bass buildup, and early reflections, your lack of room ambience at home can be acceptable. With fairly minimal investment you can address these issues in substantive ways. The raw materials of your recordings will then be good enough that they can be molded into the most desirable shape in the mix. If you are using your space to do your mixes, your frequency response will be good enough that your mixes will translate to a wide variety of situations. The room you work in is your most important recording tool, so take the time to optimize it.

STRATEGIZE GEAR PURCHASES

The gap between professional audio equipment and consumer-level gear used to be enormous, and what once set a professional studio apart from a mediocre one was nothing short of a half million dollars of investment or more. The driving force behind the music industry evolution of the last couple of decades has been the development of cheaper and better gear. Thankfully, the quality gap between consumer gear and high-end gear has been substantially reduced. Investing thousands of dollars into gear today can produce a sound that would have cost tens of thousands of dollars a decade ago, and hundreds of thousands of dollars two decades ago. High-end gear is absolutely better and always will be.

Everyone will define "high-end" cost differently, but the price-to-performance ratio is currently at an all-time low. The very definition of professional audio gear has changed dramatically throughout the last decade. My usual advice to composers is to find a balance between cost and quality. Armed with a good recording interface, a few good mics, a decent acoustic space, and some knowledge of mic placement, skilled composers can make great recordings.—**John Rodd**

For discerning musicians there is no other way to go, but it's possible to get a lot of production value out of a small gear investment if you focus your money in the right places.

When buying gear for your studio the most important place to invest your money is the equipment that touches analog audio. Once the music is in your computer, software and plug-ins can effectively replace the mixers and outboard gear of a more traditional studio. When you are trying to do fast work that's high in quality and inexpensive, mixing in the box is the way to go; however, there are certain elements that can't be replaced by a piece of software, and those are the best places to invest your money.

Microphones are at the beginning of the recording chain, and there is no good substitute for a high-quality mic. High quality doesn't necessarily mean expensive, but mics are often pricey and it's not hard to dump a lot of money into a mic locker. There is an art to matching microphones with sound sources, and one of the fundamental skills in audio engineering is finding exactly the right mic and placing it in exactly the right position. Vendors naturally want to hype their product and create a gear lust. They have practically made the use of specific mics for specific situations into a kind of voodoo. The truth is, however, that there are numerous wonderful mics on the market. As long as you have a variety of mics chosen for versatility you will be able to record most anything well.

When choosing utility mics for a basic mic locker you should get mics that are clear and don't impose a strong personality on the sound. You should have a variety of dynamic mics and condenser mics. Dynamic mics have input levels that drop off quickly when the mic moves away from the sound source, so they are great for sound rejection when you have several mics open in a small space. They also tend to have a lower signal level and are often good choices for loud sources. Condenser mics are valuable for the opposite reason. Since they are powered mics the diaphragms are more sensitive, allowing them to pick up more detail and produce hotter levels.

You should also get some variety in small-diaphragm and large-diaphragm mics. The majority of large-diaphragm mics are condensers, but some large-diaphragm dynamics are available too. Small diaphragms are lighter and move more easily, which stereotypically means that they are brighter, crisper mics that provide more detail and less warmth. Large-diaphragm mics move more slowly because of their weight and size, so they have a tendency to somewhat smooth out the sound. Depending on the music you are recording, you may want to record a given instrument with a large diaphragm one day and a small one the next, so it's valuable to have options.

If you record certain types of music consistently you may want to have a character mic or two. This may be a great vocal mic, a kick-drum mic, a tube mic that's slow and sounds dark, a pencil-sized omni that's so crystal clear it's practically clinical, or anything else you can imagine. If you will use it frequently enough that it will pay for itself, it's worth having around. Your character mics will likely get less use than your utility mics, so invest in a nice array of all-purpose microphones before you start channeling money into mics that deliver a specific sound.

Preamps are the next step in the audio chain, and they're a crucial one. If you run a mic through a cheap preamp and then through one that costs several thousand dollars, you will easily notice that there is no comparison. With mic preamps you almost always get what you pay for, but there are some great options on the market that provide a good value for a fair amount of money. Just like with microphones, you should aim to own a variety of preamps. A bank of eight identical preamps is probably less valuable than four different pair. Each preamp has a certain sound and specific strengths and weaknesses, so you want options. It is best to get a mixture of preamps made with integrated circuits and discrete components, as well as some made with transistors and some with tubes. If you have a sampling of preamps from these broad categories you'll have a good variety of sounds available to you.

Just as with your mics, don't buy character preamps until you have a collection of unobtrusive utility preamps that you are happy with.

After the preamps comes the analog-to-digital (A/D) conversion. This is one area where the cost has dropped dramatically in recent years. High-quality A/D conversion is extremely important because poor conversion distorts audio in subtle ways. Some converters have soft or hard limiting in case you overdrive the channels. This may or may not be desirable to you, so choose accordingly. There are three important factors when measuring the quality of converters, and two of those factors are almost universally present today. Every decent audio interface can run at a 24-bit depth and a 48k sample rate, which is the industry standard, and sample rates up to 192k are common. Adequate resolution is always available today, even on budget equipment. Since technological developments took care of the first two criteria, the most important thing to think about is the clock.

The clock determines the timing of those 192k sample points. If the clock is accurate you capture an accurate representation of the sound, and if it's unsteady you get a pixelated version. This pixelation is called jitter. Because resolution is always available today it's safe to say that any audio interface with a reputation for having a steady, low-jitter clock is going to serve you well. If you already have an audio interface and it accepts word clock you can probably improve its performance by adding an external clock. Doing so can make subtle improvements to good gear and dramatic ones to cheap stuff. Your A/D conversion is like the image sensor in a camera, and recording audio with a cheap interface is like taking a photo with a cell phone camera. You should invest in a good audio interface. Thankfully this no longer requires breaking the bank.

Once the sound is digitized and inside your computer, you can operate your studio extremely inexpensively. There are amazing software

> You can create a very fat, rich sound on crap equipment. It's very handy to have a ninety-piece orchestra in a big studio, but if that's not in your budget you've got to do something else. Looking for production value can be getting one great player and one great microphone. That should be within the budget.—**Stewart Copeland**

tools for audio processing, and they closely rival their hardware equivalents. The added benefit, of course, is that you don't need a studio full of wires, and you can carry your mixing gear in your laptop. Funds are always limited because recording studio gear can be a bottomless pit of expenses. If you're trying to cut costs, plug-ins are the way to go. For the price of one hardware compressor you can get several dozen software compressors, again providing you with a variety of tools for different tasks. They won't be quite as good as the real thing, but they will get the job done. When trying to build a cost-efficient studio, anything that you can do with software should be done that way.

When it leaves your computer, audio is converted back to analog, and you should consider investing in the rest of your signal path. Your amplifiers and speakers are the most important pieces of gear in the studio because they are the lens through which your music is viewed. Ironically, they are also typically the weakest link in the average composer's setup. You should buy the best amps and speakers that you can't quite afford. It is absolutely worth extending yourself a bit in those purchases because every piece of gear and software in your studio is subservient to the sound that comes out of your speakers. There is no question that you want the best, most accurate, most high-quality speakers you can justify.

When buying speakers, don't forget to think about low frequencies. Music that will be played in a theater will go through subwoofers, and you need to be aware of what your music will sound like when frequencies as low as 20 Hz are easily amplified. If you don't have a subwoofer

The greatest music is great because of the theme or concept, not because of the rack of compressors it went through. That said, experimenting with new gear and instruments can be really inspiring.—**Bill Brown**

you will have no idea what is going on in that deep bass range. When you take your music to a dub stage or theater it might shake the entire room or provide no subwoofer content to speak of, and you really won't know until you get there. If you are mixing for film, video games, or trailers you must be in complete control of your deep subbass frequencies.

Get a subwoofer to augment your speakers, and make sure that it is tailored to match their frequency response. Don't just install it and forget it. You won't really benefit from it unless you spend some time measuring and adjusting the frequency response in your room. You should adjust the volume and placement of the sub to give you the most flat frequency response possible. In a perfect world you would have a flat frequency response as low as 20 Hz, just like in most movie theaters. If you can come as close to that as possible you'll be able to control the entire spectrum of your mixes and have a much better idea of how your mixes will translate to other settings.

When collecting recording studio gear the most important elements are always going to be those that handle analog audio, and thankfully they can be reduced to the front and back end of the audio chain quite effectively. Everything in the middle can live comfortably in software and produce excellent results. Your recording signal path leading to the A/D conversion and your playback will always be crucial. If you get a utilitarian collection of mics and preamps, an audio interface with a good clock, and excellent speakers, your gear collection will be well on its way to producing amazing results. You can continue to add gear infinitely and achieve better results when you do. Nevertheless, if you invest too much money, music becomes a hobby instead of a profession. Focusing on the fundamental areas will simplify your setup and give you the most production value for your money.

PERFORMING

RECORD YOURSELF

I T'S ALWAYS BEST to have live performances in your recordings whenever possible because everyone has access to the same sample libraries. Unfortunately, budgets usually don't provide enough funding for you to hire all the players you want. One of the best guerrilla tricks for saving money on your score is to record yourself performing on many instruments acoustically. MIDI is a bit void of personality, so the more you layer yourself performing, the more acceptable and human the MIDI underneath will seem. You won't have to hire musicians. You won't have to schedule studio time. You'll be completely in control of the performance, without having to explain anything. And you can make it happen any time you want. Supplementing your MIDI and the performers you were able to afford with your own live performances can add depth to your productions and save you money at the same time.

Another valuable side effect of consistently recording yourself is that throughout time you will develop a certain sound that people will be able to immediately identify. Think of Thomas Newman's piano sound. It is a distinctive sound, and an astute listener can identify Tom's music from just a couple of piano notes, long before his writing style has a chance to be observed. When asked how he arrived at his piano sound and how he has maintained such a consistent sound throughout the years, the answer was surprising. The expected response was a technical one about the engineering of piano recordings, but his reply was far simpler and more elegant. He always uses his own piano, he places the mics close, and he plays quietly. That's it. The distinctive piano sound that has helped define Tom as a composer, a sound that has been widely copied, is a natural result of his personal performances on his personal instrument. He has been playing the same piano for decades, and it became a signature sound. If you make a point of always using your primary instruments in your scores your music can develop a similar signature.

Each music school requires pupils to specialize in an instrument—and for good reason. It is far better to be excellent at one skill than mediocre at several, and schools could not hope to teach competency in several instruments during the short period of time students are enrolled. Even if not part of a school's requirement, most musicians have one instrument that they play substantially better than any other. In the context of a score with a limited production budget, your chosen instrument should almost certainly be an important element. Your passion, love, and training are sizable resources that shouldn't be overlooked. Not all scores require an orchestra. If your primary instrument is the accordion, you should work that into as many of your scores as you can. Whatever your specialty, it can add production value.

You presumably spent many years of your life playing and practicing your instrument before deciding to become a professional composer. You should exploit that time and expertise to the fullest extent. There are many ways to extract sound from any instrument, and you should be in full control of as many techniques as possible. If piano is your instrument, you can collect keyboard instruments of all kinds to expand your sound palette. You can also get into prepared piano, use the piano resonance as a reverb, pluck the insides, and so on. If guitar is your instrument, you can collect guitars, banjos, Dobros, basses, mandolins, and other stringed instruments and use them creatively. If your instrument is flute, there are thousands of different types of flutes. As an instrumentalist you have skills and habits that are uniquely yours, and a guerrilla film composer needs to get as much mileage out of those talents as possible.

BECOME A MULTIINSTRUMENTALIST

There is obviously much to be said for specializing in an instrument and becoming an expert or virtuoso at it, particularly if you achieve expert status in many different styles; however, in the commercial world of professional composing being a generalist can almost be as useful as being a virtuoso. Most of the time your budget will be uncomfortably tight. No matter how big your budget, your goals will always be a little more grandiose. You will always want to get the most for your money, and a great way to accomplish this feat is to record yourself on as many instruments as you can play. This is not to say that you need to become a one-man band, but the more layers of yourself you record and the more varied those layers, the more diverse your music will sound and the more color it will have. Recording yourself as a multiinstrumentalist will also help your demos sound more finished and therefore help your director approve them more readily.

As a broad generalization, music for media plays a subsidiary role to the dialogue or drama at hand. It can be memorable and sophisticated, but it rarely has moments in which technical brilliance takes the spotlight. For the most part, music for media simply needs to communicate the appropriate emotion and nothing more. If a piece of music is going to have a supporting role and appeal to a wide audience base it usually can't be overly complicated. There is a good reason why simple textural pieces proliferate in scores and the Brahms string quartets are rarely heard. Functional music intended for mass consumption needs to be accessible. There are plenty of exceptions, and composers like Max Steiner, Jerry Goldsmith, and John Williams have been writing sophisticated and virtuosic music throughout the history of film; however, simpler music has a dependable home in media, and it will always be in greater demand than virtuosic music.

When the end goal is music that is stereotypically uncomplicated it becomes desirable to be a multiinstrumentalist. It's hard to be truly brilliant on more than one instrument, but it's possible to be good on many. That diversity, which is sometimes frowned upon and is a real disadvantage in the serious worlds of academics and competitions, is a big advantage to working composers. If you play multiple instruments you will write for other instruments better, can record yourself in many different contexts, can create a more sophisticated sound, and can avoid hiring some musicians. If you want to squeeze the most out of your production budget, perform on your primary instrument, along with several others. The more layers of yourself you record the less MIDI and fewer musicians you'll need, so multitracking yourself is a great guerrilla technique.

FAKE IT IF YOU MUST

The assumption thus far has been that you are indeed a specialist in your instrument and you have an adequate proficiency with several others. If neither of these assumptions is true you can still multitrack yourself playing lots of different instruments. It may not be advisable to fake your way through a lead part, but many of the supporting parts can probably be faked quite successfully. It will be a great learning experience, and there are a multitude of studio tricks available to help polish the performance. Composers and performers heavily edit their recordings, and you should use every trick available to you to increase your production values and save money.

When you record yourself playing an instrument on which you are limited, you end up writing specifically for the few things that you are capable of doing, and there's nothing wrong with that. As always, limitations can be an effective inspiration. If complexity is needed, it can come from other instruments. The added acoustic timbre of the simple part will augment the recording in a way that samples cannot. In many instances you can effectively use the timbres of instruments in your recordings with only a beginner's technique.

If the pressure of the schedule is bearing down on you or you need brilliant performances you should hire the best players you can afford. Using great players is the only way to get a great performance quickly. If the performances for those particular parts don't need to be brilliant and you have plenty of time to do lots of takes and editing you can stretch your budget and record yourself on some secondary instruments. Depending on your skill level, the loss in time and quality may be big or small, so the decision of whether to record yourself is one that has to be made contextually.

Collecting instruments is to musicians what collecting brushes is to artists. Almost all composers have a wide assortment of instruments in their studio to augment their recordings in a variety of ways. Many composers collect specific types of instruments in an effort to consciously mold and differentiate both their sound and artistic voice. The variety and individuality that is born from a specific collection of instruments and a specific set of skills and weaknesses is extremely valuable.

USE EVERY STUDIO TRICK

The tools that producers use to clean up performances are no secret. The first and most important one is isolation. If you're recording numerous layers of yourself isolation comes naturally because there is no bleed between tracks. If you plan to play along with other musicians and clean up your performance later, make sure that your sound doesn't get into their mics too much. Isolation lets you focus the microscope of your DAW on small issues and correct them without affecting the rest of the recording. If you plan to heavily edit certain parts you should record them separately whenever possible.

When paying for musicians or studio time, doing endless takes is quite costly. When you're alone, the only cost is your time. You can do an endless number of takes, which is helpful when playing an instrument that is not your forte. For sections that are particularly difficult, you can set up loops and record the same small segment indefinitely. If you need to record over and over again to get a passage right you are essentially practicing an instrument with the microphone open. That gives valuable focus and objective perspective to your practice. The deadline provides motivation for your practice, the recording is the best judge of how successful your practice is, and the time spent is bound to benefit you in the future.

Whether you are recording yourself or other musicians, you will always edit multiple takes into the final recording. Take comping is very routine, but when playing instruments that are not your primary ones you may need to do much more comping than normal. Perhaps you find the chord transitions on piano or guitar difficult, or the finger span on a bass too large for comfort, or you can't seem to get the groove on a percussion instrument to sound right. Whatever the reason, you may need to separate your takes into tiny pieces to build something usable. Don't be afraid to do microsurgery to get the best results.

Quantization moves MIDI or audio relative to the absolute time grid inside a sequencer. Quantization used to only apply to MIDI, and if you wanted to quantize audio you had to manually snip and shift each suspicious beat. Luckily there are now a number of great tools that can quantize audio effectively, and they basically do the music editing for you on the fly. If your rhythm isn't perfect or you want to align your performance with a particular groove it's not overly hard to fix it in an automated way. Audio quantization is reasonably new to the recording scene, but most of the major DAW platforms can do it, and there are great third-party plug-ins for it as well. And quantization doesn't have to be used only as a repair tool after the fact. You can also plan to use it in advance, wait for a particularly expressive performance, and move on knowing that you'll be able to make it work.

Another type of audio processing changes the timing of audio, but instead of aligning to the sequencer's grid, it aligns to another piece of audio. The original plug-in, Vocalign, was only useful for vocals. Melodyne and others like it can now do this kind of alignment with a wide variety of audio types. It is useful in creating a rhythmic consensus between tracks when instruments have been layered many times to create size and depth. It can also help solicit a better groove or feel from a performance. This is something you still need to do with plug-ins because most DAWs don't offer the functionality. There are several excellent tools that can perform this kind of alignment processing, and having one is invaluable.

Pitch correction, once an expensive and sometimes frowned upon form of audio manipulation, is now extremely common and built into the major DAW platforms. It can be an incredibly helpful tool in making a slightly imperfect performance fall into line and save you the trouble of doing take after take. When used discretely for isolated pitch problems, pitch correction can be completely invisible, and the end result is stunning. It's a fantastic productivity tool that allows you to truly "fix it in the mix." When used more forcefully, it can become a special effect. Although the popularity of its use as an effect has waxed and waned, it has been a common effect for decades. Pitch correction was once only possible on monophonic recordings. Fairly new advances in pitch correction and audio manipulation allow digging into polyphonic recordings and adjusting the pitch and rhythm of specific notes. The new generation of pitch correction software is a massive step forward, making it a more viable producing option than ever before.

Sound replacement is another great tool. If you are working with percussion, there are several great plug-ins that will allow you to substitute an instrument of your choosing for the one that was recorded. MIDI triggers for drums have been around for a long time, but they were never much more than sensors. The new breed of sound replace-

If you're a flutist you should put your flute on every cue. Learn how to record yourself playing the flute, and do it a lot. Mark Isham is a perfect example because he's a damn good trumpet player, and he puts trumpet on everything. I'd like to see more composers do that. Especially when you're younger and you don't have the budget to hire players, it's a necessity. You can always edit. The difference between myself and a virtuoso guitarist is only about two hours of editing.—**Craig Stuart Garfinkle**

ment plug-ins replace sounds on the fly, and they take latency into account so that there is no delay. You can mic a beginner's drum kit in a small room and replace the kit with the best-sounding sample library in the world. Sound replacement technologies allow you to focus on the emotional feel of a performance, capture the expressive humanity of it, and make decisions about the instruments and production after the fact. It's a fascinating reversal of the producing process and another great studio trick to help get the most out of your performances.

The tools that help us sculpt our performances are a bit like stencils or other guides in visual art. There is absolutely nothing wrong with using them. A good producer is well aware of their benefits and knows the tools well enough to use them effectively when the need arises. The first and most fundamental connection we have with music is the actual making of it, so record yourself as often as possible.

PRODUCING

CHOOSE YOUR PRODUCTION'S SCOPE

IT USED TO BE that if you had a budget for six players you wrote music for six instruments and found creative ways to contain your score within those limitations. Thankfully the confines of exclusively acoustic recordings are long gone, and composers are free to write for any size and type of ensemble via MIDI no matter what budget they have to work with. Although the budget no longer prescribes limitations in instrumentation, it still dictates what size production is possible when recording the score.

You always have the ability to write MIDI for any ensemble imaginable, but that doesn't necessarily make it a good idea to write beyond your budget's production limitations. It might be a great idea and a real lifesaver, because if you're working on a sports commercial that needs epic orchestral rock in twenty-four hours it's the only way to pull it off; however, it could also be a terrible idea because you might find yourself hopelessly chasing the production values of film scores that had one thousand times your budget. It's one thing to augment your live recordings with MIDI and quite another to completely overextend yourself. Most experienced composers prefer to decide early on what kind of production they will have and then write music that fits appropriately within the scope of the production.

129

> On the game *Journey*, Sony couldn't afford to hire orchestra for the entirety of the game. To compensate and avoid MIDI, I made the orchestra an emergent component of the dramatic arc of the score. By the end of the game it's a fully orchestral score, but it starts out with cello solos echoing amongst a whole bed of electronics. I often end up doing that sort of thing. I put all my eggs in one basket and figure out how to approach and depart from that moment to build an arc that helps the drama of the story.—**Austin Wintory**

There will be times when you are hired to fake the sound of bands and orchestras by yourself, and there's nothing wrong with doing so as long as that is the expectation. There are many mediums in which large live ensembles are rare, and yet the sound itself is frequently used. The sound of MIDI orchestra has become idiomatic of lower-budget productions of all kinds. It's like the sound of punches in movies. You know it's unrealistic, but you have heard it so much that you readily suspend your disbelief. As long as the music is allowed to have a slightly contrived sound and a less sophisticated and refined performance, there's no problem with using MIDI. Oftentimes a director will prefer a MIDI orchestra to a more realistic-sounding small ensemble. In those cases, use the full barrage of MIDI and have fun.

That is not typically the expectation, however. Many times large ensembles are faked with MIDI because there was no money to record the real thing. In those cases it's questionable whether fake instruments are the best solution, particularly because MIDI is somewhat synonymous with low budget. When the use of MIDI goes beyond augmentation of live recordings and becomes wishful thinking it is usually not the best solution. It's possible that a large ensemble of MIDI will sound like a

> A good score needs to sound like there is no more expensive version of that music that could exist. When you look back on it later you should never have a thought like, "If we'd only had a little bit more money." I don't want to punish directors because they can't afford a live orchestra, and in most circumstances I would be if I used samples.—**Austin Wintory**

> When I write I'm not fantasizing that I have a 100-piece orchestra and writing a cheap MIDI score, because no matter how good it gets you can always tell. I ask myself what's right for the project and how I can make it sound good. Always. I have never submitted a score in my life that doesn't have something recorded on it. If there's air running through a mic it sounds better. Period.—**Laura Karpman**

cheaper production than a smaller ensemble of live players. Ambitious MIDI programming could actually be a detriment to the production.

Naturally, context will determine what is appropriate, but when the number-one expectation is realism consider lowering your sights and not writing for a ninety-piece orchestra. Composing within the reasonable scope of your music budget might produce a better and more appropriate result. When MIDI and other electronics are used not as budgetary band-aids but are chosen for their strengths, the end product will be substantially better. It will most likely serve the entire project better too, because the scope of the score will be on par with the scope of the project at large. More often than not this will involve some recalibration of the expectations of the music both on your part and the part of the director, since aspirations are consistently larger than budgets.

> The need for size can be a problem, because MIDI can't replicate the combined efforts of an orchestra. You can find ways to go in another direction, but that's certainly a constraint. Not every movie wants size, but when the film is a large canvas it's a major challenge to score with limited means.—**Peter Golub**

> If a music budget can only afford a limited number of live musicians, then I always start by trying to find a musical approach that can be achieved with the number of musicians we can have. I try not to attempt something musically that we can't afford to produce. In an ideal scenario, I'd like it to feel like if we had $10 million to produce the music, we still would have done it with this number of musicians because it's right for the film.—**Ryan Shore**

CHOOSE YOUR PLAYERS

When deciding how to produce your score you need to make decisions about your recording locations and players. Those two choices will probably have more influence on your final production values than any other factor, so they deserve careful consideration. A MIDI cello will never compare favorably to a live one. A good cello player in your studio will never compare to Yo-Yo Ma in Carnegie Hall. We can now squeeze more production value out of each dollar than ever before, but the truth remains that you get what you pay for. When you are planning how to record and with whom, you should spend every penny you can afford to hire the best players. The fastest and best way to a high-quality finished product is with high-quality performers and recordings.

There are a lot of things that computers and electronics are naturally good at, but replicating acoustic instruments is not one of them. The earliest attempts at synthesizing acoustic instruments with electronics began in the early 1900s. Despite all the ingenuity of mankind, more than a century later there is still no contest between the best sample libraries and the best musicians. Composers use MIDI because it's a practical tool, but real players always bring something to a recording that virtual acoustic instruments cannot. Live players give unique performances that are never duplicated. They can be lost in a moment. They have inconsistencies and imperfections. They make additional noises that get recorded. They have breath, emotion, and life. In short, they bring humanity to recordings, and that humanity is irreplaceable.

You will always produce a better score if you record as much human performance as possible. The nature of the instruments is not important. A skilled theremin player will solicit more emotion from that

John Williams, the most wonderful composer among us, he stands on a box with a stick and has the entire orchestra in the room at the same time. That's ideal. That's wonderful. That's gold. On the other side you have situations where there's no orchestra, no live players, and you do the score all by yourself. Then you have something in the middle, which is where most scores are written these days.—**Charles Bernstein**

> When you really want your music to be good the key is to not rely on the technology, because the humanity is what really makes it good. Even if you only have the budget for one musician, use that one musician.—**Craig Stuart Garfinkle**

purely electronic instrument than most composers could extract from a theremin plug-in. Every composer interviewed for this book and probably every successful composer out there will agree that music is better when the performances are captured instead of artificially re-created. Even if the part is a synth bass line or an electric organ, play it in, and don't quantize your MIDI perfectly. The subtle differences cannot only be perceived by fellow musicians. Your clients will hear it and feel the difference viscerally. Even though they may not know why, the live performances will speak to them more effectively.

The quality of the room and the gear you use is secondary to the performances you capture in your sessions. If your budget is tight and you have to choose whether to spend it on your players or slightly better studio context, prioritize the players. No matter what your budget and ambitions, try to record at least your principal instruments live. When your featured instruments have the humanity of a live performance, the ear more readily believes the artificial layers underneath it.

When working with players you don't necessarily need to have them come to your studio, nor do you need to meet at another studio. Remote collaborations are very common, and for many kinds of music they can work extremely well. The number of home studios has been steadily increasing for decades now, and there are many excellent players who are capable of recording themselves at home. It can be a fantastically efficient way of collaborating. You both work in your separate studios on your own time, and after a little back and forth you download finished performances of your music. This model is not only for low-budget productions and players. There are many well-respected studio musicians who do this to get a little more work and serve a wider client base.

It is extremely common in the scoring world to have a base of sampled instruments and a handful of live players on top of it to make the MIDI sound more realistic. Sometimes it is samples augmenting the

> My job as a composer is to find the exact intersection between what we can afford and what we creatively want, because they do intersect. If you think of supply and demand curves in economics, they always meet somewhere. Similarly, what we can afford and what our creative musings lead us to will also meet somewhere. You can produce the perfect score for that budget, you just have to figure out what it is. I've found it often ends up being the most creatively stimulating work, because you wouldn't think that way if someone said money is no object.—**Austin Wintory**

players and sometimes it is the other way around, but it's a common approach to balancing budget and quality needs. You get the cost savings of MIDI and the quality of live performances, and at some point it's either good enough or it's all you can do. There are naturally limitations on how much realism you can achieve when trying to create a large ensemble sound, but it's a middle ground that's so run of the mill it's more the rule than the exception.

Restrictions in the scope of your production will obviously get in your way to some degree, but like all restrictions they will also foster ingenuity and creativity. You always need to find ways to work around your budget and maintain your artistic integrity. The key to that integrity of production, just like in writing, is to embrace the restrictions instead of pretending that you are in a more grandiose situation. Use your creativity and intuition to create the perfect music using the resources you have. The solution may not be immediately obvious, but limitations can force ingenuity and sometimes lead to greatness.

> The first time I did a large string group in my living room it wasn't because I couldn't afford a studio, it was that I literally didn't have the time to prepare and move my sessions from my studio to another one. I decided do to it in my living room because it would still sound better than it would have without. Much to my surprise it sounded great, ergo a new discovery that my living room is a fabulous string room. Necessity is the mother of invention.—**Laura Karpman**

TAKE OFF YOUR COMPOSER HAT

The quality with which music is performed and recorded during record-ing sessions has more impact on the final production values of the score than anything else. If your score is brilliantly performed and recorded it will be difficult for you to mess it up completely, even if you mix it yourself on headphones. On the other hand, if your recordings are me-diocre, even the best mix engineer won't be able to fix them. Mixing and mastering will help you polish the recording and bring out the nuances of it, but they can't create quality that isn't there in the first place. The key to making great recordings is to be a great producer.

The world of music for media never adopted the record industry's habit of separating the roles of artist and producer. There are few pro-ducers dedicated to scores for film, television, and video games, and most composers produce themselves. Other members of the music team certainly contribute to the recording's production value, most notably the sound engineer and mixer, but if you have them on your team they work under you and within the parameters that you establish for bud-get, time, and studio location. As the producer of your scores, you will always have more influence and power over the production values than anyone else.

Producing is nothing like composing or performing. A producer is often a dispassionate third party who can objectively critique and im-prove the music, and that objectivity is a valuable asset. You will never be able to take a truly objective perspective of your own music, but the more analytically you can think about it, the better. To produce well you need to be able to see the big picture, and to do that you must distance

A composer who is producing their score needs to constantly make creative decisions that will shape the music. They have to find a way to deliver a good-sounding end result regardless of their budget and schedule. The more a composer knows about music mixing, the better they can produce a superior end product. That's true if they are doing the mixing or if they are hiring a professional music mix-ing engineer, because the composer has to give revisions and over-all sonic guidance to the engineer for the end result.—**John Rodd** yourself somewhat from your composition and the minutiae of it. To be a great producer you need to set aside your pride of authorship and think about bettering the music instead of creating it.

PUT ON YOUR PRODUCER HAT

To take your music to a higher level during your recording sessions you need to assume the various roles of a producer. As producer your most important job is artistic director—and sometimes cheerleader. You must provide the focus and direction for the both the studio work flow and the performances of your musicians. You need to be deeply connected as a listener and musician to guide and coach your players toward the ideal expression of your ideas. During recording sessions you are the leader, teacher, and source of inspiration that focuses the artistic vision. You must discern the essence of the music, bring focus to those elements, and strip away elements that distract from it. Third-party producers provide a critical ear, experience, and objectivity that artists often lack on their own. When you are producing your own music you need to strive to provide the same for yourself and your musicians.

The most fundamental way to focus your musical intent is through arrangement. Many producers believe that their main job is to simplify, carving away layers of music the way a sculptor carves away stone. It can be helpful to take a few steps backward and look at your composition as large building blocks instead of seeing the gritty composer details. By adding and removing layers of music you can change the overall effect by focusing the ear on particular elements.

While in a session your ears have to be turned on and working at red-alert status at all times. You can't afford to miss the subtle details that come from the technical or performance sides. You need to hear the mic selection and signal path just as clearly as you hear the articulations and intonation of your players. Once the players leave the studio you're stuck with whatever material you captured, so you need to be hyper-aware of details and engage in laser-focused listening the entire time. The training of your ears only comes through experience and lots of time spent experimenting. The best producing experience comes from doing it in the studio, but if you're listening critically you can learn a lot from recordings too.

The producer is also the project manager, encompassing all the logistics of scoring, from software updates to equipment rentals to final delivery. You need to be in complete control of the master schedule and ensure that every step of the process stays on schedule. You must clearly communicate that schedule to everyone so that expectations stay in line with reality. You need to plan and maintain the budget. You have to assemble your team. No matter how big or small your team, you need to be the head of communications within it and the main liaison to your collaborators outside of it. You also need make sure that your team members always have what they need to stay productive and on track. There is a lot to manage. You need to be extremely organized and make sure that none of the details slip through the cracks. You are responsible for the mundane organizational details. Within those details lies a structure that is needed to support the artistic integrity of your music.

A producer is the financial manager of a production, and a big part of managing finances is being skilled at negotiating. There is rarely anyone else managing the budget in score production, and you need to have tight control of the finances. This is especially true because most productions today are package deals, and costs that exceed the budget come out of your pocket. It's not hard for productions to go over budget, especially when you have larger groups of players and a larger team in the studio. You might negotiate ways to get a single player into your studio cost effectively, or shop around for a studio that will give you good rates because they're trying to fill their calendar, or buy soundalike mics for a third of the price of the name brands. On a larger scale it could mean negotiating your contracts with production companies, bargaining for equipment rental, finding a cost-effective mastering engineer, or anything else. Composers often have to put on the business negotiator hat, and many aren't great at it. Remember that if you negotiate well, you can make more money in those minutes than you can in many hours of writing music. Smart negotiating is really where you make your profit and how you keep a production's budget lean.

Communication skills are key because producers are supervising and overseeing the recording process, much like a director guides a film shoot. They need to connect with everyone in the studio to instruct them, communicate the intent of the music, inspire the players, and manage the variety of personalities present. Without good communication the recording process can be slowed or get misdirected, and it

> Part of my job as a music producer is to keep things completely focused on the task at hand, which is to actualize the music so that it works perfectly with the picture. We've worked for months together, the filmmaker and I, to make it perfect. The recording can't go off track from that, and it has to be an actualization of our particular creation. There are an infinite number of decisions, so you have to be assertive, let go of things, and move on as soon as you hit your goal.—**Miriam Cutler**

can be frustrating for everyone when needs or goals are not well understood. Few things will help achieve speed and quality in the studio more than clear communication, which, of course, saves money.

Producers must make many decisive choices about what will excite and move the music. The decisions are both practical and artistic, ranging from choosing signal path and mic placement to assessing phrasing and emotional content. Money and time are always an issue, so decisiveness and clarity of purpose are important, and they translate directly into high production values. Good producers know exactly what they want and know how to achieve it, and they move forward confidently when they have met their goals.

KNOW THE GEAR

As the producer you are the intermediary between the musicians and the gear. Depending on how you are recording you may or may not be operating the gear yourself. In either case you need to be the person with the ideas. The best recordings are made when the producer has already envisioned the end product at the time of recording and each track is individually produced with that end product in mind. If you are also the engineer you need to implement your sonic concepts. If you are working with a recording engineer you must clearly communicate the concepts to him. In either scenario, you need to translate your intent as a composer into reality through the means of recording studio techniques.

Along with focusing the vision of the production you need to fully control the sonic qualities of your recordings. The effect a recording has on the listener is only half about the writing. The other half is about the sounds, production value, and textures. The qualities of the

In the early 2000s music was by and large very meticulously produced, as evidenced by hip-hop, trance, house music, and film composers of the time. It was heavily edited, tightly controlled, and totally flawless. Now we've swung the other way, and widely popular bands like the Black Keys and many other indie rock groups keep the chair squeaks, the page turns, and other little flaws. People suddenly have a newfound appreciation for recordings that are produced in a way that's less sterile. The umbrella of acceptable production decisions has gotten a lot wider, and the benefit is that your production decisions can be more a part of your aesthetic expression.—**Austin Wintory**

sounds are just as important as the musical content. Even with fairly inexpensive equipment it is possible to make decent recordings. Thus, production values are not only about getting the best sounds. You need to choose the specific types of sounds you want for creative reasons and find technical ways to produce those results. If your ensemble is small you might have the luxury of exploring during recording sessions and experimenting with different sounds or approaches. As your sessions grow, time becomes more valuable, so the larger your sessions the more important it is to know what sound qualities you want and how to achieve them. Choosing the production approach for each sonic element is a subjective and creative process, but implementing those choices is a highly technical one.

When you also assume the role of recording engineer, a technical and methodical approach is essential regardless of the artistic context. When engineering it's important to be very familiar with the gear you are operating. You already have your hands full managing the sessions from a practical and artistic standpoint, so you don't want to waste any energy fiddling with gear or problem solving technical glitches. If you are engineering you should be so fluent with the tools that you don't think about them, you just use them to accomplish what is necessary. It's only through a deep familiarity with your gear that you will be able to free yourself to be an effective creative leader during the sessions.

POSTPRODUCTION

12

MUSIC EDITING

KNOW THE MUSIC EDITOR'S ROLES

MUSIC EDITING can mean many different things, including compiling takes, synching scores, cutting songs, and organizing paperwork. A music editor's tasks are closely related to composing and include many technical aspects of audio preparation and delivery. On larger productions, composers can benefit immensely from working with a music editor; however, the budget is often too small to justify the cost. In those cases, as usual, the guerrilla composer has to do the job himself.

A music editor's tools were once very different from a composer's, and that meant that the composer and music editor were generally two separate people. Thankfully the razor blades, hole punches, and Auricle machines that were part of the editor's trade are long gone. Today the work is customarily done in Pro Tools, but all DAWs have similar capabilities and can get the job done. Because the composing platform can also be the music editing platform, it's possible for composers to take over the job and do so effectively. The fact that separate tools are no longer required makes music editing more accessible to the masses of composers, but the job remains a specialized and technical one that can be quite time consuming. Although all composers these days have the tools required for music editing, they don't necessarily have the experience and knowledge to do the work efficiently and at the highest level.

There are many advantages for having a music editor on the composer's team. In addition to working directly with the composer, the music editor is the point person for all the licensed music in the movie, and the production team benefits from knowing all the music will be handled properly. A key factor adding to the difficulty of music editing is that the picture can change at any moment, and it often does, even through the final dub. The music and all the sound then need to be conformed and edited to resync to the picture. This in itself can be a major challenge for the music editor or composer doing their own music editing. When you add all the additional responsibilities of temping, spotting, song editing, on-camera music editing, managing score demos for the director, conforming and delivering all the music, and making cue sheets for royalty reporting, it can become a very challenging job.—**Steven Saltzman**

Music editors are normally paid by the production company, and the money does not come out of the music production budget or the composer's fee. In fact, the Motion Picture Editors Guild requires that the music editor not be paid from the composer's budget; however, the prevalence of package deals is making it increasingly common for composers to hire their own music editors, particularly for indie films and documentaries. When you are forced to hire your own editor it may appear to be a financial burden, but that's not necessarily the case. Music editors can save you time and increase the quality of the production, both of which could quickly translate into cost savings.

Music editors provide technical support that allows you to focus on the creative side of writing, but they do more than that. The music editors that I've worked with are really fine musicians with really great ears, and they have great knowledge and sensibility about how music works with picture. I can run cues by them before I play them for my director. We'll discuss scenes, try music options here or there, and it's a creative collaboration. It's like having a friend with great ears in the room with you to bounce ideas off of. I consider them creative partners, as well as technical people.—**Peter Golub**

I work with music editors, but I inevitably do a lot of music editing myself too. A composer is constantly editing his own music.—**Stewart Copeland**

I do all of my own music editing. I would love to have help, but that's something where there's nothing in the budget—ever.—**Miriam Cutler**

I hire a music editor to do all of my session prep because he's much more fluent in Pro Tools than I am. He'll make sessions that we can just fire up and hit record. He'll change all of the I/O and get it all set up for whatever studio we're going to, and then it's good to go. He will always be better at that than I will because I just won't commit the time to learn Pro Tools to the degree that he has.—**Austin Wintory**

When you have the luxury of working with a music editor you will be able to delegate a sizable number of tasks. By taking care of the technical work, interfacing with your clients, and giving insightful musical advice, they can free you up for the more creative and big-picture jobs. Editors can work on several projects at once. Hence, they tend to work on far more films in a year's time than a composer can. It's a safe bet that your music editor has worked with a wide variety of composers and has experience you can benefit from. If you're not sure how to best use editors, they will be able to guide you and make it as easy for you to delegate tasks to them as possible. If you are composing for the short forms of commercials, trailers, or music libraries, music editors are usually not necessary.

LEARN THE EDITOR'S TASKS

If you are going to do your own music editing, there are many chores that you will be unable to delegate. The job starts with the spotting

session, in which you decide with the director precisely where music
will play throughout the film. That meeting is usually run by the director or composer, but the music editor is typically the one taking notes
and making detailed spotting notes after the fact. Without an editor
you have to document that meeting yourself and have a good intuition
about how to spot music that is appropriate for the picture. You have to
communicate well with the picture editor and speak the picture editor's
technical language. You need to properly prepare clicks and, if you're
using them, punches and streamers for your sessions. You need to
handle the documentation and note taking while you produce your live
sessions. If the picture changes you will have to conform the music to
it. You need to deliver the right formats to the dub stage or production
company. Finally, you'll need to know how to make and submit a cue
sheet to the performing rights organizations.

The job of music editing has been an important one in the film business ever since movies had sound, but it is still extremely rare to find
any university or trade school courses that focus on the topic. Music
editing skills, if they are taught formally at all, are usually taught as incidental elements of other courses. The craft of music editing is almost
entirely taught on the job, as a practical skill. Composers who have
focused on other areas of study are unlikely to truly understand the
subtleties of a music editor's work.

Video game music is handled differently from film and television. In
games there is no dedicated music editor, and the composer is always
heavily involved. The composer typically delivers the music in several
layers that represent different game states. The number of layers and
complexity of assembling them depends entirely on how the music will
be implemented in the game. The composer and his team help assemble
the audio deliverables, and there can be incredible amounts of editing

There are very few schools that teach music editing. There are more
postproduction audio programs popping up throughout the country,
but they often focus on all the other sound elements in a motion
picture, such as location recording or editing dialogue and sound
effects, and often leave out music editing. If you can find a course
on music editing it can teach you the basics, but it's best to learn
by doing and mentor with a music editor.—**Steven Saltzman**

and organizing that take place during this stage. Once the music has been delivered to the game company, their audio director is responsible for audio implementation. They might spend a considerable amount of time further editing the audio to suit the game's needs, and they will often create new cues from the source material the composer delivers. The composer is responsible for the music editing prior to delivery.

MAKE GREAT SPOTTING NOTES

The spotting session is important to the beginning of the scoring process because you and the director must be in agreement about the dramatic and musical goals. You need to have a consensus about exactly where music is going to start and stop, what the music is going to do, and how much music is required. Sitting down with a director to watch the film for the first time can be a lot of fun, but because of its implications to your work, it's also an important meeting that needs to be carefully documented. The process is somewhat technical, but it also has substantial creative implications.

The task of creating spotting notes and more specific timing notes used to be a huge and detailed task for music editors. Those notes were long, technical lists chock-full of precise numbers. These days much of that information can initially be contained in the marker window of a DAW, particularly if there are adequate notes on the markers; however, there can still be great value in keeping detailed spotting notes. The marker window, with its timings, cue titles, hit points, and notes, should

I recommend that composers working on their own pay attention to the details spotting notes can provide. After the spotting session with the director there is value in knowing each scene that has music and what the director or producer feels about the emotion of the scene. If there is already temp music for them to respond to in the film, then this is particularly true. Get in the habit of using proper cue numbers and time codes. Spotting notes can be used for organizing the recording session, music changes, and the final music cue sheet. All the composers that I work with appreciate a more detailed spotting note list in this way, even if they started with their own simplified version.—**Steven Saltzman** be formalized in a separate document that can be further developed. Only after carefully reviewing the spotting notes will you be able to create a realistic schedule for your work.

Spotting notes can evolve and grow into a master cue sheet that helps you keep track of titles, versions, instrumentation, duration, start times, and dramatic notes. That list can expand and also track the stages of the cue's progress as it moves through composition, demos, approval, revisions, orchestration, score prep, recording, mixing, and mastering. Each cue will progress at a different pace, and you will vastly improve your organization and efficiency by keeping that document current.

USE TEMP MUSIC EFFECTIVELY

One of the first music editing jobs for a film is the creation of a temp score. Temp music is incredibly helpful in the production because it gives the illusion of a completed film. In the early stages it can help the director and picture editor get a better feel for the emotional content and pace of the film as they work. As the film progresses, it can help refine the tone and communicate the director's intent to the composer. Later in the process temp music can function as a score in screenings for the production company, test audiences, and marketing people. Although the composer community often grumbles about temp tracks and the creative problems they can present, they are valuable and functional tools.

Temp tracks are one of the important areas in which a dedicated music editor can substantially elevate a production and speed up the scoring process. Music editors have a good working knowledge of how music works in film and what kinds of music work well in different dramatic situations. To do their jobs they also need to have a large library of music from which to draw. The best music editors know their library well and can quickly find the perfect music for a scene. They are both film music connoisseurs and historians, and they have specific knowledge of the musical vocabulary of genres and composers. The creation of a temp score is a highly creative, subjective, and interpretive process. It can be likened to painting with large brushstrokes. If the job is done well, you can follow and refine the concept, but if the job is done poorly, you may have to start from scratch with a new concept. A good temp score also takes the music budget into consideration, uses music

The temp music is often a love–hate experience for the composer. They need to listen to it, but at the same time they must write their own music that they feel is right for the film. The most important elements to glean from a good temp score are which cues the director likes and dislikes, the tempo of the music, the style and orchestration, the musical emotional arc of each cue, the thematic choices that were made, and any hit points the temp addresses.—
Steven Saltzman

that is within the appropriate scope, and does not create unattainable expectations. The music editor has the ability to help you get on target from the very beginning of your writing process. This can be priceless in time-pressured situations.

If the film production or your package deal can't support a music editor, the job of creating a temp score usually does not fall on you. This is one of the rare instances when you are typically not required to bear the additional workload and responsibility that's forced by a smaller budget. When money is scarce, the picture editor usually creates the temp score. This is both good news and bad news.

The good news is that additional responsibility is avoided. The bad news is that the picture editor probably does not have the music library, fine-tuned ears, or skill to create a temp score of the same quality. Less experienced directors and picture editors have a tendency to use too much music or put it in inappropriate places, which can make scoring more difficult because the temp score is a road map for you to follow. Since temp music never makes it into the final version, the film editor's work might be good enough to help the film progress, but it usually will not focus and shape the musical vocabulary and dramatic arc in the same way as an excellent temp score.

PREP YOUR DAW FOR RECORDING

Sometimes you will record at home in your own studio and with your own DAW. In these instances, you may not have much prep work to do before you record. Your I/O can already be set up, your sequence can be tracking with the picture correctly, and you won't need to build new sessions for each cue that have your audio, video, markers, MIDI, and tempos. Recording using your writing setup makes your session prep simple.

Even if this is your situation, you should take the opportunity to triple-check the session and make sure that it is set up correctly. As discussed earlier, frame rates can be tricky, and controlling this esoteric detail is one of the most important tasks of a music editor. Large errors in frame rate are easy to catch and fairly uncommon. If your video file is in twenty-four frames, you will quickly notice when your session is running at 29.97. If your frame rate is wrong it will most likely be wrong by 0.1 percent, which is the NTSC pull-down rate, and you may only see the effects of that drift when you try to marry your recorded music to the final picture. That small percentage will make your music drift out of sync surprisingly quickly. There are many reasons why this error could happen, and they are not all within your control.

Everyone on the postproduction team needs to be clear about the frame rate of the source material, work prints, and final delivery. They are not always the same, and there are plenty of reasons why any one of these might be different from the others, either intentionally or unintentionally. The music editor must understand the subtleties of time code and the conversions that may need to happen, ensuring that the composer can record his music with correct sync. If you are working without a music editor you need to carefully supervise the frame rate details. Be wary of the possibilities for error and the NTSC pull-down trap. If you have a bad Quicktime export and don't know it until after recording, you will be forced to time stretch your audio.

The other most common tasks that a music editor will need to carry out in recording session prep are ones that will come much more naturally to the guerrilla composer. Printing clicks to audio is simple to do. Organizing the existing audio for playback and headphone mixes is also simple busy work. If new tracks need to be set up and I/O adjusted, it's also not a huge task. Your markers and MIDI will already be in your sessions. When recording in your own studio, it's usually quite easy to handle these music editor's tasks.

It gets more complicated when you take your music elsewhere to record. Your audio and MIDI needs to be exported cleanly and your sessions rebuilt in the platform in which you will record. That usually means Pro Tools in this context. Specific knowledge of the other studio is required to make sure that your I/O, headphone mixes, and other sends are working properly. Luckily there are always ways to import the I/O settings and additional tracks on which you will be recording. Once you get one cue fully set up in the new studio you can import that I/O and the new tracks to your other sessions. It's not a difficult process, nor is it an artistic one, but it needs to be done.

When working in outside studios your MIDI system will be unavailable. If you have not already done so, convert your MIDI to audio, which you must do at some point anyway. Import the video again into every cue and confirm that the sync is correct. Also confirm that the bar numbers in the sessions match the bar numbers that your musicians will see on paper. Working in outside studios is a little more technical and setup more detailed, but if you can't afford a music editor the skills required to set yourself up are very accessible.

EDIT THE TAKES

In a more traditional setting or larger-budget one, there is usually a music editor present at the recording sessions to make copious notes about each take that can be referenced during postsession editing. If you don't have a music editor at your sessions, you will need to devise a method for keeping track of which takes are your favored ones. Some people comp their takes in real time or during breaks so that there is a complete and finished performance to listen to by the end of the session. Other people take notes to keep track of what has been done. Others make notes inside the DAW via region file names, take names, or other internal labels.

It doesn't matter what method you use as long as you follow a consistent method of note taking. If, after a recording session, you are left with piles of takes and no notes, you will most likely have to listen to each take again when comping them together. Accurate note taking during your recording session will save an enormous amount of editing time.

When comping takes together, there are really only two secrets to achieving great results quickly. You need to know the software you're using and the material. It is much more efficient to build an edit based on good notes and only go back to listen to the other takes when you discover something that needs to be patched up. Knowing your software will help you to edit quickly, particularly the keyboard shortcuts that can speed up your editing processes. Edit as soon after your recording sessions as possible so the information will be fresh in your mind, and make an edit based on your take notes before you start to spend time listening back.

The editing is often more involved than simply choosing good sections and cutting them together. It's not uncommon for rhythm, pitch, timbre, dynamics, interpretation, attacks, releases, and room noises to need editing too. These are highly context sensitive, so there is no way to quickly describe how to edit your takes to perfection. Something you can reliably count on is that audio editing will always sound better than audio manipulation. Editing in a note or phrase with better pitch will always be a better choice than using pitch correction software. Editing to clean up rhythms will always sound better than audio quantization plug-ins or time stretching. There are some amazing audio repair tools on the market, but the final product is much better when the audio is good on its own, without processing, because audio processing leaves behind artifacts.

On occasion, and for a variety of reasons, it is necessary to reedit the music after recording. The most common cause is that the picture was changed or music is needed in a scene that previously didn't have it. It could be a dramatic choice in which you or the director want to reshape a scene, either for emotional reasons or to avoid dialogue. It's also possible that you didn't have the time and money to score all the scenes specifically and need to edit new cues after a recording session to stretch your budget as far as possible. It's not unusual to have to reshape music after recording it, so leave time for it in your schedule.

FINISH AND DELIVER

When time is in short supply, new cues can be built, new scenes filled, and credits covered, all with music editing. If you have recorded in layers, which almost everyone does, it requires minimal effort to change some of the layers around and make a cue work well in a couple different places. If the editing happens in the raw tracks instead of the final mixed audio you can easily add or remove layers, which makes it more like arranging than just music editing. This technique won't always work, but once in a while you will be able to fill a scene with edits of

There have been a couple times when I got called for a TV movie, and, I'm not kidding, they wanted eighty minutes of music in seven days. There's no way I'm writing eighty minutes of music. It's physically impossible. What I'll do is purposely write a theme that has a lot of levels to it. When I start a new cue I may bring in all those tracks, knowing that I'm going to start stripping away stuff. That's sort of like composing with music editing.—**Nathan Furst**

your own music instead of composing, squeezing some mileage out of your budget.

After you have completed your writing, made your recordings, and edited your takes into brilliance, the picture will change. This is basically a guarantee, so don't be fooled by the old rule that composers are supposed to work to a locked picture. The editor can export a final locked picture the day before the final dub, and everyone knows it. The picture is always in flux, and there's nothing you can do about it. When the picture changes you need to conform your music to it. Because music is so dependent on time this always creates extra work. You should always add a little extra time into your schedule for changes. You also have to surrender any idealistic ideas you may have about your music and its perfection because you'll need to chop it up and force it into a space where it was not designed to go. During this process it's nice to have a music editor because the music editor will hear the intent of the music and cut it to fit without remorse. If you aren't able to hire a music editor, adopt the same ruthless attitude toward your music.

Prepping your sessions for the mix is the next task for a music editor. If you're still in your studio and mixing on your own setup,

Often in a television series a composer may write a few episodes from scratch. Then, as the season progresses, they can begin to reuse some of the music that had been written for previous episodes. As their library grows these pieces can be recut for future episodes. Essentially this is when the composer puts on the music editor hat, and that can save them writing time and production costs.—**Steven Saltzman** this again may be incidental. In fact, if you're planning to mix in your own studio, you should already have a mix template in place by the time you begin writing so there is nothing to set up. If you'll be mixing outside your studio, the sessions will need to be prepped for the mixer, which again requires some specific knowledge of the other studio. The mixer will need all the sessions laid out in the same manner, with the same track names, and set up to use the same I/O. Just like before the recording sessions, make sure that mixing can start as soon as your sessions are opened so you don't waste time. Sometimes the setup can be as straightforward as adding outputs to tracks; however, many times it will also involve grouping and bussing things in a way that suits the mixer's taste or his specific setup. Just as with your recording session prep, there are ways to import your I/O and any necessary tracks. Be consistent, be thorough, and confer with the mixer to make sure that he has everything he needs.

After the mix is done a music editor will typically prep the sessions for delivery and then attend the film's final audio dub. If you're working without a music editor you'll need to deliver the audio yourself, and it would be wise to attend the dub. The dub is the last chance for the music to be cut or for changes to be made to the volume, EQ, balance, and so on. If you have delivered stems, which is common, it is particularly important for you to be present. Stems give more control, but it may also be necessary to protect the music from bad edits and remixes. There is almost always a need to advocate for the music's volume because it tends to get buried. If any music editing is necessary you want to be sure that you approve of how it's done and how your music will be presented in the finished product.

The last step of finishing is making the music cue sheet. Cue sheets are often mishandled by small production companies. Because the cue sheets become legal documents, it's crucial that the music editor or composer oversees them. Although the performing rights societies prefer that the cue sheet come from the production company, composers are increasingly assuming this responsibility. That is particularly true for productions that do not have a music supervisor or music editor. An accurate cue sheet is the source of all future royalties, so it's important that this paperwork be filed promptly and accurately. It is best if you don't trust the filmmakers to do this and better yet if you shoulder the cue sheet duties.

Sometimes a small indie production will approach my song catalog, and they don't have any clue about how music licensing works or what a music cue sheet is. Composers need to stay on top of the cue sheet. They may need to create the cue sheet themselves to ensure that all the music is credited properly, including third-party source cues, and that the cue sheet is submitted to the performing rights societies.—**Cindy Badell-Slaughter**

The cue sheet needs to include the cue number, cue title, total time of each cue, publisher, composer, PRO affiliations, royalty splits, and specific type of music usage. Along with the composer's music it also needs to include any source music that was used in the film. The PROs provide sample cue sheet templates, and they must be filled out meticulously to ensure proper royalty payment. The logging of music is a rather dull administrative task but an important one that cannot be overlooked.

MIXING AND MASTERING

PURSUE MIXING SKILLS

WHEN MIXING your score you have the opportunity to make it shine or let it fall flat. Even if you are working with a mix engineer you're not free from responsibility. You can't take off your producer's hat until the final masters are done. The mix is where your score fully comes to life, so the production values and attention to detail are paramount to success. Mixing is like sculpting in the sense that you are taking the raw materials of your recording and carving them into a final shape. The tools you use, the level of detail, and the level of expertise employed make a big difference in the impact of the final product.

When you begin mixing your score, it's important that you turn off your composer brain as much as possible. Composers do not listen to music the same way a mix engineer does. Instead of listening to melodies, harmonies, and form, mix engineers are listening to timbres, gestures, and dynamics. They listen to sound spectrums and colors, but they listen to them in terms of frequency as much as instrumentation. They listen to performance nuances but also to the nuances of the various audio processes they employ. Although mixing is a subjective and artistic process, it is also a methodical and scientific one. The part of your brain that wrote the notes and is connected to the composition itself will not help much in the mix because mixing has nothing to do with composing and everything to do with sonic sculpting.

> The foundation of producing good-sounding music is critical listening. When using faders, panning, automation, compression, EQ, reverb, or any other audio processing, decisions are constantly being made during the process. Hundreds of tiny decisions all add up and make or break the sound of the end result.—**John Rodd**

Mixing music is a bottomless craft. It can be pursued and practiced for a lifetime and with active learning the entire time. Composers don't have the luxury of devoting that much time solely to mixing, and most don't even have the luxury of formal training or apprenticeship in it. Because composers have an incredibly wide array of responsibilities they have to be a jack-of-all-trades. The problem is that their music needs to compare to and compete with music mixed by expert craftsmen who have devoted their lives to mixing. Today's mixing tools are fairly inexpensive, but they are only as good as the user, and becoming a good mix engineer is a sizable endeavor.

Although it's possible to dedicate an entire lifetime to the craft of mixing, it doesn't take nearly that long to achieve an understanding of the fundamentals and a solid proficiency. The core concepts can be learned fairly readily and refined as you continue to gain experience. As with everything else in music, improvement comes from practice and repetition.

LEARN THE FUNDAMENTALS

Just as with the rest of music education, you can learn to mix either from formal studies, an apprenticeship, or practical experience. All three methods have value, but unlike the rest of music studies, there seems to be a consensus about the best way to go. Most engineers will agree that practical experience trumps everything else. That's not to say that universities, trade schools, and books have nothing to offer. They provide concentrated and focused learning in a short period of time and teach theoretical concepts, both of which always have value; however, the cliché "If you've seen one you've seen them all" doesn't apply anywhere in mixing. Every piece of music is different, as is every instrument you'll record and every studio you'll work in.

It's important that composers develop a solid understanding of and experience with the fundamentals of mixing because the composing and mixing processes are intricately linked. The majority of composers mix while they're writing, going back and forth between the two processes so that their demos will sound good. Once a cue is recorded most composers do their own mixes. Mastering is a highly specialized craft that requires different rooms, equipment, and software, but many composers find themselves mastering their own music as well.

The reason the fundamentals of mixing are so important is that you can't mix music with your eyes. That may sound obvious, but it's a surprisingly easy trap to fall into. There is a vast amount of visual feedback coming from software and plug-ins. There are meters, settings, and curves to look at everywhere. Many people fall into the trap of mixing music visually. The very act of staring into a computer monitor while attempting to mix creates a level of distraction that can lull you into passive listening. The visual feedback is highly relevant and gives valuable information about how everything is working, but it should not be the basis for decision making. You should make mix decisions based on what you hear and only use your eyes to put a name to what you did and to help you remember it.

One of the great things about the fundamentals of mixing is that they are totally free to implement. The necessary tools are already in every DAW on the market. No matter what your studio setup, you can get a better sound from having a more thorough understanding of the fundamentals. No matter how expensive your gear, you will not get a great sound unless you know how to use the tools well. Knowledge is power, and in this case knowledge is a better final mix. Mastering the fundamentals of mixing will help you mix faster and better without having to spend one extra penny.

> I never wanted to be an engineer or mix my own music. It wasn't even something composers thought about because when I started we had a different job. Now we've been forced into engineering, recording, and mixing our own music, and it has to sound great.—
> **Garry Schyman**

Level Management

One of the most important fundamentals is that of level management. In digital audio, there is no saturation of circuits or tubes like there is in analog circuits, and no soft distortion. Instead there is an absolute maximum volume level and harsh distortion when that level is exceeded. If a sound wave is too large for the digital dynamic range, the top of the wave will be cut off by the guillotine of the digital threshold, resulting in a sound wave with a squared-off top. Mixing is additive, and each new track increases the overall level. Your final mix with all tracks combined needs to fit comfortably under the digital threshold, so level management throughout each step of the mix is important.

The first waves to be chopped by the guillotine are the transients, the fast, high-intensity sounds that begin a waveform. Transients usually live in the first few milliseconds of a sound, and digital level meters move much more slowly than that by design. If digital meters moved in response to every sample they would show only a blur. Thus, they are designed to react in a slower and smoother manner. If transients pass quickly enough they may not register on the meters, and you might unintentionally use the guillotine on your audio. This could introduce distortion without it being seen visually on the meters, and if it's subtle you also may not hear it. Audio should come nowhere near being clipped unless you are consciously using it as an effect.

Avoiding the guillotine means giving yourself enough headroom. Your headroom begins during the recording process, when your individual tracks should have their average levels at about two-thirds of the full dynamic range. This gives plenty of volume and plenty of headroom at the same time. A common mistake composers make is recording with their levels on each track approaching full scale, meaning that there is a good chance that some transients have been chopped off. It also means that during the mix process the faders will need to be toward the bottom, where small movements make big changes, or you will have to put trim inserts on the tracks. It's easy enough to turn the tracks down, but once your transients are chopped by the guillotine nothing can be done to get them back. It's best to turn down your gain before anything is recorded, as you'll simultaneously make the mix easier and capture better audio.

You should have headroom in each step of the audio signal path and every plug-in that processes the audio. Be sure that you are not peaking and introducing distortion into the sound in the signal chain. When you run your levels too hot, the distortion might be subtle and it could go unnoticed, but it will still reduce the audio fidelity. Many interfaces, plug-ins, and DAWs introduce hard limiting to avoid harsh digital distortion, which can be helpful, but it also camouflages technical errors. To preserve your transients, your final mix should have at least five dB of headroom, and more is acceptable. If you work to keep your tracks and your mix at moderate levels, you will preserve your audio fidelity.

Panorama

One way to make a mix more clear and effective is to carefully control the pan and consciously place each track in a specific physical place in the left-to-right spectrum, or the 360-degree spectrum if you are mixing in surround. The intent of pan is to give each track exactly the right physical location to help it interact with some tracks and avoid others. Two instruments that tend to step on one another sonically will be much easier to hear in the mix if they are not in the same physical space. To blend sounds do the opposite and put them on top of one another. Pan is setting the physical stage left to right, and to a certain degree it determines which sounds will need to blend and which ones will not interact as much.

Pan is not only the left-to-right adjustment that you see just above the fader. When working with stereo sounds, proper control of pan means you are also controlling the width of the sound. The effects of adjusting the stereo image width are completely contextual. In one situation a narrow stereo field may suddenly make a sound more audible, and in another the narrowness may bury it beneath other sounds. An electric guitar with two mics or a string section sample might have an extremely wide stereo image, which might take up too much space and obscure other audio in your mix. In a different musical context you might need to spread the stereo image of the same sound wider to avoid obscuring audio. The context dictates everything.

Any time you are working with stereo audio you must consider the width of the stereo image, in addition to where the center of that image will be placed. If you only have a single pan knob at the bottom of your mixer you are only adjusting the center point of the sound. You will need to insert a plug-in to control the stereo width. If your

DAW doesn't provide an easy means, there are plenty of plug-ins to compensate.

Focal instruments should usually be in the center, and less important instruments can be spread freely throughout the physical spectrum; however, bass sounds should more or less stay in the middle. It is much more difficult for our ears to determine the specific spatial location of low-frequency sounds, and those sounds also carry the most energy. This is why subwoofers typically sit in the middle without disturbing the stereo image of music. It is most common to keep the low-frequency elements of the mix toward the middle, partly because they tend to be foundational, important sounds, and partially because we want to preserve our mix headroom by distributing the low end evenly between left and right channels. Bass management is always a challenge, and it gets even more difficult to manage if the bass energy is coming from just one side.

Depth

Every mixing board has a pan knob on it, but pan only covers one dimension of the stage. A great mix also carefully controls depth because the apparent distance of a sound from the listener has a profound impact on the mix. It's only with good control of pan and depth together that you can truly control the use of space in your mix. The front-to-back dimension of a mix is trickier to control, but, thankfully, it has gotten easier in recent years.

Reverb is often used by itself to create depth, but reverb alone only creates a poor illusion of it. If you have a close-miced cello track and you put a huge hall reverb on it, the end result for the listeners is that they feel as though they are sitting right next to a cellist who is playing in a big room. Adding reverb does not create distance from the listener, it only increases the apparent size of the room. When controlling depth you are deciding how far away from the listener the cello player should be. Unfortunately we don't have convenient near and far adjustments on our mixers because depth is more complicated than pan.

There are four main elements required to make something sound farther away. The first is a delay of both the sound itself and the early reflections of that sound. Delays of milliseconds can make a surprisingly large difference. The second is volume because things that are farther away get quieter. The third is pan because the farther away something is the more monophonic it sounds. The stereo spectrum of a distant sound is much narrower than one close by. The fourth is EQ, because high frequencies dissipate more quickly than bass sounds. These four elements, combined and carefully controlled, can create a sense of depth. The difficulty lies in the fact that they need to be controlled in specific ways that are closely related to one another. Creating depth with delay, volume, pan, and EQ quickly becomes a technical and fiddly process.

Fortunately some wonderful plug-ins have been developed in the last few years that handle all four of these elements simultaneously—and handle them well. Many reverbs now integrate stage positioning into the plug-ins, which means you no longer need to know how many milliseconds it takes for sound to travel thirty feet. The new breed of stage positioning plug-ins let you drag an icon across the stage and control both pan and depth at once—a brilliant new ability in mixing. The four parameters of depth are always linked the way they should be. It is simple, visual, and usually far superior to any attempts you would make on your own to replicate the same thing.

These stage positioning plug-ins are the fastest, best, cheapest, and easiest way to get depth in your recordings. You should get the best one you can afford because it makes getting physical separation and depth in your mixes simple. You can visually move instruments around your virtual stage, and the adjustments are no more difficult than moving the pan knob. You don't need to understand how it works and don't need a signal chain of four processors to make it work. For the guerrilla mixer this is without a doubt the best solution.

If you don't have a stage positioning plug-in and still want to create depth, you can do a pretty good job of faking it. Although reverb is not depth, people have been faking it that way for quite some time, and it can work in a pinch. To push a track backward in your mix, turn it down, reduce the width of the stereo image, roll off the high end, and start adding reverb. Add the reverb last because you want to control the elements that genuinely create depth first. The reverb has some delays in it, and they are rather complex, so it can do the trick. As long as you are conscious of the four elements of depth you can fake it fairly well without sophisticated delays or fancy plug-ins.

Equalization

A smooth, even-sounding mix makes good use of the entire frequency spectrum without overcrowding it. Careful control of the frequencies of each individual element makes space in the spectrum for all of them to coexist. As you EQ your tracks, think about the frequencies that are characteristic of that sound and about other tracks that use the same frequencies. You may need to reduce those frequencies elsewhere to make room for the character of the track you're working on. Moreover, think about the less-characteristic frequencies and ask yourself if they might conflict with other tracks. You may want to pull those back. Each instrument needs a clearly defined place on the EQ stage so that all of them can be heard well. EQ can be used in many subtle (and not so subtle) ways, but in its most basic function, it offers a highly effective method of cleaning up mix elements to help them sit together better.

Fixing the EQ of an individual track when it's soloed can be a helpful starting point, although you should have already gotten the best sound during the recording process. Nevertheless, the big picture of mix EQ matters more. Getting impressively boomy percussion might be inappropriate next to your bass, and getting wonderfully sizzling cymbals might be inappropriate if you have a singer and need to hear consonants. A track that is perfectly balanced in the mix may sound like it is lacking something when soloed because that missing sonic space is filled by another element. EQ is about the staging of the entire sound spectrum.

The guiding motivation behind your EQ adjustments should be the sharing of the spectrum. This means that you need to listen to your music in a different way than you did while composing. Listen for missing frequencies or overcrowded ones, properly diagnose them, and move tracks into or out of those spaces. When a frequency band is crowded decide which track needs that band most and carve those frequencies out of the conflicting instruments. When your mix has a hole in it, determine which track is the best candidate for filling that space and boost those frequencies. For most musicians the process of listening to frequencies instead of notes is very foreign, and it takes a lot of practice to get good at it.

Overcrowded EQ is usually a bigger problem than holes in EQ. Combined with the ever-present goal of keeping the mix at moderate levels, subtractive EQ is usually more effective at fixing issues than boosting frequencies. Our ears register EQ boosts much more readily than dips, especially if the region being treated is very narrow. A narrow midrange boost, for example, may sound like a wah-wah pedal stuck midway, whereas a cut at the same frequency and of the same width might be much harder to hear. The reason for this is that our ears always bias themselves toward louder sounds, meaning that subtractive EQ is a better choice because the end result has a better chance of sounding natural. At first, subtractive EQ may be harder for you to hear and identify, but most great engineers will agree that it's the best starting point. Each track will have a certain range in which it speaks most eloquently, and you want to give it space to speak in those frequencies. Some instruments will already have a specific frequency range, but many have a broad spectrum that needs to be controlled.

When one track is taking up too much space it is harder for everything else to cut through the mix. If you have tracks with a particularly broad spectrum you should be prepared to cut nonessential frequencies. The solution is to either carve out some holes to make space where necessary or add shelving EQs to bracket the sounds within a certain frequency range. The point is to carve away enough conflict that the tracks can speak readily in their most characteristic frequency range. These kinds of EQ adjustments will bring an incredible amount of clarity to the mix, while also allowing individual tracks to be heard in the most ideal manner.

Compression

Compression is one of the most valuable tools in mixing. It is also one of the less readily mastered elements, and thorough control of it is one of the skills that sets great mixers apart from the rest. Compressors are dynamics processors that control the volume of a track, but they do it in minute ways. Putting a compressor on a track can be likened to adding volume automation with unique fader moves every few milliseconds. Contrary to popular belief, compression is not simply a way to make things louder, nor is it a substitute for the proper use of the other elements of mixing. Although it can raise volume, so can the faders on your mixer. The true value of compression is the way in which it can modify and control the dynamics of the recorded performance. The purpose of compression is control, not loudness.

You shouldn't be mixing with your eyes anyway, but your eyes are less helpful with compression than with any other element of mixing. You are mostly flying blind when using compressors. They act so quickly that the meters will never show you everything that is happening. As you change the settings you will not get enough visual feedback to help you make objective decisions about the results. Good control of compression must come from understanding the controls and deep, critical listening.

To learn to listen for all the control points of a compressor and how they affect your music the only thing you can do is spend time fiddling. If you experiment enough you will begin to hear the individual controls of a compressor as separate processes. There is no other way to learn other than by spending time experimenting and listening, but a few key areas help make the controls more obvious for learning.

If you are focused on learning about attack and release times, choose a sound that has both a sharp attack and a long decay, perhaps a piano or a snare with a long reverb. If your compressor has a knee adjustment, try it on both soft and aggressive sounds, perhaps strings and percussion. A soft knee is nice for smoothness, and a hard knee is good for volume control. The compression knee can be tricky to hear, and you need to know when it's helpful and when it's not. Any kind of audio is good for learning about threshold levels and compression ratios. Take a variety of different audio tracks and experiment with the entire range of compressor settings to learn what each one does on its own. Do this in a methodical way, and take notes if it helps. Compressors are sophisticated audio processors, so try to focus on one setting at a time until you begin to hear how it affects the sound.

There are no shortcuts for learning dynamics processing. The only path to mastery is to throw a lot of music at as many different compressors as possible and learn from the results. More than any other aspect of mixing, good use of compression requires experience. Lack of experience is the reason that composers, who have to multitask their mixing skills, along with all their other responsibilities, can't get the same quality out of their compressors. Compressors are also an area where additional investment in gear pays off. If you can set yourself up with a nice selection of aftermarket plug-ins you will be much better off than if you use the generic ones that come with your DAW. No matter what tools you have, you should feel free to jump in and compress with authority because it's the only way to learn.

Reverb

Reverbs are an important element of mixing, and another factor that separates great mixers from the rest is the expert use of high-quality reverbs. The way effects and processors are used can make or break a mix, and since reverbs are the most common effect they deserve special mention. Reverbs usually add the characteristics of an acoustic environment, but sometimes they add simulations of electronic or mechanical reverberation instead. The reason reverb is so important when mixing is because in most projects the individual tracks don't share a common sense of space. As a result they sound scattered rather than seeming to belong to the same recording. The primary objective of reverbs is to connect tracks that have no inherent connection by giving them some shared acoustic characteristics. Reverb can, of course, be used as a special effect as well, but its primary function is ambience and cohesion.

Reverb can also be used as a creative effect, bringing life and interest to individual elements of a mix. There are six main types of reverbs. Room, chamber, and hall reverbs are simulations of small, medium, and large acoustic spaces. Plate and spring reverbs are simulations of mechanical reverbs. Algorithmic reverbs are created purely mathematically, and while they are often emulating one of the five other reverb types they can sometimes have a distinct sound of their own. There is enormous variety within each type of reverb, and you can sometimes choose from hundreds of presets with just one sophisticated plug-in. The use of reverb is a subjective process, and just like everything else, the best way to learn is to experiment for hours on end.

Reverb is not necessarily a plug-in or hardware effect that you apply to audio. When you record in a good-sounding room, you can use room mics as your ambience source and completely forgo the use of artificial reverb. You could also forgo the use of room mics and move your close mics farther away until you have the room sound you want. Assuming you are in a good space, ambience that is recorded live is often highly preferable to an artificial one. It is intricately connected with the ambience on every other open microphone. Hence, it has a much more natural and believable sound. Any time you are able to capture room ambience while recording you should do so. Those tracks are always valuable somewhere in the mix. If you are in a room that sounds decent but is too small or doesn't have enough of a reverb tail you can split the difference and put your room mics through an artificial reverb to broaden the ambient sound a bit. Sometimes this can be the best of both worlds.

When setting up reverbs in your DAW you will usually need many tracks to use the same reverb. It's best to set your reverbs up on aux channels instead of as inserts on specific tracks. It's likely that the same reverb won't work well for all of your tracks. A frequently used technique is to set up several different reverbs that sound similar enough that they will blend together well. As a starting point, if you have short, medium, and long reverbs set up you can send instruments to any one of them based on what sound you are trying to achieve. If your mix template has this basic setup it can work for a wide variety of music.

The most fundamental reason that you add reverb is so your tracks can share the sonic footprint of a space you didn't record in. Just as with everything else in mixing, be aware of how one track's reverb works in relationship to the entire mix. Part of that process is closely monitoring the reverb levels, but another part is the consideration of the sonic qualities of the reverb sound. You don't necessarily want the full stereo spectrum that most reverbs provide or the full EQ spectrum. There are many occasions when you might want to narrow the width of a reverb's stereo field or limit the frequencies it reverberates. Presets can be nice, but you should always tweak them to suit your particular needs.

Reference Mixes

The use of reference mixes is a valuable part of mixing. If you find a couple of recordings that you like in genres similar to your own and reference them throughout your mixing process you can save a lot of experimentation time. This is a common practice in mastering, and it can be helpful in mixing too. When importing a reference mix into your mix session, be sure to level match the track with your mix. The commercial recording will probably be substantially louder than your own, and you should compare it to your own in a level matched way. Only

The best way for composers to study the production values of other mixes is to take a great-sounding score cue from a big-budget film score and load it into their DAW, match the overall volume with their mix, then compare back and forth between their mix of their cue and the overall sound of the big-budget score cue. It takes some time to learn to disregard the expensive-sounding live orchestra and focus in on such things as amount and quality of reverb, overall brightness and bottom end, midrange clarity, and the like. If a composer can learn some critical listening skills by comparing high-end mixes to their own they can begin to work toward having more balanced, polished, and commercial-sounding score mixes.—**John Rodd**

then should you begin to compare the two to find solutions to your mix problems.

High-quality reference recordings provide a perspective and goal for your mix, and they alleviate some of the guesswork. They allow you to pursue specific goals in your sounds instead of the abstract goal of a good-sounding mix. You can compare specific elements and act on what you hear. Any time you find yourself struggling with a mix, either for technical reasons or because of time, a reference mix can be a great help.

By the time you are mixing your cues it's likely that you are weary from an intense writing schedule and your ears are completely fatigued from hearing the same music over and over again. Using a reference track gives you a much-needed new perspective on your mix. It helps you see what's lacking in your mix and reveals inconsistencies that you otherwise wouldn't have noticed. This can be extremely valuable under any circumstances, but especially when plagued by the pressures of time and fatigue.

Relative Balance

The relative balance of tracks is one of the last things that needs attention during the mixing process. As you work through the fundamentals of mixing, the faders can stay set in one place and remain without automation almost until the end of the mix process. Most of the mixing happens in good level management, pan, depth, EQ, compression, and reverb. Once your spatial stage is set, your sound spectrum is balanced, your dynamics are controlled, and your effects are judiciously working to your advantage, and there will be little left to do. When thinking about mixing many people immediately think about moving track faders, but it's probably the most incidental aspect that still qualifies as a fundamental. The heavy lifting of mixing happens in all the other elements, and volume rides just add the nice finishing touches.

The relative balances of tracks are easy to manage because they are totally open for adjustment based on taste and the expressive needs of the music. In the final stage of volume automation you may be setting overall levels, finessing phrases, or fine-tuning the attacks and releases of notes. It is much less technical than any of the other mixing fundamentals and marks a return to the expressive nature of the music. Volume automation is the last chance you have to make elements more prominent or hide them, to finesse a sound or make it blunt. You could tinker for hours, but it's enjoyable, easy work, and you can't go wrong as long as your levels stay moderate.

MASTERING

Mastering is a highly specialized craft and requires specialized tools. The most important element in mastering is the engineer. The engineer's ears and experience will make all the difference. The second most important is the room. A well-balanced room free from standing waves or resonant frequencies is essential. The room should not alter the music's frequency spectrum in any way. The third most important element is the loudspeakers. They should be of excellent quality, with a ruler-flat frequency response throughout the spectrum. This usually means the speakers are large and expensive. Near-field monitors will not do the job. The fourth most important element of mastering is a high-fidelity audio signal path and gear that can make precise changes in pleasing ways. Only with these four elements in place is a studio ready for mastering.

Clinical precision and high-quality gear is important in mastering because you never know on which platform your music will be played. It might come through a cell phone, boomy stereo, or well-balanced theater system. Mastering requires a flat and clinical frequency response in the speakers and the room. The finished product must be balanced so that it will sound as good as possible on as many varied systems as possible. State-of-the-art equipment is required for the same reason that a finish carpenter uses the finest sandpaper at the end. It is the last link in the sonic chain, the most delicate, and the most refined.

When mastering is defined as polishing a mix using the absolute best engineer, room, and equipment there can be no guerrilla shortcuts for mastering at home. There is no way to fake a perfectly flat frequency response in your speakers and room. There are some good mastering plug-ins, but they're not as good as their hardware equivalents. There is no way to replicate the specialized experience of a professional mastering engineer. If you can afford it you are always better off going with a professional. Unfortunately that's often not an option, and you will need to deliver finished masters yourself. When this is the case, you need to do your best at mastering using the skills, studio, and equipment that you have. For guerrilla composers, the definition of mastering needs to broaden to encompass anything you do to make a mix ready for final delivery.

On the bright side, although proper mastering is preferred, not all music for media needs to be mastered perfectly. Your score is always going to be underneath other audio elements, so if your mixes are good then mastering from home can often be good enough. Scores for film and television generally just need to sound natural and unaffected. The EQ spectrum needs to be well shaped, but music mixes often sit better in the final product when they are minimally compressed or limited. Most music libraries only accept finished masters, but a few do the mastering themselves. If you're writing for commercials or trailers, you definitely need to deliver finished mastered tracks that will be pleasing to the ears. Video game scores are often delivered as multiple layers of music, in which case each one needs to be independently mastered.

If you have to master on your own, the best approach is to always use gentle EQ curves and make small changes. As a general rule, you probably don't want to make changes greater than three dB in mastering. Any compression should be gentle and more focused on the control of dynamics than loudness. The score will sound better and more natural when all of the dynamics of your mix are intact, so don't overcompress. Because the music will probably never be at full volume in the context of the film's complete audio mix, you don't need to compress or limit your music much, if at all. Light limiting to reduce a few notable peaks is often all that's required.

Listen to your masters on as many different speakers as possible. The drawbacks of not having perfectly flat speakers in a perfectly flat room can be somewhat mitigated by listening in different environments and taking note of the differences. By doing so you can get your master closer to the middle ground, which is, of course, the goal of a proper mastering setup. Composers produce their own masters all the time, and like any other craft, they get better with experience. It is always worth considering hiring a mastering engineer, however. A mastering engineer can do the job correctly and better five times over in the time it will take you to check your mixes on five different systems. They can put a final polish and shine on your music that makes it tickle the ear in a much nicer way.

DECIDE IF YOU WILL MIX

Composers constantly juggle a wide variety of skill sets and responsibilities, and amongst all of them, none are more disparate than those of composing and mixing. The skill sets required and the perspective when listening to music are wildly different. Both roles are simultaneously art and craft, and both are limitless. Few people achieve mastery of one, and far fewer acquire a mastery of both. The irony is that the two skills

> The quality of the mix is extremely important. It's important for the composer to have a capable production team and work with a professional engineer if the composer is not a sound engineer.—**Ron Mendelsohn**

> On most projects, the reality is that any engineer who is better than I am is going to cost so much money I can't get near them. I hate to say it, but if you want to be a film composer these days you're not going to get the budgets to hire great mix engineers.—**Craig Stuart Garfinkle**

There are a new host of plug-ins for fixing things, so I'm now doing a lot of recordings in my living room which sound fabulous. I know that if somebody bumps into something I can use a plug-in to get rid of that. I can pull a single instrument out of a track, tune it, and put it back. These things are possible. In the old days I would stress every time I recorded. Now I'll put anybody anywhere in the house, and I know that it's going to be okay, which is a beautiful feeling.— **Laura Karpman**

are inextricably linked and often happen simultaneously. In the commercial world excellence in both is usually the expectation.

The complexities and sophistication of the two crafts present composers with an important and difficult question: To mix or not to mix? The desire for quality dictates no, but the budgets usually dictate yes. Your music will always sound better if an expert craftsman mixes it; however, this oftentimes means that you either make no money on the project or are actually investing in it. There is frequently no right answer to the question of whether to hire a mixer. Sometimes a composer will gladly go out of pocket and over budget on a project that he believes in just to make sure that the music sounds amazing. That's usually for career building or artistic reasons. In other situations the same composer might have equally legitimate reasons for not hiring a mixer.

The need for composers to mix and master their own music is a burden that didn't always exist, and for that reason it's a negative. On the other hand, the tools are a lot cheaper than in the past. Hence, the ability and skills are substantially more accessible than they once were. The current factors that limit a mix are primarily the mixer's ability and

The best experience for mixing is doing it, comparing your work to recordings that you like, and engaging in tactical exercises to try to get those same results. You have to spend time with it. You have to twiddle knobs. You have to learn what 2.7k sounds like, when you need to take it out, and when you need to boost it. It's learning by doing.— **Yoav Goren**

> I have no desire to master. There's lots of software out there and I could learn how to do it, but I'd rather go to someone who is good at it. I think it's really important when you have such a huge workload to understand how to delegate and where you should delegate. Mastering is a good place to spend money. But that said, on most of my scores I don't master them unless they're going to be an album.—**Miriam Cutler**

experience, not the hardware or software. High-end equipment makes a difference, of course, but nowadays a skilled mixer can produce great results with fairly modest resources. It is up to you to determine if you are going to pursue excellence in the art and craft of mixing or outsource it for the sake of focusing on your composition. Even amongst the best there is no consensus.

FINDING WORK

THE ULTIMATE QUESTION

THE QUESTION "How do I find work?" is one that can baffle even the most successful artists. Any industry relating to the arts is whimsical. Styles, tastes, personalities of creators and consumers, and the arts themselves change. It can be difficult to pinpoint a need and position yourself to fill that need. Even if you're able to do so, it can still be difficult to monetize what you have done. The methods of finding work are constantly changing, and the type of music that sells is changing even faster. No matter how long your music career lasts, the difficulty of finding work will persist for all but a lucky few.

If you are in search of a dependable, sustainable, well-paid career, pursuing music is a bad idea. Everyone needs running water, a place to live, clothes to wear, ways to communicate, and methods of transportation. There are many offices that need help and many products that need to be sold. If you want a stable lifestyle, pursue something else. As a composer you might eventually become well paid, but you will never have a steady or predictable career path.

> I don't think anybody who is just starting realizes just how hard it is to be a professional musician, how much you need to put out there.—**Craig Stuart Garfinkle**

VIDEO: FINDING WORK. Pictured: Yoav Goren. www.vimeo.com/
guerrillafilmscoring/findingworkteaser

> You never know where your next job is coming from. You just never
> know.—**Jack Wall**

> It's an art-based career. There are no guarantees in any culture in
> the world that art is going to be sustainable and provide you a good
> living.—**Yoav Goren**

At least half of a composer's job is simply finding work, and finding
work can be harder than doing it. Jobs will come and go. Some months
you will be busy beyond belief, while at other times you won't have any
projects and will need to create work for yourself. It is a volatile industry, and you usually won't be able to choose when those times come
upon you. If you want a career as a composer, you must be prepared to
expend considerable energy finding work.

LOTS OF WORKERS, LITTLE WORK

It would be nice if there were clear and dependable steps that composers could take to get reliable work that pays well, but they don't exist.

I don't even really submit demos anymore unless it's for a specific reason or project. When you submit a demo, you need to know that you only get ten seconds, and that's optimistic. They're going to click on something, choose five or six seconds, and then say, "Okay, I get what that's doing. Next." You're going to get five seconds a cue, and that's if they're even listening to the demos they receive.—**Nathan Furst**

In many other industries, if you are qualified and experienced, you can get a job. If you lose one job, you can take predictable steps to find another. The process of submitting resumes, filling out job applications, and going to job interviews reliably leads to consistent employment. People can get degrees or other training certificates to pad their resume, make themselves more hirable, and increase their wages. This process is highly effective for the vast majority of fields.

None of these approaches work for musicians. Being highly skilled and experienced is not enough. A resume is unlikely to help you as a composer, although a credits list may. Submitting demo reels is the composer's equivalent to submitting a resume, but unsolicited demos typically get minimal attention. Formal interviews are few and far between, but chance conversations at parties can be pivotal. Degrees and certificates don't make you more hirable, but the knowledge and experience gained certainly does.

Instead of a corporate ladder, musicians have a huge rock face to climb. It's difficult. Yes, you can move in any direction at any time, but you can also fall from great heights very quickly. Few have the fortune of finding a niche in the rock face that lets them climb to the top swiftly and with ease. The result is that composers have to find their own ways of getting or creating work; therefore, the process of finding work becomes highly creative and entrepreneurial.

DIVERSIFY YOURSELF

There are few musicians who find work doing one specific thing their entire careers. Only the most successful are able to be exclusively composers, performers, or bandleaders. If you want to stay gainfully employed, you need to be a Swiss army knife of musical skills. That

> The key to getting the big gigs is being able to do it entirely on your own, any way you can do it. I spent years doing that, and throughout time it conveyed that I know what I'm doing. That's the only way you're going to land a big studio picture.—**Nathan Furst**

way when one doesn't keep you busy the other can. As your career develops, you may be able to specialize more and focus on specific aspects of music, but in the beginning you need to exploit your skills in every way possible.

Being multitalented is the musician's equivalent of padding a resume. It's nice if you're a great producer, but if you're also a recording engineer, play several instruments, and can arrange you become a much more interesting package. Good composers have value, but composers who also orchestrate, do music copyist work, perform, mix, and master have more value. Even if a project does not require your whole package of services your expertise will usually be appreciated, and you should be able to charge more as a result.

The composers who readily find work are the ones who are a one-stop shop. Producers and directors usually don't want to be bothered with the details of the scoring process, and especially not with the problems. They want their composer to handle it, get help if necessary, and deliver a great product. If you are able to take a score from concept to completion quickly, cost efficiently, and with high quality you will get work. It doesn't matter to your director if you do it alone or with help.

> In years past, there was more of a division between composers based on the mediums they were working in. Composers were often thought of predominantly as a television composer, or a film composer, or a game composer, or a composer for advertising, and those composers were often not thought of for the other mediums. Fortunately, during the past decade or so, some very talented composers have been working to break down those barriers by working actively in different mediums. Being diverse can open doors for opportunities. I've always been interested in all kinds of projects and mediums.—**Ryan Shore**

> To stay busy you should have different piles of music. You could write songs for Heavy Hitters, for films, for a client that does commercials, for an advertising agency, for a trailer music company, etc. You need to be constantly writing.—**Cindy Badell-Slaughter**

In the beginning of your career you will not be able to hire many people to help you, so to get work you almost have to have the ability to do everything by yourself.

There is a well-known catch-22 in the music industry: You will never be hired to do something until you have already done it successfully. If you want to score a network television show, you need to be able to point to previous network experience. If you want to write an orchestral score for a film, you need to have created other orchestral film scores. Thankfully, the catch-22 is only the front door to success.

By diversifying your skill base and the types of work you do professionally, you enable yourself to work for and with more people. As your group of colleagues expands, you will gain closer associations with the type of work that you want to be doing. Your connections will get better, your credits will grow, and little by little you will gain the legitimacy that people seek before they will hire you. By doing jobs that support and surround your specific composing goals you can sneak past the catch-22 and get in through the back door.

BE PREPARED FOR AUDITIONS

One of the keys to finding work is remembering that composers, no matter how established, are always auditioning. Each piece of work is a calling card and an audition piece for the next project. Each performance is a representation of your artistry. Each person you work with is an opportunity to leave a good impression. Everyone you know outside of work might know someone in the industry. Each event in your musical life has the opportunity to be an impression that leads to future work.

You never know when an old track will resurface or someone's impression of your live performance done years ago will suddenly have profound importance. Career opportunities can come just as easily when you're at a party or buying bread as they can when you're at a

> The community of employers is who is really going to help you out in terms of keeping you on a job, but you need to be a good friend to everybody. That's really what I think it comes down to.—**Craig Stuart Garfinkle**

film festival or industry event. Social connections are the fuel behind music industry opportunities. Thus, you can never predict when an opportunity may arise. If it goes badly, you may never even know it was an audition. No one is judged only by what he chooses to present to the world. You might be judged by the sum total of your music or a single piece of music that you would prefer to forget. Although there is much you can do to put your best foot forward, you are, in fact, judged by any and all of your work.

You can't constantly pretend that you're onstage, and you shouldn't constantly pitch yourself to everyone around you. People who try this approach come across like disingenuous used car salesmen. There are a couple of things you can do, however. First, make sure that no matter what you work on, you put your absolute best into it. Remember that

> We're always auditioning. It doesn't matter how long you've been composing, because people want to see what you would do for their project. It's like an actor. You might be the best actor in the world, but if you're not right for a project it's not going to work.—**Jack Wall**

> The best working relationships are the ones with people who you have worked with before. When working on a second, third, or fourth film with somebody, there's a level of trust that there isn't the first time. I find that the further down the line you are, the more trust there is. They tell me what they want, they come back, they give me notes, but it's not the feeling that I'm auditioning or that I could get fired. I also have gotten work through picture editors, more than any other route of getting work. When I hit it off with an editor that oftentimes leads to another picture.—**Peter Golub**

everything with your name on it needs to represent you as fully as possible, so treat your compositions as if you are making audition pieces.

Be open, honest, and excited about what you do. Enthusiasm goes a long way, and yours can impress people long before they listen to your demos or talk to you about a potential project. You shouldn't be in the music industry if you don't love it. If you love what you do, let it show. A genuine, honest expression of passion and expertise will excite and impress the people around you. This enthusiasm can garner results from the most unexpected places.

MAINTAIN DIRECTOR RELATIONSHIPS

The need for trust and mutual creativity leads directors to search for composers in personal ways because those types of connections can't come from credits, education, ability, age, or celebrity. Personal relationships trump credits every time. When directors hire composers they need someone who they can trust with their art. The two need to have a simpatico relationship, a mutual understanding of the music the project needs, and a working relationship that both parties enjoy. If the interpersonal aspect doesn't work, the creative relationship will fail. Any other credentials can be negotiated if need to be, but a shared artistic vision and constructive working relationship are not negotiable.

> The first time working with a director is always difficult. It's important to develop an open line of communication, because 50 percent of what we do is about the relationship. We need to instill trust and have a deep level of communication right away. I often describe it as marrying someone that you've never even gone to bed with, and you're supposed to know what they like without ever having any experience.—**Miriam Cutler**

> Credits and experience are the first thing potential clients look at if they don't know you, and sometimes if you're lucky enough they'll listen to your music and like it enough to keep pursuing you. Most of your work will come from relationships, however, so building those should be paramount.—**Bill Brown**

> You don't really get paid for what you do. You get paid for the relationships that you have. To get paid for anything, you have to have somebody fighting to get you paid. That's the nature of the economy almost everywhere, but in the music business especially. Your goal is to go into a project where you have powerful friends and allies that you've been working with for a long time who take it as a personal affront if you don't get a decent salary.—**Craig Stuart Garfinkle**

Successful directors return to the same teams over and over again because those teams worked well in the past, and they are comfortable with the teams they built. If you have maintained a good relationship with a director your competitors will never even hear about the opportunity when the director is in need of a composer. Once a bond is formed and trust is established, the diector has no reason to go elsewhere.

Your goal is to make yourself indispensable to directors and fill their needs so fully that they never consider going to someone else. When you successfully serve the specific project's needs, as well as the director's needs, the director will almost certainly return to you with more work in the future. A strong relationship with one director can also lead to work with one of his friends or colleagues. That relationship could develop into a reputation within an entire community, and it can open a lot of new doors when it reaches that tipping point.

> If you want to start in this industry some great places to begin are in an office, a music department, a recording studio, or assisting another composer. You can learn a lot there and build connections at the same time. You have to have the right skills to get your foot in the door, and the skills are probably going to be administrative or technical, not compositional. It's more about how fast you can type something or fix a broken plug-in. You have to be able to supplement your income because your scoring won't pay very much at first.—**Cindy Badell-Slaughter**

BUILD A NETWORK THAT ENDORSES YOU

If a director needs a composer and doesn't have the right one, he will almost certainly begin his search by asking colleagues for recommendations. It's rare that people will begin by cold-calling agents or putting up advertisements. People seek personal recommendations because their options are vast. There are tens of thousands of composers to choose from, the process of starting a composer search from scratch is daunting, and no one has time for it.

Asking friends and colleagues for recommendations does two things for directors. First, it reduces their options from infinite to a number they can probably count on their fingers. Second, their colleagues act as a trusted filter, and they can be confident that the short list is a good one. When someone can simply ask around, follow up on some recommendations, and get exactly the right composer for the job, he will use the same method every time. Only if that doesn't work will he begin to approach agents or place notices in industry publications.

That moment of personal recommendation is gold to a composer. If you can be the name at the top of someone's list, the website a person happens to remember first, or the inspired genius that someone raves about, you will be head and shoulders above the rest of the crowd. It doesn't mean you'll get the job, but it opens a door for you in the most flattering of ways. When you are recommended to someone, your first interactions will be preceded by a benefit of the doubt, and you will have that person's full attention. The moment in which your friend recommended you is the moment in which your art is monetized, or at least gains the potential for it.

Recommendations will never come if you actively try to sell yourself all the time, nor will they come from "networking" for the purpose of self-promotion and handshaking for the sake of furthering your own needs. Using your relationships for active marketing strains and diminishes them. It doesn't matter if people have your contact information and know your work. What matters is that they like and respect you and know your abilities. The best way to monetize the relationships you have is to consciously not try to monetize them at all, because genuine relationships are, without fail, the most reliable conduit to work opportunities.

> I made a rule for myself that I wouldn't network with people that I didn't want to be friends with. I don't want to be careerist and befriend people just because I think they will be really successful. I only connect with people who I love and understand me as an artist.—**Laura Karpman**

The kind of networking that works most reliably is drawing connections for other people, not for yourself. If you know one person who has a need and another person who can fill that need, connect them with one another purely for the sake of helping two of your friends. When you are the voice giving the personal recommendation, you are strengthening your relationships with those individuals, building your community, and forming new bonds that hold it together. Your contribution to the success of others will not be forgotten. Your thoughtfulness and good intentions will leave an impression—one of gratitude and trust. The trust and connections that are born out of those actions will eventually come back to you at some unknown time. The best way to propel your career forward is by generously pouring yourself into your community.

On rare occasions you can ask for introductions or recommendations, asking someone you know to connect you to someone you don't know, but do so with caution. In these situations you need to be able to represent yourself well, represent your friend well, and be a valuable resource to the third person. If the exchange will not offer benefits to all three people, particularly the person you are trying to get to, you would be wise to wait until it will. People sniff out name droppers and celebrity hunters very quickly. If you are using your existing relationships to get to bigger and better ones, that too will become obvious faster than

> I think part of why I've succeeded in reaching my goals is that I've identified and tapped into a community that I wanted to be a part of. I made a major investment of my time and energy into developing relationships in that community, and it's really made me a part of it. I'm reaping many, many benefits from being part of that community and being seen as a person who truly is committed to that community.—**Miriam Cutler**

I can't think of the last time I cold-called a project. All the work I get these days comes through a person that I already know somehow or another, even if it's distantly. Many directors will call around to their director friends and say, "Who have you worked with that you like?" and they'll get a recommendation. So if you want that job, you won't even know about it unless you have worked with someone in their circle already, which becomes a chicken-and-egg scenario. You have to have already had work to get that work. Personal recommendations are without a doubt the strongest credential, and I find that some variation on that ends up being more and more true the better you do.—**Austin Wintory**

you may think. If you have something valuable to offer, offer it proudly. If you're only trying to ride coattails, be discreet.

BUILD COMMUNITY

Since relationships are so crucial to the career path of composers, it's important to think about how you want to go about forming and maintaining those relationships. The soft skills connected to interpersonal relationships are just as influential in your career as the hard skills of music that you are hired for, maybe even more so. It's not that you need a strategy for your relationships, because if you implemented a strategy you would become like that used car salesman, but you should have some philosophies about how you want to build and develop your work relationships. The relationships need to be genuine, but because you are also working on career development they need to be genuine in a conscious and directed way.

Composer careers grow organically. The growth may be fast or slow, but it is never random. New growth and opportunity springs from what is already there. If your music stands on its own and speaks well for itself, and if the composer does the same, opportunities and relationships grow naturally. Throughout time a career increases in size and substance. At some point a snowball effect begins, and the ball can begin to roll on its own, increasing in size and speed without minimal effort. The key to growth and the snowball effect is that the core must be strong because otherwise it can't hold itself together.

Careers develop on their own, and you have to be unafraid of the fact that you don't know how long it will take. That's the part that's really daunting. Some people meet someone in school that ends up setting their career off. Before you know it they're doing massive stuff, and it seems like they came right out of the gate doing really big things. But John Williams was forty-three when he scored *Jaws* and forty-five when he scored *Star Wars*. He had almost two decades of experience that no one knew anything about. He was just biding his time.—**Austin Wintory**

For composers, the core is made of relationships. If you maintain and strengthen connections your career will be strong enough to survive. If the relationships are weak and people consistently fall away it will be much harder to gain mass and achieve a snowball effect. The relationships are not only with clients, but with colleagues, competitors, friends, acquaintances, and admirers. The solid core of a successful career is an entire community, and it's for that reason that you need to spend time thinking about and maintaining your connections with your community.

One of the most tried and true ways to develop a career is to find directors who are working at your level and grow with them. If you can maintain your working relationships as you walk the bumpy road of the industry together your successes become mutual. Most collaborations are only there for a season, but there are numerous stories of collaborations that became lifelong and highly successful ones. It is difficult to work as an equal with people who are much more successful than you are because they usually don't feel a need to reach down and pull you up to their level. In the same way, you should avoid working with people who you feel are below your own level because they will diminish the quality of your work. You need to start working with people at your own level, grow with them, and make yourself indispensable to them so that they bring you into new projects.

On a practical level, there are many ways in which you can position yourself for new relationship opportunities. The most obvious is to surround yourself with people who might want to hire you. If you're selling water, you want to be where people are thirsty. If you're a composer, you want to be where people are making products that need music. The fastest career development happens face-to-face, person-to-person. In a perfect world you would be the only composer in a community of potential clients, and throughout time you would get to know all of them. If you choose a group of creatives and make yourself part of that group, you will eventually be recognized as the composer of the group. Being recognized as such can eventually turn into work opportunities.

The musician community is another important source of work. Although it might seem like other composers are your competitors, this is not really the case unless they write music similar to your own. Musicians hire one another back and forth all the time. The opportunity for learning is also a key factor that makes your community of musicians significant. Whether it is a professional organization like the Society of Composers and Lyricists or a group of band buddies that meets at a bar, having a community of other musicians can give you support, knowledge, experience, and sometimes additional work.

If your goal is to score for video games then you need to meet game designers. The video game world is inherently more tech oriented than films, so online approaches can work well in the beginning. There are several game designer forums and social media groups, and it's possible to get work by being an active member of the online community of designers. Even better are in-person opportunities like the Game Developers Conference, where you can meet people face-to-face and interact with a large number of individuals in a short period of time.

If you want to score for film and television you should become acquainted with filmmakers. Film festivals are wonderful places to meet people who work in film. Many cities have organized groups of filmmakers that meet to discuss their industries and share their work. There

---

The most reasonable way to build a career is to find directors and producers who are working at your level, and collaborate. It's very possible those friendships could become lifelong collaborations. Also, if you're able to help someone with a spec project, if it goes really well, there's a good chance that person will come back to you for the next project. That worked for me in one very key instance, which eventually led to me scoring *CSI: NY*.—**Bill Brown**

> Having a director that perceives you as a partner is ideal. I scored many USC and UCLA thesis films when I was coming up. I cut my teeth on a ton of those. I would do anything to do them. I also wrote music for the UCLA sitcom, and I ended up doing sitcoms for ten years. My focus was on building those kinds of relationships. I also built up relationships with other composers.—**Craig Stuart Garfinkle**

is a steady stream of hopeful new filmmakers coming out of universities, and scoring student films can be a great way to build new relationships. A less obvious way of getting film scoring work is through picture editors and music supervisors. They can recommend you directly or drop your music into a work in progress.

Music libraries are the easiest contacts to form. If you want to write for music libraries all you need to do is start writing. You can literally write anything you'd like. Build up a nice collection of tracks with a similar vibe and start reaching out. The most high-end libraries don't accept unsolicited submissions, but many others will. With music libraries you don't need much of an introduction or sales pitch. You can simply present your package, describe it clearly, and ask if they want to publish it. If they say no you can shop it to another library. It's not unlike selling Girl Scout cookies door-to-door. When they say no it's not personal, and if you knock on enough doors someone will buy.

> If you're in video games, people are impressed with your credits, but also with what they hear in your demo. They're always looking for something new. It's very different from film and television, which is very credit driven. Game music is more about your sound and how it can benefit the world that they're building. It's more driven by creativity than credits.—**Jack Wall**

> I will always help my friends. Career development isn't only about clients. It's just as much about the community of artists and trying to share with other artists.—**Craig Stuart Garfinkle**

Sometimes a director has no money, but you like that person and you believe that what they're doing is worth some time. Maybe you're not going to write a whole eighty-minute score for them, but you'll say, "I know you can't afford music, but let me write you a couple themes, because I think what you're doing is cool." I think that's really important, and you never know. Maybe that person will keep you employed for decades.—**Nathan Furst**

My involvement with the Sundance Film Festival has been very fruitful for me. I think we create our own opportunities. Because I was very committed to pursuing that, it has been truly opulent. I first went in 1997, and as soon as I got there I realized that the documentary film community was what I had been looking for and Sundance was a place where they gather. For me, it's just like heaven. Everything I am interested in and care about, I can find there. It's been wonderful because it was a mutual love. We found each other, me and Sundance.—**Miriam Cutler**

The key to finding work as a composer is unquestionably the relationships you have with people. You cannot take them for granted or draw on them in a way that makes the give-and-take unbalanced. The relationships that will lead to long-term success are loyal ones based on mutual respect, generosity, common interests, and shared passions. When you build a real community and pour yourself into it you will find yourself in fertile soil where your career can grow freely and with support.

CAREER DEVELOPMENT

BE PATIENT

UNLIKE POP STARS, composers become more important and more legitimate as they age. The skills, artistic voice, technique, professionalism, and industry knowledge required in scoring for any kind of media take a long time to build. It takes more time to build up credits and longer still for those credits to be weighty enough to form a firm foundation for a career. Once a composer has been around for a while clients can work with that composer from a position of trust, whereas it requires a leap of faith to hire a recent graduate for a big project. If two composers have similar credentials and relationships with the director, the older composer will usually get the job.

Developing a career as a composer is an endurance test. If you maintain a certain level of productivity for a lengthy period of time, much of your competition will drop out of the race. Older composers will vacate their positions; younger composers will stop nipping at your heels; and you will, by default, become one of the experts. If you have been scoring films for three years, you are a beginner no matter how brilliant you are. If you have been doing it for thirty years your clients take you more seriously.

No matter how technology develops and how the industry evolves there will always be a limited number of big-budget gigs that pay composers well. The group of A-list composers will always be limited,

VIDEO: CAREER DEVELOPMENT. Pictured: Stewart Copeland.
www.vimeo.com/guerrillafilmscoring/careerdevelopmentteaser

and the B-list will always be an insider's club. There's no reason you shouldn't aim to be an A-list composer, but it will not happen quickly because it takes more than a few big movies or games to build a solid reputation. In the meantime, composing will probably not pay you much. In the scoring industry, big money and fame generally come at the end of a career, if at all. Even the guys at the top are feeling the budget pressures of today's industry. The lack of reliable income is a persuasive reason for composers to choose other career paths. If you want to be a composer, be prepared to supplement your income in other ways as you wait for time to be on your side.

> After twenty years of film scoring I'm now focused on concert music instead. I love scoring film and I love working with directors, but it's a classic scenario in which the work is brilliant and the business sucks.—**Stewart Copeland**

> I've been working in the game industry since 1996, and I've out-lasted everybody I've worked with. I'm still doing it, and everyone else is doing other things.—**Jack Wall**

> You don't know how long it will take to launch your career, which means that the people that don't make it haven't failed, they just end up quitting. The only people that make it are the ones that stick it out long enough. There's no way to go for the rest of your life and not make it, because there are too many people quitting all around you. If you stick it out it's because you love it, and people who love it draw others who love it too. I know it sounds very naive and idealistic, but it's the only thing in common I've seen about every composer who's successful.—**Austin Wintory**

ADOPT CAREER-SUSTAINING QUALITIES

The qualities that sustain a composer's career are not related to the art of music. Your music needs to be brilliant and original, but that alone is not enough, just like a great steak doesn't keep a restaurant in business. A product by itself does not build or sustain a business, a fact that is often misunderstood by artists in all mediums. Musicians are usually focused on the creative process and making an end product that is high quality and has integrity. They hope that their art will speak for itself and draw attention to them, but that is usually a false hope. There is too much music in the world and too much media being consumed for that hope to be realized, except in a handful of cases. Making a high-quality product and dropping it into film festivals or iTunes is like putting a message in a bottle and throwing it out to sea. Only one in a million will have any result. Your music needs to be great, but other things build and sustain your business.

Relationships are just as important to sustaining a career as they are to finding work. Being a film or video game composer is more than

> To sustain your career, you have to be very honest to yourself and let yourself be vulnerable to others. Directors will want to work with you when they've made a legitimate connection and you're not just the music guy in their life. Otherwise, they'll eventually meet someone that they like better who they actually connect with and is equally qualified.—**Austin Wintory**

What's been the driving force behind my career development—and it's spanned almost thirty years—is I love what I do, and I love the world of film and television music.—**Cindy Badell-Slaughter**

a career choice, it's almost a lifestyle choice. The community around you has a huge influence on the trajectory of your career, as does the strength of your bond with that community. If you are an earnest and accessible member of the filmmaking and music communities you will find work, helpers, education, and counsel. Legitimate and meaningful connections to those communities will go as far as anything else in sustaining your career.

Passion is another essential. The people who have sustained successful careers as composers have a deep passion for their music and the mediums in which they work. They have fun doing what they do, and their passion creates a better product. The industry is volatile, trying, and unpredictable. The hours can be long and the schedules short. It is increasingly difficult to make a good living as a composer, particularly in the early stages of your career. The process of composing has to be fulfilling in and of itself. People without a true passion for composing tend to abandon ship in pursuit of other careers. For those who deeply love it, the difficulties are worth it.

When scoring for media you are a service provider. A consistent thread that connects successful composers is that they fully embrace

I think the bottom line is you've got to have fun or none of this is worth it. If you don't love it, then go be a lawyer. If it's all about money, do something else.—**Jack Wall**

What keeps me going is the honor and privilege of being a working musician. It's absolutely extraordinary for a man, a woman, anybody of any race, color, or creed to make a living as a composer. It is an extraordinary accomplishment, and I'm very proud of it.—**Laura Karpman** their supporting role. They do not have the ego of a diva that always wants the spotlight, and they are eager to provide good customer service to their directors and producers. When scoring for media, you are far removed from the purely artistic world of concert music and never esoterically writing something for the sake of self-expression. You must recognize that film scoring is a craft and not pure art. There is always a product to sell, and you serve both the product and the product's creators. To sustain your career, keep your ego in check and maintain a service-oriented attitude.

As a service provider, you must be able write great music fairly quickly. The writing needs to happen on command. There are instances where it may be rejected just as fast as it is written, so the flow of new ideas must be constant. Fluency in writing is essential because you will not survive the deadline-driven scoring world without it. You need to write music as fluently as you can talk over coffee. The first step in achieving that fluency is simply to write a lot. The more you write, the more your process and templates will be refined, and little by little you will start to write better music in a more efficient manner.

To write quickly you must always have a fountain of new musical ideas. You need to be able to put those new ideas into tangible forms and mold them to suit the task at hand. You need to write for wildly different projects on time lines that are out of your control. Thus, the breadth and depth of your musical ideas must be vast. To become an overflowing fountain of musical ideas there are really only two requirements. You need to habitually feed your creative side. Study and listen to keep that part of your brain full, fertile, and inspired. You must also keep the fountain flowing. If you don't write for a while the pipes may get filled with debris, and your fountain of ideas may be slowed or blocked.

> The critical factor that makes me a composer, and that you can't really be a composer without, is a river of music going through my head almost 24/7. It's just a fact of my life that there is music in my head. Writer's block? What's that? It's more like I just open up the gate and it pours out. I can't really explain where that comes from or what that is, but without that, I can't imagine doing this job.—**Stewart Copeland**

PREPARE FOR THE ENDURANCE TEST

Willpower is crucial to career building, just as it is in any other long-term endeavor. Opportunities will come and go, there will be good times and bad, and your passion will naturally ebb and flow. You will be physically and mentally weary at times, and it will take determination to move onward. The voice inside that suggests quitting has a different volume for everyone, but it's always there. Quitting doesn't necessarily mean you quit the career. It may just mean that you stop working too easily and let yourself be distracted too often. At some point, it takes nothing more than determination and discipline to keep going. You can achieve greater discipline in two basic ways: internal motivation or external motivation. Internal motivation is the longest lasting, so making your own goals and a plan about how to accomplish them is the best solution. That being said, no one has an endless supply of self-discipline, and outside accountability is helpful. Outside motivators can come in a million forms and assist in keeping you on track. Industry meetings, small business support groups, classes, books, seminars, movie screenings, film festivals, and conventions are a few examples of external motivators that might be valuable to you.

Another factor that sustains a composer's career is productivity. A large, actively growing catalog and a growing list of credits is proof of success and promotes more of the same. There is a reason that the term *one-hit wonder* is pejorative. It suggests that if someone is only known for one thing that person has never accomplished anything else that

This is not a logical profession to enter anymore. It really isn't. You have to go through a lot of disappointments and struggles to survive a career as a composer, so it's dependent on your own personal, private motivation. How important is it to you to achieve this? You may be thirty-five or forty and your friends, who are lawyers or doctors, are living a pretty full life while you're still struggling. You better be sure this is important enough to you to be in that position. It's a high-risk business, and it has to be a passion for you. You have to have certain blinders on and really want to achieve this in your life, but it's a sacrifice and you may or may not be successful.—**Garry Schyman**

In regard to career development, if I encounter a roadblock I always ask myself if those challenges are specific to music or if they are perhaps more universal. For example, if I were to open an unrelated business outside of music, would I run into those same challenges? If so, it would be better to try to learn those lessons in this career, rather than pursuing something else only to encounter the same roadblock in a different career years later.—**Ryan Shore**

was good. If you have done a lot of great things but nothing recent it may be assumed that you have gone out to pasture. To create a snow-ball effect in which your career achieves self-perpetuating motion, you need to give it momentum. Keeping your productivity high and your achievements coming is how you push your career through the snow and gather momentum.

BE IN THE BUSINESS OF MUSIC

Most people get into professional composing because they like the work and want to get paid for it. Most focus on the music-related work, but if you are a freelance composer you own and manage a small business. Even if you excel in the skill areas that composing requires, it's not enough to produce success. The hard skills of business development are required for career growth just as much as musical skills. A restaurant owner will not be able to grow his business if he keeps his head down in the kitchen. Likewise, a composer can't grow his career if he ignores his business management responsibilities.

Musicians are notoriously disinterested in accounting, business, and marketing, and as a result they are consistently bad at these aspects of running a business. A mind that thrives in accounting is very different from the mind of a creative. The strategic, legal, and numbers-oriented aspects of being a small business owner are highly logical, ordered, and pragmatic. Composing couldn't be more different. It's abstract and requires free association of sound and emotion. For a mind that is drawn to music, the business side can be a heavy weight that steals joy and bogs down the creative process. Hence, most composers learn only minimal information about entrepreneurship and

> The aim of the musician is music. The aim of the professional musician is business. This is not to say you neglect music and strictly become a businessperson, but it does become, and needs to be, a major focus.—**Timothy Andrew Edwards**

spend much of their time trying to get gigs, which they misinterpret as business development efforts.

An easy way to gain an advantage over your competitors is to thoroughly study the business aspects. A great composer will not be able to compete with a great composer who also has a well-formed business plan and the skills to execute it. This is not to say that you should get a master's in business administration, but if you have a working knowledge of contracts, accounting, royalties, taxes, payroll, marketing, public relations, and other business concepts, you will be better prepared to establish and build your composing business. Don't just be a musician. Be strategic and savvy in business too.

In the United States there is a government agency called the Small Business Administration. It has been around since the 1950s and is designed to protect and assist small businesses with everything from education to loans to influencing government policy. There are Small Business Development Centers in major cities nationwide that provide assistance to small businesses and aspiring entrepreneurs. There are many other small business groups available as well, ranging from support groups to seminars to business schools with an entrepreneurial focus. The information you would learn and guidance you would receive could not be further removed from what you would learn in music school, and yet that knowledge is highly relevant to composers. Fill in your knowledge gaps.

> Managing the business side is hard. We're trying to cultivate ourselves as composers, and that's a full-time job. Composition is a time-honored craft that needs to be nurtured. You have to live it. When you're distracted with all these other things trying to make a living, it's a hindrance.—**Yoav Goren**

BRAND YOURSELF

Branding is the process of differentiating a product from the competition to make it more memorable. Your brand tells the world what they can expect from your music and services, and it succinctly shows what you're about. Branding is about meaning and connections. Your brand is the emotional connection people make with your music and you personally. The strength of the brand is ultimately what determines if your clients will become loyal customers.

Branding yourself is not about getting work, it is about packaging yourself in a recognizable way. It's not about finding your voice, it's about concisely communicating your voice and what kind of composer you are to others. Your name and photo differentiate you from other composers, but having a name and a face is not branding, it's just labeling. Your brand is the sum of others' experiences with you. Effective self-presentation shapes their experiences so that your name begins to have meaning and symbolizes your career goals. You need to have an image, a genre, a persona, and a style. Branding is about building your own pigeonhole instead of letting other people choose one for you.

Because a brand is a collection of experiences, you already have a brand even if you have never consciously thought about it. Anyone who has met you or heard your music has an impression of you. If you are not thinking about how you want to present yourself and your music to the world, your brand could be growing in a direction that does not support your goals. You should not let your branding happen accidentally or let yourself be passively categorized by other people. It is important to maintain a consistent image of yourself and your career during public appearances, online forums, and industry events.

Discovering and defining your brand is a journey that will take some time. It can be difficult, time consuming, and uncomfortable. It requires, at the very least, that you know your career goals, what you have to offer, what type of clients you want, how people already perceive you, and what qualities you want people to associate with you. This involves a discovery process, and some of your specs will change throughout time. As they do, your branding should change too, because you should project the image of your business goals and not your current reality. For example, B. B. King's "King of the Blues" wasn't a reality when he first started having his band introduce him that way.

The composers that really have been successful and have maintained success throughout many years have built up the brand that is Hans Zimmer, Thomas Newman, David Newman, Danny Elfman, Chris Young, etc. You know what you're getting when you buy a certain brand. They have a certain identity. They have a certain type of sound. They've cultivated their persona through their music, and I think it has truly helped them sustain their careers.—**Craig Stuart Garfinkle**

With consistent branding, however, it first became a trademark and then a reputation.

Your efforts at branding have to be credible and authentic or they will be ineffective. The image you project has to be believable because people will compare the branding to the real thing when they encounter you. If your branding creates expectations that you can't fulfill, the brand that sticks will be that of a fraud. You have to live up to the promises of your brand.

Each encounter leaves an impression on people, so you must always project the character of the career you are trying to build. You should have a visual branding that applies to your websites, printed materials, personal style, and everything else visual. Research your competition and see how you can brand yourself differently and better. Personify yourself in everything.

Even if you're just starting out, you don't necessarily have to work for small money. Think about Rolls Royce. They didn't start at the bottom as an everyman's car and work their way up. They always produced

When I first started scoring I went from being a respected performer in my field to being a nobody. Nobody knew who I was, and I was working on terrible projects as a composer. I wanted to develop a respect for my work, and the only way to do that was to always do my best work. I realized early on that I wanted to invest in my name meaning something. I wanted it to mean high quality, connection to the material, commitment to the community, commitment to the subject matter, respect for the subject matter, all these things. Everything I do feeds into that.—**Miriam Cutler**

> I don't brand myself. I don't advertise myself. I don't spend any energy in that department. I do recommend meeting people and dealing with individuals, because it's an individual that will hire you. You don't get hired by a community, you get hired by one person. The bigger the crowd of composers they audition, the more devalued you become. If they test the waters with thousands of composers, you're devalued. If you meet people, you talk to them, you get to know them, and they get to trust you, you'll get work.—**Charles Bernstein**

first-class products and demanded corresponding prices. Honda will never be able to compete with Rolls Royce because they are already established as an affordable, common car.

If you charge too little money for too long, you will be branded a budget composer. The market needs both inexpensive composers who crank out music and A-list composers who make a first-class product. Be clear about your goals, ensure that the quality of your product matches your goals, and charge accordingly from the beginning. You are the only one who creates value for yourself, and when you say no to work you are branding yourself too. Know your own value.

BE VISIBLE

Just as musicians are generally not drawn to business, they are rarely drawn to marketing, and many feel like it is disingenuous or selling out to consciously market themselves and their music. There is some room in the market for idealistic composers who quietly write great music and let it speak for itself, but not much. An active desire to avoid marketing is too impractical for most businesses to survive. The majority of composers need to make efforts to be visible and create opportunities for their names to be remembered and their brand reinforced.

Since a brand is a collection of experiences you need to invent reasons to interact with people. You can do that with a music release, a blog post, an e-mail list, a private party, or any other way you can imagine. An obvious first step is to build a web and social media presence that reflects your career goals. You need good demos that are targeted at the kind of work you want to pursue.

> Creating awareness of your work can be very important for building a career. Hopefully some degree of awareness of one's work will happen naturally as a career grows; however, it can be helpful to make concerted publicity efforts as well.—**Ryan Shore**

Creating those moments of interaction is marketing, but traditional marketing doesn't work for composers. Composers are not hired by the general public, so broad approaches like billboards or commercials are out of the question. Even targeted online ads are too imprecise. Composers are hired by a single person. It's usually a film or game director, or it may be a producer or music library, but it always comes down to a single person doing the hiring.

On the bright side, this is great news for composers who don't want to market themselves. For a composer, marketing is primarily about creating opportunities to meet people one at a time and make a connection. It comes back to community, connection, and relationships of substance. Work with as many different people as possible, make yourself visible in the community, and invest yourself in that community. You have to make the phone ring, which happens by building and maintaining your network of people, one person at a time. Perhaps the building of genuine interpersonal connections doesn't deserve to be called marketing, but it will have a marketing effect. Whatever you call it, be proactively genuine and valuable to the community in which you want to work.

BE AN ENTREPRENEUR

It's rare that people fall into scoring because of a good business opportunity. Trent Reznor of Nine Inch Nails is one example of a composer who entered the film scoring world because of a business opportunity. His first film score was for *The Social Network*, which had a budget of $40

> Being in business for yourself and being an entrepreneur, you have to figure out how to make a living when things aren't happening.—**Craig Stuart Garfinkle**

> Regretfully, I think I'm more of an artist than I am an entrepreneur. I really wish it was the other way around, because I have to fake being a businessman.—**Nathan Furst**

million. Ryan Amon, who scored *Elysium*, is another. That was his first film score, and the film had a $115 million budget. Both men stumbled upon good opportunities and gladly took them; however, now that they have a foot in the film scoring world they still need to be as entrepreneurial as everyone else. It's hard work, even for composers who have a good head start.

Most composers will readily admit that they are more an artist than an entrepreneur. The foremost reason they chose scoring as a vocation is because they love it, and then they tried to find work doing it. A few lucky composers will find a network television show that sustains them for many years or a few directors who are productive and loyal enough to keep them busy. These people can settle into their jobs as composers and not worry too much about finding work, but this is not the case for most. The hardest work for composers is finding work. If you want to work consistently you need to be an entrepreneur. This point is consistently overlooked by individuals and education systems alike, but it is a crucial one. Great composers who are not clever entrepreneurs will not succeed.

The key to entrepreneurial thought is putting yourself in the shoes of your client. An employee mentality asks what needs to be done, and an entrepreneur mentality looks for what can be created. If you are focused on what you can build for your clients and how you can fulfill their needs you are on the right path. You need to see what they see and think the way they think. You can't start a business with a product that is arbitrary, that is, your favorite kind of music to write or the

> Unfortunately, I'm purely an artist. I would love to have a magic wand that could hit me on the head and make me a better businessperson, but I'm an artist to my core. I grew up wanting to be a composer from the time I was seven years old. I didn't grow up wanting to be an entrepreneur.—**Laura Karpman**

> I think that entrepreneurial behavior is inherently creative, extremely creative. Composers who just want to write music all day probably have an inaccurate notion of what it is to be entrepreneurial.—**Austin Wintory**

> I think I'm both artist and entrepreneur because being a musician wouldn't be enough for me. I have to be more. I am always looking for this larger purpose. Following my interests keeps me stimulated. I'm always excited. I couldn't be more excited. My career has been very satisfying. It's been fantastic.—**Miriam Cutler**

music that is popular at the moment. Both of these have a good chance of being unwanted, the former because it may not be marketable and the latter because the market is already saturated. Instead, understand your clients' needs and problems, and determine which need is underserved by other composers, and pursue that. If you create solutions for your clients that make their lives easier, you are more likely to have a successful business.

When you are actively working on a project you have great insight into what your client wants and needs. It is the best testing ground you could ever want for business development and long-term business planning. Your professionalism and creative problem-solving abilities during the working process are entrepreneurial too, and the solutions you find on one project could become the basis of your business model in the future. Include the opinions and reactions of your clients into your branding and business model whenever possible.

MUSIC LIBRARIES

LEARN THE INSIDER'S SECRET

THE EXISTENCE and workings of production music libraries are largely overlooked in formal music education programs and almost all literature about music and film scoring. If they are mentioned at all, it is sure to be more of a footnote than a focus. Music libraries possess vast amounts of music, generate huge sums of money from license fees and royalties, and control a sizable share of the market; however, understanding of them does not extend far beyond industry insiders. They are unknown and essentially invisible to most educators and the general public.

Music libraries are publishers of music that specialize in licensing ready-made music for productions. The concept of production music libraries has been around since the 1920s, when wax records were first made for radio broadcasters. Production music later transitioned to television and then film, so production music has been around for almost 100 years. Long ago library music had a negative connotation because it was perceived as canned or cheesy music, but that's no longer the case. Those limitations are gone, the production music industry is mature, and music libraries are a powerful force in the industry. The music caters to the needs of commercial broadcasting both in content and length, making it easier for clients to search and edit the music to picture. Libraries fill a need in the marketplace for music that can be

VIDEO: MUSIC LIBRARIES. Pictured: Cindy Badell-Slaughter.
www.vimeo.com/guerrillafilmscoring/musiclibrariesteaser

cleared instantly; is organized by mood; is designed and conceived for
use in film, television, and radio; and can be licensed for reasonably low
fees.

Music libraries have vast collections that are meticulously cataloged, cross-referenced, searchable, and carefully curated just like any
other library. The size of the catalogs and output of new music can be
staggering, and big libraries like Megatrax may have an output of 100
albums or more per year. They go to great lengths to create thorough
metadata about each of their tracks so that the catalog can be searched,
cross-referenced, and parsed in many different ways. Since music must
serve a specific need in productions, the libraries can be searched by
genre, tempo, mood, instrumentation, length, and other factors. Music
supervisors can find numerous options for their specific needs in a reasonably short amount of time, making it easy to find exactly the right
music for a particular purpose.

There is an incredible amount of media content that requires music
but not a custom score. There is an equally large amount of media content for which a composer might be considered desirable if there were
time, but the time is always too short. Music libraries fill those needs
and provide a hefty percentage of the music content for television, cable, film trailers, and advertising. They play a role in film when source
music or songs are required because composers typically don't write

those portions of the score. Libraries will occasionally provide source music for video games as well. Some other types of clients that use music libraries are advertising agencies, radio stations, corporations, government agencies, ringtone companies, recording studios, film studios, educational institutions, post houses, web developers, and much more. If music is involved, production music libraries can likely be used in some capacity.

Outside of music libraries it can be difficult to authorize the use of music. Publishing rights are typically owned by the publisher, while the master recording rights are owned by the record label. Sometimes use of a piece of music also requires permission from the artist. It can be hard to track down the publisher of a particular song or the owner of the recording because catalogs and companies are sold all the time. Some artists refuse to let their music be used in commercials or television at all. Even once those who own rights have been identified, negotiating the use of individual pieces of music can be cost prohibitive. The license fees for a pop or commercial song, especially a well-known song or band, can reach into the tens of thousands or even hundreds of thousands of dollars. Even if all parties are in agreement, there is rarely time for that process to play out in today's world of production.

> Libraries are great for productions because they come with ready-made music in all genres. The one-stop aspect is a big deal for the buyer, as is the nonunion aspect.—**Cindy Badell-Slaughter**

Libraries provide controlled pricing and convenient licensing because they own the copyrights of their music. Unlike traditional publishing they are able to license the music without the composer's permission, which gives them great freedom and speed. They are able to negotiate autonomously and serve their client's needs directly without

> Although I do not have specific numbers to back up this assertion, it is my understanding that production music represents the largest share of music on television, without question. Custom scored music and licensed commercial music represents a much smaller share.—**Ron Mendelsohn**

> At Immediate Music our tracks have been customized for trailers, and it's ready to go. When people are cutting a project they have a wealth of material to choose from. There's no reason for them to think about a custom score.—**Yoav Goren**

involving a third party in the negotiations, which is a major advantage greatly appreciated by productions. The various libraries operate differently, but because they can license music autonomously it's possible that a composer would not know his music has been licensed until receiving a check. It's no surprise that libraries are so predominant.

LIBRARIES ARE YOUR COMPETITION

As a composer, whether you are in direct competition with the music libraries depends on what medium you are pursuing. In long-form projects, particularly video games and feature films, there is little competition between libraries and composers. Long-form mediums require a musical voice, through line, and dramatic development throughout time, which library music can't provide. There's no way to cobble together a good ninety-minute film score from library cues. The implementation of audio in games can oftentimes be intricate, and big games might require 200 or 300 minutes of music. Only the simplest and shortest of video games can use library music. In film and video games, the role of production music is primarily to provide source music, which does not compete with the composer at all.

In shorter forms like a television episode, commercial, or trailer, libraries are dominant and can represent significant competition for an individual composer. The production companies often work exclusively

> Libraries provide an outlet for composers who write for them, but they can also definitely give composers a run for their money. If a library has underscore, or if the library is offering custom music, then they are going to be competition for a single composer. That's why composers need to be prepared and need to have their own arsenal, their own catalog to license.—**Cindy Badell-Slaughter**

> Libraries are definitely competition in television because so much of television today is reality television and unscripted. There really is no thread. There's not as much artistry in it, it's more of a product. Libraries are indeed doing the bulk of the heavy lifting in television today because it's quicker, probably cheaper, and they provide a lot more options.—**Yoav Goren**

with libraries and not with individual composers, which means there is typically no way for you to get those gigs directly. Most television shows have a composer, but they usually also work with libraries or the composer has a library of his own. In shows that don't purely use library music it's common to use a hybrid approach in which important scenes are scored and unimportant ones use library cues. The convenience and speed of the libraries trumps everything else. A sole composer is at a significant disadvantage when a client requests ten options for a scene or thirty minutes of music by tomorrow.

The best way to compete with libraries and differentiate your services as a composer from those a library provides is to write music that is highly specific. Your director has a vision and is collaborating directly with you to define characters, stories, and emotions in the film. Make the most of each collaborative opportunity. Involve the director so much that he feels as if he helped create the music and it says exactly what he wants it to say. You can compete with a library on the basis of your service, your relationship with the director, the development of thematic material, and the specificity of your score. These have always been the core duties of a composer, and they are the areas in which libraries cannot compete with an individual who is writing a custom score. Composers and music libraries can both provide music for all forms of media, but they often have different functions and serve different needs in the marketplace.

LIBRARIES ARE YOUR PARTNERS

The composers that think poorly of libraries probably don't understand them well or have outdated perceptions. Music libraries need composers, and their businesses rely on them. Instead of thinking about production music libraries as competition, it's smarter to acknowledge the

A library is a modern-day benefactor, if you will, like the old days from the fifteenth, sixteenth, seventeenth centuries, the court. Who hires composers today and pays them to write music? Who gives them commissions? These days, a lot of libraries do.—**Yoav Goren**

place they have in the market. They can be your partners and provide opportunities for you.

For example, well-known film composer agents will not add a composer to their roster until the composer is already doing quite well. There are hard costs associated with keeping a composer on the roster that make it impractical to sign smaller composers. Music libraries, on the other hand, will gladly work with anyone who creates good music that fits their needs. Their business is all about pitching and selling music, and in that way they function a little bit like agents. The more prominent libraries have hundreds of composers in their catalogs, and that variety is a strength. Libraries are all about the product, so your career status and credits almost don't matter. If you have good music that they need, they will accept you into their catalog. Once that relationship starts you have people working on your behalf to license your music and provide passive income for you.

Productivity is integral to the growth of a composer's career, and a consistently growing catalog is essential even if you don't currently have a project. In a perfect world you would move from project to project with little downtime in between, but the reality is that the fluctuation of work can leave you with substantial amounts of free time between gigs. This is where music libraries come in. Few composers work only for music libraries. Writing for libraries is most often a supplemental activity instead of a primary one. They provide an outlet for you to continue being productive, continue practicing, and make a living during the times that you have nothing else going on.

In the early part of your career the biggest hindrance to being a composer is how sporadic the work can be. You might score a film; write for a video game; do a couple of commercials; and then, after a good run, find yourself without work. This lull is the perfect time to write for libraries because you can convert your valuable skills into money. Some will write music first and then pitch it to the libraries,

The role that we fill as production music libraries is to give composers steady work that can tide them over between their other projects. Most of the composers we work with are also working in film, television, and recording, and the work they do for us really helps level out their income and keep them busy year-round. It's very much a complementary activity to their other work.—**Ron Mendelsohn**

while others will first find out what a specific library needs so they can fill that void.

There are libraries that focus on every niche you can imagine, so concentrate on your strengths, create a great product to the best of your ability, and work with as many libraries as you can. If the material is good you will be able to convert it into a supplemental cash flow. Over time it can become a significant portion of your income.

WRITE FOR LIBRARIES

There are many different music libraries with varying business models. One thing that most of them have in common is that they work with finished tracks. A select few are involved in mastering, and many will give feedback or comments on tracks. But for the most part, libraries are not involved in the creative process. The first step in working with music libraries is to compile a collection of your best tracks.

By definition, library music needs to be precisely cataloged and organized, which means that it needs to fit neatly within its box. Individual tracks need to have variety in energy level and instrumentation, but the scopes of styles and emotions need to be tightly focused because licensed music needs to fill specific dramatic needs. The duration of the music might need to be ten seconds or three minutes, and it will be different each time the piece is cut into a project. Your cues need to communicate the same type of emotion throughout. If the sections within the cue are too musically disparate the cue is less functional for music editors. Transitions that change the mood too much will get in the way. It is better for the music editor to have two different cues that are internally consistent because the editor can cut them together and create transitions as needed. The cues absolutely need to have shape, direction, variety, and multiple energy levels, but the emotional effect of the music should be focused.

Just as the individual cues need to be focused, libraries prefer that a composer is also focused. Composers oftentimes like to show off the breadth of their abilities in their demos, but this is the worst possible approach when pitching to a music library. It's more ideal to present a tightly focused package of tracks than a broad variety of styles. Library music tends to be emotionally specific, so limit your stylistic offerings. If you tell a library that you can do every style they won't be impressed. When the music you submit is easy to put into a stylistic box, it will be better received.

The most highly respected libraries do not accept unsolicited material because they don't have time to listen to all the submissions they would receive; however, most libraries will listen to your tracks if you approach them. The more targeted your focus and more intriguing your pitch, the better chance you have at getting their attention. You can shop your music around to different libraries quite readily. Libraries are always on the lookout for new talent, and they're quite happy when new composers with new sounds approach them. There is no mystery or secret to getting your music into a music library, you just have to knock on a lot of doors until you find someone who wants to listen. If you produce good music you will find a home for it. If you're fortunate, it can earn money for you for many years.

Don't forget that "listen" means something different in the context of a music library that rabidly consumes music. When a library is deciding whether to work with you, it's likely that they will listen to five to ten seconds at the beginning of a track and another five to ten seconds somewhere in the middle. They will get through only a few tracks, and if you're lucky they'll leave your music playing while they write you a two-sentence e-mail. If your music is accepted, the library's clients will give it just about as much time when they're browsing through the library, maybe less. The production values need to catch ears immediately, and the content of the cues must be so focused that five seconds anywhere in the cue can represent the entire cue reasonably well.

The good news is that nowhere in the industry are the barriers to entry lower than with music libraries. No matter what genre you prefer, there is a music library somewhere that specializes in that part of the mar-

> The majority of our composers work in some kind of team situation where either they've teamed up with an engineer, or they've teamed up with cowriters, or they've teamed up with someone who has a studio. It is much easier for us to work with a composer who can deliver a finished product than with a composer who comes in here with a handwritten score that we have to produce. We do have studios here on the premises, and there are a lot of albums that we do record here in-house, but for the majority of our projects we prefer the composer to deliver a finished product.—**Ron Mendelsohn**

ket. Musical style is not a barrier. The classic catch-22 exists throughout the rest of the music industry: You can only get work if you've already had it before. But the production music world is so focused on the product and its ability to be licensed that credits and reputation are much less important. If you're looking to supplement your income or break into the scoring industry music libraries are a fantastic place to start.

BUILD YOUR OWN LIBRARY

In the past, film and television usually used work-for-hire agreements, which means that although the composer keeps the writer's royalties, the company owns the music. A composer working under such agreements often enjoys a separation of his fees from the music production costs, which are covered by the production company. Video game agreements tend to be buyout agreements, meaning that the composer receives money up front and has no ownership or rights.

Package-deal agreements have largely taken over in the film and television industry. In a package deal the production company pays a fixed fee to the composer for finished recordings. The composer therefore is responsible for all production costs and pays for them out of that fee. Any money not used for production is the composer's income, so package deals encourage low-cost productions. These agreements also typically originate from the production companies and can also be work-for-hire agreements; however, ownership of the music can sometimes be negotiated. When the budgets are small it is possible for composers to retain ownership and control of their music.

Here's a typical scenario. You're hired on the spot and you start on Monday, but the picture's in and they want you to move fast. They can't afford to pay you very much, but they've got lots and lots of picture. So what do you do? There needs to be music in the bin, so build your library and be the bin. You don't want them to go shopping anywhere else but you.—**Cindy Badell-Slaughter**

Budgets are shrinking consistently throughout the industry, and because of this a new model has slowly been emerging. It is increasingly common for composers to also be music publishers, retain all rights, and license their music to productions. The motivation for this is twofold. First, taking the publishing rights off the table allows the budgets to be smaller because the composer no longer needs to surrender ownership of the asset he creates. Companies that cannot afford to own and control the music can still use a composer and get a custom score. They get the rights they need for their film, but ownership and control remain with the composer. Second, it allows composers to build their own music library. Composers can exploit their music freely by licensing it to other projects, creating sheet music, releasing soundtrack albums, or anything else.

Along with working for music libraries, it is a good idea to build your own library of music. If you have a back catalog of music that you can license you might be able to fulfill a client's needs despite a lack of money or time. If producers know that you come with a catalog of music it can make you much more attractive to hire because you will be able to work quickly and inexpensively. This is particularly true if you are pursuing mediums that tend to use extensive amounts of library music. Your catalog can be handed to editors and some of your music can be cut into the project before you start writing, making the work process faster and more efficient. If your catalog is targeted and lends itself to licensing, building your own music library could create substantial long-term income.

It's very important for composers to start building their own libraries, especially in genres like reality television.—**Garry Schyman**

> The industry is tough, and we have to find every possible way to make a living. Things like passive income and the ability to reuse or relicense music are far more important than they used to be. Whenever you can, keep your publishing rights. You have to think of all kinds of ways to make each note stretch as far as it can.—**Nathan Furst**

CONSIDER THE LIBRARY'S BUSINESS MODELS

Twenty years ago there was never any question about clients paying a sync license fee for a song or master recording. Each track warranted a license fee, even the most basic demo that made it into a show, and those licenses often had to be renewed every five years. There were always broadcast royalties attached to each license, and at the end of the day it was possible to get a nice paycheck from a well-placed track. But as the music industry has evolved, the production music business has been forced to evolve as well. Music libraries cannot command as much money as they used to, and there are several business models that threaten the long-term health of the business.

The conventional business model for music libraries is that they commission new music from composers and license it to productions. There are three potential sources of income for the composer. The library may pay a fee to the composer for the commission, the library may share sync fees with the composer when a piece is licensed, and performance royalties are paid from the performing rights organizations after a piece is broadcast. Depending on their business models, some libraries may omit either the commission fee or the sync fee from the agreement with their composers. In the conventional model the libraries are exclusive distributors of original content. The music is unique and screened for quality, their composers are vetted, and the music has been properly cleared for licensing. The music also tends to be fresher and interesting because it is newly commissioned. The library knows its content, carefully curates the catalog, and can help its clients find the perfect track.

As the industry has evolved the value of recorded music has decreased, and the business models of some music libraries have correspondingly changed. Another model that is becoming increasingly common is aggregation. Aggregators indiscriminately collect content from as many sources as possible to assemble a large library. An important distinction from the conventional model is that aggregators do not commission the music, and they often distribute the material nonexclusively. They may also let composers anywhere in the world upload their music to their library, where it can be searched and potentially licensed. They are simply brokers and have no connection to the material.

The problem with this model in production music is that the tracks are seldom screened, and the composers are not vetted. No one knows if there will be property infringement issues or if the rights have been properly cleared. As you would expect, the catalogs tend to be lower quality, outdated, more difficult to search, and, of course, cheaper. The aggregation model reduces both quality and price and can cause legal ramifications if music is found to be infringing on someone's copyright, so it is not good for the long-term integrity of the production music industry.

A more destructive business model for music libraries is that of nonexclusive licensing. The philosophy is similar to aggregation in the sense that they assume more is better, and many nonexclusive libraries are also aggregators. Nonexclusive libraries allow you to place your music with them and other nonexclusive libraries. You can still also license the tracks yourself. In theory, if your music is available from more outlets it has more opportunity to be licensed. It sounds good on the surface. The library will simply take your track, give it a new title, and send it out into the world with their best wishes.

Royalty reporting is increasingly done with audio fingerprinting technology, in which computers analyze the sonic fingerprint of music that is broadcast and report it to the performing rights organizations automatically. It is a much more sophisticated version of the technology used in the popular mobile phone app Shazam, which can identify any song in less than ten seconds. When identical master recordings are registered under multiple titles with different rights associated with them, accurate royalty reporting is extremely difficult. Nonexclusive libraries that retitle their tracks run the risk of several parties claiming the publishing rights to a piece of music, creating a confusing and expensive legal exploration with the potential for copyright infringement claims. The duplication of tracks pitched by several libraries can also be an annoying time waster for music supervisors.

A third new business model is called the synchronization license free model, or free sync. The idea is that the performance royalties should be valuable enough on their own, and clients should not need to pay an up-front sync fee. In other words, the opportunity to be broadcast and receive royalties should be payment enough. When this business model emerged, paying license fees was universal and no one was asking for free music. This model was offered as a strategy for undercutting the competition so that new libraries could gain more market share, but it threatens to make the sync fee obsolete and take away reliable income from composers. The stability of this business model may be especially precarious because the royalties, which are the primary revenue path, are under attack and shrinking consistently. This business model has identified a saturated market and has little concern for the well-being and earning power of composers.

In the most recent and destructive business model, other libraries have taken the opposite approach to building market share by declaring their catalogs free of performance royalties. The idea is that networks can renegotiate the blanket fees they pay to ASCAP and BMI because they are broadcasting some performance-free music. This model takes a pessimistic view of the future value of performance royalties and discards them in favor of cash up front, namely, the sync fees. Just as in the free sync model, the performance-free model consciously eliminates one component of the composer's income stream.

The music licensing and clearance budgets are really shrinking. On many occasions a music supervisor will say, "I have no budget." The first few times I was shocked, but now I'm just sad because every single other department has a budget. Why was music left out?

Catalogs like mine are not free. I think that any time it's your business model to give away something for free you're devaluing yourself, devaluing music, and eroding the business. Do you want to start at zero, and do you have to start at zero? I don't think so. It's time for artists to see further down the line and protect the industry. They need to protect their performance rights. If they're not protecting their income and valuing themselves, no one is going to value them.—**Cindy Badell-Slaughter**

> Some parts of the industry are in a race to the bottom. The high end of the market, clients in film, television, and trailers, generally respect the value of music and insist on a high level of quality and service. There will always be a viable market for high-quality productions and personalized service.—**Ron Mendelsohn**

These are the four main business models that are threatening the traditional production music business today, and they are becoming increasingly common. They are not inherently evil, nor is the old way always the best way, but when compared to the conventional business model they put the composer's income, as well as the library's income, at serious long-term risk. The Production Music Association alone has more than 670 member libraries to choose from, and they each make their own terms for their composers and clients. When you begin to work with libraries be sure to educate yourself about how their business works.

Performance royalties and intellectual property copyrights have been protected by law for quite some time as a result of many hard-fought battles, and there is no good reason to voluntarily throw those rights away. The models that undercut the traditional model are likely to be unsustainable because they deprive the libraries of the money required to hire quality composers, create quality content, and deliver good customer service. Make a decision about what kind of business you want to do, and explore the library's business practices before you begin to collaborate.

SAMPLE CONTRACTS

COMPOSERS ARE traditionally not the ones to provide legal agreements. When working with television networks, film studios, or video game developers, the contracts are usually generated by the companies and given to the composer or the composer's agent for review; however, when composers retain full control of their music and license it to productions, they are often responsible for providing the agreements.

The music that is licensed may be written specifically for a project or it may be preexisting in their library. The same type of agreement is used in both cases. The rights to two things are needed when a production company wants to use music: rights to the intellectual property of the composition and rights to the recording. A sync license covers the composition and is required for anything that is not in the public domain. A master use license covers the recording.

This appendix contains two sample agreements. The first is a combined sync license and master use license, an example of what a composer might use when licensing recordings of his own music to a production. The second is a master use license, an example of what a composer might use to license his own recordings of public domain music. When other types of agreements are required, they will probably be generated by the production companies, not the composer.

These samples were generously offered by Mark Litwak, a veteran entertainment attorney with offices in Beverly Hills, California, who is also the author of six books. One of the books is *Contracts for the Film and Television Industry*, which is an extremely valuable resource and highly recommended.

In reviewing these contracts please note that the information provided is not a substitute for consulting with an attorney and receiving counsel based on the facts and circumstances of a particular transaction. The terms in these sample agreements are not always appropriate, complete, or up to date.

SYNCHRONIZATION/PERFORMING/MASTER USE AND MECHANICAL LICENSE

THIS SYNCHRONIZATION/PERFORMING/MASTER USE AND MECHAN-ICAL LICENSE is made and entered into as of _____, by and between _____ ("Licensor") at _____ and _____ ("Licensee"), at _____. The parties hereby agree as follows:

1. GRANT OF RIGHTS: Licensor hereby irrevocably grants to Licensee the nonexclusive right to include in the photoplay tentatively entitled "_____" (the "Film") and in promoting, advertising, and publicizing of the Film that certain musical compositions written and owned by Licensor (the "Compositions") and the recording of an instrumental and vocal performance thereof owned by Licensor (the "Recording"). This license shall continue in perpetuity and be effective for any and all media, whether now known or hereafter devised, throughout the universe. The license shall include, but shall not be limited to, the following:

(a) Use of the compositions, and any recording and any performance thereof, in synchronized or timed relation to the Film and any remake or remakes thereof for exploitation in any and all media now known or hereafter devised (including, but not limited to, audiovisual devices), including the recording and distribution of the Film on DVD, videocassette, videodisc, by television (including cable, pay-per-view TV, and broadcast TV), electronic publishing rights, theatrical and nontheatrical exhibition, and in advertisements in-context and out-of-context, trailers, music videos, and other promotional and ancillary uses of the Film or such other audiovisual work.

(b) Use of the compositions, any recording and any performance thereof, on a soundtrack album including CDs, tapes, and all manner of digital track and album distribution ("Album") and to manufacture, sell, distribute, and advertise copies of the Album embodying the Compositions and Recordings by any methods and in any configurations now known or hereafter devised; for the release of same under any trademarks, trade names, or label; to perform the Compositions and Recordings publicly; and to commit to public performance thereof by radio and/or television, or by any other media now known or hereafter devised, and to permit any other person, corporation, or other entity to do any or all of the foregoing. Licensor shall have the right to release the Recording as a so-called single ("Single").

(c) Right to make, import, and export copies of the Composition and Recording in the Film.

2. NAME AND LIKENESS: Licensor hereby grants to Licensee the irrevocable universe-wide right, in perpetuity, to use and permit others to use Licensor's name, voice, approved photograph, likeness, and biographical material concerning Licensor in connection with the Film, Album, and any music recordings in any format derived therefrom and any promotions and advertisements thereof. Any photograph, likenesses, or biographical material submitted or furnished by Licensor to Licensee shall be deemed approved, and, promptly following the execution of this Agreement, Licensor shall submit to Licensee a reasonable assortment of approved photographs, likenesses, and biographical materials for use by Licensee in connection herewith. All such materials submitted by Licensee to Licensor for approval (which approval shall not be unreasonably withheld) shall be deemed given in the event Licensor fails to submit written objections thereto within five (5) days after the applicable photographs, likenesses, and/or biographical materials have been submitted to Licensor for approval.

3. RERECORDING: Licensee shall have the right to rerecord, edit, mix and remix, dub and redub the Recording in Licensee's sole discretion, and nothing contained herein shall be construed to obligate Licensee to employ Licensor in connection with same.

4. COMPENSATION:
   (a) Provided Licensor fully performs all material obligations under this Agreement, and in full consideration of all rights granted herein, Licensee shall pay or cause to be paid to Licensor, within thirty (30) days of the initial commercial release of the Film, the sum of $_____.
   (b) It is specifically understood and agreed that the sums set forth in this clause 4 and the record royalties set forth in clause 5 below shall constitute payment in full to Licensor, and to all persons or entities deriving or claiming rights through either Licensor.

5. ROYALTIES:
   (a) With respect to the exploitation of the Recording if embodied on the Album, Single or an individual download, or other phonograph records derived therefrom, whether in disc, cartridge, tape, magnetic, electronic,

or other form, Licensee shall pay to Licensor a basic royalty at the rate of
_____ percent (___%) (the "Basic Album Rate") of the suggested retail list
price ("SRLP") or wholesale equivalent in respect of net sales of Albums
sold through normal retail channels in the United States (including, without limitation, physical retailers, e-retailers [e.g., Amazon.com] and digital
music retailers [e.g., iTunes]) in the form of CDs, vinyl discs, cassettes,
and any other configuration, prorated by multiplying the applicable royalty
rate by a fraction, the numerator of which is the number one (1) and the
denominator of which is the total number of master recordings, including
the Recording, contained on the Album (the "Licensor Fraction").

(b) The royalty payable to Licensor hereunder for singles, budget records, foreign record sales, and other sales of records or exploitations of
the Master shall be reduced and prorated in the same proportion that the
basic U.S. Album Rate payable to Licensee in respect of the Album (the
"Basic Distributor Rate") is reduced or prorated pursuant to Licensee's
agreement with the applicable Distributor, provided that with respect to
such sales of records or exploitations of the Master for which Licensee
receives a royalty, which is computed as a flat fee or as a percentage of
the Distributor's net receipts from such use, Licensor's royalty hereunder
in respect of such sale or use shall be equal to the amount of Licensee's
flat fee or net receipts, multiplied by the product of the following:

$$\frac{\text{Basic Album Rate}}{\text{Basic Distributor Rate}} \times \text{Licensor Fraction}$$

(c) Except as otherwise provided in this Agreement, Licensor's royalties hereunder shall be computed, determined, calculated, and paid
to Licensor on the same basis (e.g., packaging deductions, free goods,
reserves, definition of suggested retail list price, percentage of sales,
discounts, returns policy, taxes, etc.) and at the same times as royalties
are paid to Licensee by the applicable Distributor.

(d) Notwithstanding anything to the contrary contained in this Agreement, (i) Licensor shall not be entitled to receive any record royalties at all
with respect to records sold prior to the recoupment of all Recording Costs
for the Album, if any, and Conversion Costs from the royalties otherwise
payable to Licensor hereunder; and (ii) following such recoupment Licensor's royalties shall be credited to Licensor's account hereunder solely in
respect of records thereafter sold that embody the Recording. The term
"Recording Costs" shall mean all direct costs incurred by Licensee in the

course of producing and recording any master recordings, including the Recording embodied on the Album and including, without limitation, the cost of studio time, musician fees, union payments, instrument rentals, producer's fees, and advances and the costs of editing, mixing, remixing, and mastering and other similar costs customarily regarded as recording costs in the recording industry. The term "Conversion Costs" shall mean all direct costs incurred in connection with the conversion of the Recording from use in the Film to use in the Album, including, without limitation, new-use, reuse, remixing, and reediting costs and all other costs, which are now or hereafter recognized as conversion costs in the recording and motion picture industries.

(e) Licensor shall be deemed to have consented to all royalty statements and all other accounts rendered by Licensee, unless specific objection in writing, stating the basis thereof, is given by Licensor to Licensee within one (1) year from the date such statement is rendered. During this one-year period, Licensor may, at its expense, but not more than once annually, audit the books and records of Licensee, solely in connection with royalties payable to Licensor pursuant to this Agreement, provided such audit is conducted by a reputable certified public accountant, during business hours and upon reasonable written notice. Licensor shall be foreclosed from maintaining any action, claim, or proceeding against Licensee in any forum or tribunal with respect to any statement or accounting rendered hereunder unless such action, claim, or proceeding is commenced against Licensee in a court of competent jurisdiction within one (1) year after the date on which the Licensee receives the Licensor's written objection.

(f) Licensee shall account to Licensor upon a semiannual basis within 90 days of June 30 and December 31. Licensee shall have the right to rely upon Distributor's accounting and statements.

(g) Licensor shall be entitled to inspect such books and records of Licensee relating to the Album during regular business hours and shall be entitled to audit such books and records of Licensee relating to the Album upon reasonable notice to Licensee and provided that not more one (1) audit is conducted every calendar year and further provided that such audit shall last not more than thirty (30) consecutive business days once begun and does not interfere with Licensee's normal operations. Within thirty (30) days of the completion of the audit, Licensor will furnish Licensee with a copy of said audit. All audit expenses shall be borne by the Licensor.

6. CREDITS:

(a) If the Recording and/or Composition is contained in the Film, Licensee shall accord Licensor a credit in substantially the following form in the end titles of release prints of the Film approximately adjacent to the titles of the Compositions and Recordings:

"WRITTEN BY _____"
"PERFORMED BY _____"

The type, size, shape, color, placement, duration, and all other characteristics of the credit shall be at Licensee's sole and absolute discretion. Without limiting the generality of the foregoing, such credit may be shared with and/or adjacent to credits relating to other contributors to the Recording and/or the Compositions.

(b) No casual or inadvertent failure by Licensee or any failure by a third party to comply with the provisions of this clause 6 shall constitute a breach of this Agreement.

7. WARRANTIES: Licensor, on its own and on Licensor's behalf, hereby warrants and represents that:

(a) It has the full right, power, and authority to enter into this Agreement and to grant all rights granted herein, that it is not under, nor will it be under, any disability, restriction, or prohibition with respect to its rights to fully perform in accordance with the terms and conditions of this Agreement and that there shall be no liens, claims, or other interests that may interfere with, impair, or be in derogation of the rights granted herein;

(b) The Album shall be freely available for use by Licensee, music recordings in any format derived therefrom and in the Film in any and all media (whether now known or hereafter devised) in which the Film is to be distributed (and in any and all publicizing, promoting, and advertising therefor), throughout the universe including, without limitation, in theaters, free and pay television, in-home video devices, and in radio, television, and theatrical trailers, without further payment by Licensee, except as set forth herein;

(c) Any party who may be entitled to Licensor's exclusive recording services shall have given a written waiver of such rights in connection with Licensee's exploitation of the Recording as herein provided;

(d) Licensee shall not be required to make any payments of any nature for, or in connection with, the acquisition, exercise, or exploitation of rights by Licensee pursuant to this Agreement except as specifically provided in this Agreement;

(e) Neither the Recording, nor the Compositions, nor any other material supplied by Licensor will violate or infringe upon any common law or statutory right of any person, firm, or corporation including, without limitation, contractual rights, copyrights, and rights of privacy.

(f) Licensor owns or controls 100% of the Recording and the Composition.

8. INDEMNITY: Licensor hereby agrees to indemnify Licensee, Licensee's successors, Licensee's distributors, subdistributors, and assigns, and the respective officers, directors, agents, and employees of each of the foregoing, from and against any damages, liabilities, costs, and expenses, including reasonable attorneys' fees actually incurred, arising out of or in any way connected with any claim, demand, or action inconsistent with this Agreement or any warranty, representation, or agreement made by Licensor herein.

9. REMEDIES FOR BREACH: Licensor's rights and remedies in the event of a breach or alleged breach of this Agreement by Licensee shall be limited to an action at law for damages, if any, and in no event shall Licensor be entitled by reason of any such breach or alleged breach to enjoin, restrain, or to seek to enjoin or restrain, the distribution or other exploitation of the Film, Album, or other work that may embody the Recording and Licensee shall not have the right to rescind this Agreement. This Agreement shall not be deemed to give any right or remedy to any third party whatsoever unless the right or remedy is specifically granted by the parties hereto in writing to the third party. Licensor shall execute any further documents necessary to fully effectuate the intent and purposes of this Agreement.

10. ASSIGNMENT: Licensee shall have the right, at Licensee's election, to assign any of Licensee's rights hereunder, in whole or in part, to any person, firm, or corporation including, without limitation, any distributor or subdistributor of the Film, Album, or other music recordings in any format derived therefrom, or other work that may embody the Master. Licensor shall not assign rights without Licensee's prior written consent, and any attempted assignment without such consent shall be void and shall transfer no rights to the purported assignee.

11. ENTIRE AGREEMENT: This Agreement sets forth the entire under-standing of the parties thereto relating to the subject matter hereof and supersedes all prior agreements, whether oral or written, pertaining thereto. No modification, amendment, or waiver of this Agreement or any of the terms or provisions hereof shall be binding upon Licensor or Licensee unless confirmed by a written instrument signed by autho-rized officers of both Licensor and Licensee. No waiver by Licensor or Licensee of any terms or provisions of this Agreement or of any default hereunder shall affect their respective rights thereafter to enforce such term or provision or to exercise any right or remedy upon any other de-fault, whether or not similar.

12. RIGHT TO CURE: No failure by Licensee to perform any of Licensee's obligations hereunder shall be deemed a breach hereof, unless Licensor gives Licensee written notice of such failure and Licensee fails to cure such nonperformance within thirty (30) days after Licensee's receipt of such notice.

13. NOTICES: All notices hereunder shall be sent certified mail, return re-ceipt requested, or delivered by hand to the applicable address set forth below, unless and until written notice, via registered mail, to the contrary is received by the applicable party.

If to Licensee: _____ (Licensee), _____ (Licensee Address); courtesy copies to _____, _____.

If to Licensor: _____, _____.
Notwithstanding the foregoing, all accounting statements and payments may be sent by regular mail. Except as required by law, the date of mail-ing of such notice shall be deemed the date upon which such notice was given or sent.

14. APPLICABLE LAW: This Agreement has been entered into in the State of _____, and its validity, construction, interpretation, and legal effect shall be governed by the laws of the State of _____ applicable to contracts entered into and performed entirely within the State of _____.

15. ARBITRATION: Any controversy or claim arising out of or relating to this Agreement or any breach thereof shall be settled by arbitration in accordance with the Rules of the American Arbitration Association. The parties select expedited arbitration using one arbitrator as the sole forum for the resolution of any dispute between them. The venue for arbitration shall be _____. The arbitrator may make any interim order, decision, determinations, or award he deems necessary to preserve the status quo until he is able to render a final order, decision, determination, or award. The determination of the arbitrator in such proceeding shall be final, binding, and nonappealable. Judgment upon the award rendered by the arbitrator may be entered in any court having jurisdiction thereof. The prevailing party shall be entitled to reimbursement for costs and reasonable attorney's fees.

IN WITNESS WHEREOF, the parties hereto have executed this Agreement as of the year and date first above written.

"Licensor"

_____

(Licensor)
ACCEPTED AND AGREED TO:
"Licensee"

_____

(Licensee)

MASTER USE LICENSE TELEVISION

1. The Television Program covered by this license (hereinafter referred to as the "Program") is: _____
(show name) Episode #_____

2. The Master Sound Recording (hereafter referred to as the "Master") covered by this license is: _____ (master title) recorded by _____ (artist name)

3. The master owner of this master is: _____
_____ (master owner)

4. The type and maximum duration of the master to be recorded are: _____ (type of use and timing)

5. The administrative interest and territory covered hereby is: [percentage controlled]% worldwide

6. IN CONSIDERATION of the sum of [dollar amount in words] ($[dollar amount in numbers]), receipt of which is hereby acknowledged, _____ (licensor name), _____ (licensor address) (hereinafter referred to as "Licensor") hereby grants to _____ (licensee name), _____ (licensee address) (hereinafter referred to as "Producer"), the following rights:

(a) The nonexclusive right, license, privilege, and authority to fix and record in any manner, medium, form, or language, in each country of the territory the master, in aforesaid type and use, in synchronism or time-relation with the Program, and to make copies of the Program containing the recordings of the master in the form of negatives and prints necessary for distribution, exhibition, promotion, and exploitation in all media irrespective of the means or method of delivery including, but not limited to, all Media now known or hereafter devised (including all forms of in-context trailers and promos) but excluding theatrical, out-of-context, and nonsequential/nonlinear uses. Producer further has the right to import said Program containing the recording of the composition and/or copies thereof into any country throughout the territory all in accordance with the terms, conditions, and limitations hereinafter set forth;

(b) Producer shall supply Licensor with a cue sheet of the Program promptly following the first public exhibition of such; provided, however,

Producer's failure to do so shall not be deemed to be a breach of this agreement.

7. The term of this license shall be in perpetuity commencing with the execution of this Agreement.

8. Licensor represents and warrants that it owns or controls the master licensed hereunder and that it has the legal right to grant this license and all the rights herein stated, including all performance and master use rights, and Licensor has secured and owns any and all rights from third parties (e.g., lyricist, musicians, performers, record companies, publishers) needed to grant the rights granted to Producer under this Agreement. Producer warrants and represents that it will obtain a synchronization license from the copyright owners of the composition(s) embodied in the master.

9. Licensor shall indemnify and hold harmless Producer, its successors, assigns, and licensees from and against any and all losses, damages, liabilities, reasonable attorney's fees and costs, actions, suits, or other claims arising out of Producer's exercise of such rights, or any breach or alleged breach, in whole or in part, of Licensor's representations and warranties.

10. All rights granted hereunder are granted on a nonexclusive basis. Producer is not obligated to use the master or exercise any of its rights hereunder. Licensor reserves all rights not expressly granted to Producer hereunder. Without limiting the generality of the foregoing, the following rights are specifically reserved to Licensor and may not be exercised by Producer:
(a) All rights of reproduction or use of the master on CD, tapes, and any other types of sound reproduction, in all media, whether now or hereafter known or in existence. Without limiting the generality of the foregoing, Producer shall not have the right to include or authorize the use of the recording or any portion thereof in any music recordings in any format of the soundtrack of the Program.
(b) The right to use the master, in other Programs or television programs, including uses similar to that authorized hereunder.

11. Producer shall have the right to perform, reproduce, rerecord, edit, mix and remix, dub and redub the Master in Producer's sole discretion.

Unless otherwise specifically provided for elsewhere in this license, this license does not authorize or permit:

(a) any changes to be made in the master other than to shorten same as contemplated hereunder utilizing a contiguous portion thereof; or

(b) any other use of the master not expressly authorized hereunder.

12. Producer shall have the power and authority to assign its rights and obligations under this license to any party whatsoever without consent. This license shall be binding upon and shall inure to the benefit of the respective successors, assigns, heirs, executors, and administrators of the parties hereto.

13. In the event of any breach of any provision of this agreement by Producer, Licensor's sole remedy will be an action at law for damages, if any, and in no event will Licensor be entitled or seek to enjoin, interfere, or inhibit the distribution, exhibition, or exploitation of the Program.

14. No failure by Producer to perform any of its obligations hereunder shall be deemed a breach hereof, unless Licensor has given written notice of such failure to Producer and Producer does not cure such non-performance within thirty (30) days.

15. All notices hereunder required to be given to the parties hereto and all payments to be made hereunder shall be sent to the parties at their addresses mentioned herein or to such other addresses as each party respectively may hereafter designate by notice in writing to the other.

16. This license shall be governed by and subject to the laws of the State of California applicable to agreements entered into and wholly performed within California. This Agreement sets forth the entire understanding of the parties thereto relating to the subject matter hereof and supersedes all prior agreements, whether oral or written, pertaining thereto. No modification, amendment, or waiver of this Agreement or any of the terms or provisions hereof shall be binding upon Licensor or Licensee unless confirmed by a written instrument signed by authorized officers of both Licensor and Licensee.

IN WITNESS WHEREOF, the parties hereto agree that the foregoing terms and conditions are effective as

of _____ (initial airdate).

_____

(Producer)

By: _____

_____

(Licensee)

By: _____

COMPOSER BIOS

CINDY BADELL-SLAUGHTER

www.heavyhittersmusic.com

Cindy Badell-Slaughter is president and coowner of Heavy Hitters Music, which, for decades, has been a leading provider of vocal and instrumental songs for film, television, and advertising. A twenty-five-year music industry executive, she was director of Music Operations for CBS Broadcasting Inc. for ten years. Prior to that, she worked as director of Music Clearance for EMG Inc., Warner Bros Television, and Lorimar Productions. Throughout the years, Badell-Slaughter handled music administration and/or music clearance for soundtrack albums, movies, and miniseries; such highly rated television shows as *CSI*, *CSI: NY*, and *CSI: Miami*; and on-air promotion for FOX, CBS, and UPN television networks.

CHARLES BERNSTEIN

Charles Bernstein has been a composer of film and television scores for more than four decades. He has composed scores for more than 100 motion pictures, including *A Nightmare on Elm Street*, and was a musical contributor to Quentin Tarantino's *Inglourious Basterds*. Bernstein has one Emmy win and two nominations. An educator and member of the Hollywood community, he is currently elected to the Board of Governors of the Academy of Motion Picture Arts and Sciences, the Board of Directors of the Society of Composers and Lyricists, and the Board of Directors of the ASCAP Foundation. In addition, Bernstein is the author of two books about film music and a regular columnist in the *Score*, the quarterly publication of the Society of Composers and Lyricists.

www.charlesbernstein.com

BRUCE BROUGHTON

With a career spanning more than forty years, Bruce Broughton is one of the most successful television composers in the world. He has received twenty-three Emmy nominations and won a record ten times, most recently for his score for the HBO movie *Warm Springs*. One of the most versatile composers working today, he writes in every medium, from theatrical releases and television feature films to the concert stage and computer games. Broughton's first major film score, for the Lawrence Kasdan western *Silverado*, garnered him an Oscar nomination. His next project, Barry Levinson's *Young Sherlock Holmes*, earned a Grammy nomination for the soundtrack album. Broughton is a former governor of the Academy of Motion Picture Arts and Sciences, a board member of ASCAP, and a past president of the Society of Composers and Lyricists.

www.brucebroughton.com

He lectures in music composition at the University of California, Los Angeles, and teaches film composition in the Scoring for Motion Pictures and Television program at the University of Southern California.

BILL BROWN

Bill Brown recently completed scoring his ninth season of the hit CBS series *CSI: NY* and has composed scores for numerous films, including *The Devil's Tomb* and *Dark Prophecy*. He also continues to write powerful orchestral and electronic scores for hit game titles, with a wealth of credits that include *The Incredible Hulk: Ultimate Destruction* and *Captain America: Super Soldier*. Brown's scores have been nominated by the British Academy of Film and Television Arts, *L.A. Weekly*, and GANG, and have won awards from the International Television Association and BMI, as well as the Music-4Games Editor's Choice Award.

www.billbrownmusic.com

STEWART COPELAND

A member of the Rock and Roll Hall of Fame, Stewart Copeland has spent three decades at the forefront of contemporary music as a rock star, acclaimed film composer and filmmaker, and sought after composer in the disparate worlds of opera, ballet, world music, and chamber music composition. His list of achievements is indicative of an artist who has truly done it all. He is a founding member and drummer of the multiple-platinum-selling group the Police; composer of music for such films as *Rumble Fish* and *Wall Street*; and composer for television shows, video games, movie trailers, ballets, symphonies, operas, and more. His awards include six Grammys, two BRIT Awards, and nominations for a Primetime Emmy and a Golden Globe.

www.stewartcopeland.net

MIRIAM CUTLER

www.miriamcutler.com

Miriam Cutler is an Emmy-nominated composer with an extensive background in scoring for independent film and television projects, as well as two circuses. She is a member of the Academy of Motion Picture Arts and Sciences Documentary Branch. Her extensive film and television credits include *Ethel*, *Lost in La Mancha*, and the Oscar-nominated *Poster Girl*. Cutler has served as lab advisor for the Sundance Institute Documentary Composers Lab, as well as on documentary juries for the Sundance Film Festival, Independent Spirit Awards, International Documentary Association Awards, and American Film Institute's Film Festival Awards. Furthermore, she is a longtime board member of the Society of Composers and Lyricists. Cutler has also coproduced two Grammy-nominated live jazz albums.

TIMOTHY ANDREW EDWARDS

www.taemusic.com

Timothy Andrew Edwards has nearly seventy-five film and television credits to his name, and he has scored more than 100 trailers and promos for successful feature films and television shows. He has collaborated with almost every major television network, including NBC, CBS, and ABC. Edwards is a "go-to composer" in the world of television, with compositions on such shows as *Keeping Up with the Kardashians*, *The Bachelor*, *Ellen*, and *TMZ*. His themes for *Extra*, *Leeza*, and BBC's *My Genius Idea* have become enduring signatures for all three programs. Edwards's songwriting contributions to *The Vampire Diaries*, *Smallville*, and *CW Now* have solidified his status as a master of all formats.

NATHAN FURST

www.nathanfurst.com

Nathan Furst is one of Hollywood's elite young composers. He has composed the themes and scores for more than fifty films and television shows, most notably *Act of Valor* and *The Need for Speed*. He has been honored with three nominations for his outstanding original scores, including an Annie Award for his score for the Max Steel series, and has six soundtrack albums released with major record labels. Furst writes and produces his scores at the production facility at Bandito Bros., where he is able to score in a collaborative environment. He is a self-taught musician and began composing music at a young age. After attending Los Angeles County High School for the Arts, Furst left college to accept offers to score film and television projects.

CRAIG STUART GARFINKLE

www.craigstuartgarfinkle.com

Craig Stuart Garfinkle is an award-winning music producer and Emmy-nominated composer. His career includes work on feature films, video games, trailers, documentaries, multimedia, network television, commercials, stage musicals, and albums. Garfinkle is currently part of the composing team for the forthcoming *World of Warcraft* expansion, *Warlords of Dreanor*. In the film and television music world, his music has appeared in hundreds of projects, for example, NBC's *The Office*, *Lost*, and countless others. He best known, however, for his musical contributions to film trailers with partner Simone Benyacar. Some of their recent projects in this genre include J. J. Abrams's *Star Trek*, *Sin City*, the last three *Harry Potter* films, and *Spider-Man III*, just to name a few. Garfinkle was part of the composing team for Disney's *Raw Toonage* and the composer for the KAET/PBS production *Visions of Arizona*. Both programs received Emmy nominations for Outstanding Original Score.

PETER GOLUB

www.petergolub.com

Peter Golub is a multifaceted composer who works in film, theater, and concert halls. Since 1999, he has been director of the Sundance Film Music Program, where he runs the yearly Composers Lab. Film scores include *Frozen River* (which was nominated for Academy Awards for Best Actress and Best Screenplay), *The Great Debaters* (directed by Denzel Washington and cocomposed with James Newton Howard), and *The Laramie Project* (for HBO, directed by Moises Kaufman). Recent Broadway scores include *The Country House*, *The Heiress*, and *Time Stands Still*. Golub has written numerous chamber music works, as well as vocal and orchestral concert works. He has taught composition at both Bennington College and Reed College.

YOAV GOREN

www.immediatemusic.com

Yoav Goren is a cofounder of Immediate Music, one of the most influential companies in the industry, providing high-end trailer music for commercial motion pictures. Since 1992, Immediate Music has licensed music from its library to hundreds of theatrical trailers and television spots for all the major Hollywood studios. The company's music has been featured in the trailers for such films as *Hellboy II: The Golden Army*, *Avatar*, *Iron Man*, *Pirates of the Caribbean: At World's End*, *Coraline*, *Kingdom of Heaven*, *Dante's Peak*, *Cirque Du Freak: The Vampire's Assistant*, *X-Men: The Last Stand*, the *Matrix* films, the *Spider-Man* films, *The Wolfman*, *Assembly*, and the *Harry Potter* films. In 2007, Immediate received an Emmy for Outstanding Music Composition in a Sports Program for their work on the broadcast of the 2006 Winter Olympics. The firm has its own band called Globus that fuses cinematic orchestral music with contemporary and world music rhythms.

LAURA KARPMAN

www.laurakarpman.com

Laura Karpman is one of only a handful of A-list female composers with an active career in film and television, winning four Emmys and receiving an additional seven nominations, an Annie Award nomination, and a GANG Award and nomination for her video game music. She was named one of the most important women in Hollywood by *Variety* magazine and is a professor at the University of California, Los Angeles, in the School of Theater, Film, and Television. Karpman has scored dozens of game titles, including the large orchestral scores for Sony's *Everquest 2* and many of its updates. An active concert composer, her epic multimedia work *Ask Your Mama* was commissioned by Carnegie Hall.

MARK LITWAK

www.marklitwak.com

Mark Litwak is a veteran entertainment attorney and expert witness based in Beverly Hills, California. He is the author of six books, including *Reel Power, Dealmaking in the Film and Television Industry*, and *Risky Business: Financing and Distributing Independent Film*. He is the creator of Entertainment Law Resources. Litwak has achieved the highest Peer Review Rating (AV) from Martindale-Hubbell and been designated a Southern California Super Lawyer multiple times by Thomson Reuters. As a law professor, he has taught at Loyola Law School and the University of Puget Sound School of Law, and he is currently an adjunct professor at the University of Southern California Gould School of Law. Moreover, he taught a variety of entertainment law seminars at the University of California, Los Angeles, during a span of twenty-five years. Litwak has been interviewed on more than 100 television and radio shows, including *ABC News*, *The Larry King Show*, National Public Radio's *All Things Considered*, and CNN.

RON MENDELSOHN

www.megatrax.com

Ron Mendelsohn is cofounder and CEO of Megatrax, a leading independent production music library and custom music house based in Los Angeles, California. Established in 1990, the company has earned a worldwide reputation for high-quality music coupled with unparalleled service and innovation. In addition to managing business operations at Megatrax, Mendelsohn is an accomplished pianist and composer who has composed hundreds of cues for the Megatrax library and scored numerous film and television projects ranging from promos to feature films. A tireless advocate for music rights, he is a founding member of the Production Music Association (PMA) and has served on the PMA board since its inception. Mendelsohn is also a member of numerous other professional organizations, including the Society of Composers and Lyricists, Vistage, and ASCAP.

JOHN RODD

www.johnrodd.com

John Rodd is a music recording, mixing, and mastering engineer with decades of experience in all genres of music. He has worked at the world's finest studios, including Ocean Way and Abbey Road, and he was on the staff at 20th Century Fox's Newman scoring stage for seven years. Rodd recently opened his own studio, Clearstory Sound, in Los Angeles, California, where he records, mixes, and masters for some of the top composers in film, games, television, and albums. He has worked on hundreds of film and TV projects, including *Elysium*, *Breaking Bad*, *The Lincoln Lawyer*, and *Justice League: The Flashpoint Paradox*. Video game credits include *Call of Duty: Black Ops II*, *Mass Effect 3*, *Star Wars Kinect*, *StarCraft II: Heart of the Swarm*, *Assassin's Creed Brotherhood*, *Assassin's Creed II*, *Avatar*, *Alice in Wonderland*, *The Golden Compass*, *Conan*, and *Socom 3: U.S. Navy*

Seals. Rodd works extensively with Blizzard Entertainment on the *World of Warcraft* series.

STEVEN SALTZMAN

www.saltzmanmusic.com

Steven Saltzman, MPSE, is a music editor and composer based in Los Angeles, California. He received his bachelor of music in composition and film scoring from Berklee College of Music and is a certified Avid Pro Tools instructor. He has been editing music for film and television for the past eighteen years. In addition, Saltzman has lectured nationally, and he has created and taught numerous music editing courses. A recipient of a Golden Reel Award for music editing, he is also a member of the Motion Picture Editors Guild and the Society of Composers and Lyricists, and he sits on the board of the Motion Picture Sound Editors Guild.

GARRY SCHYMAN

www.garryschyman.com

Garry Schyman is one of the most impressive scoring voices in the genre of video game music with his acclaimed scores for such series as *BioShock*, *Dante's Inferno*, and *Destroy All Humans!* His work also encompasses prime-time television, miniseries, and feature films, adding to a decades-long body of work that has seen him conduct orchestras on sound stages throughout the world, as he has scored some of pop culture's most iconic characters. Schyman's video game scores have brought him critical acclaim and industry recognition, including Outstanding Achievement in Original Music Composition from the Academy of Interactive Arts and Sciences, Best Original Score from the Spike TV Games Awards and Game Audio Network Guild Awards for *BioShock*, as well as their nominations for *Destroy All Humans!* and *Destroy All Humans! 2*, amongst many other awards.

RYAN SHORE

www.ryanshore.com

Ryan Shore is a 2013 Emmy Award and 2012 Grammy Award–nominated composer for film, television, games, records, and theater. His ability to collaborate and compose memorable music in a wide range of styles has made him one of today's most sought after composers. Shore has also received the Elmer Bernstein Award, adjudicated and presented by Academy Award–winning composer Elmer Bernstein. His scores include *Prime, Harvard Man, The Shrine, Sesame Street, Numb, The Girl Next Door, Cabin Fever 2: Spring Fever, Scooby-Doo!, WrestleMania Mystery, Spy Hunter, Jack Brooks: Monster Slayer, Lower Learning, Vulgar,* and *Stan Helsing*. Shore is currently scoring Disney Television Animation's upcoming series *Penn Zero: Part Time Hero*. He also plays the saxophone and has performed with such artists as John Williams, Matchbox Twenty (U.S. tour and the *Late Show with David Letterman*), Barry Manilow, Johnny Mathis, Dave Koz, Natalie Cole, Arturo Sandoval, and Gerry Mulligan.

JACK WALL

www.jackwall.net

Jack Wall's distinguished musical career includes such popular video game franchises as *Myst, Splinter Cell,* and *Jade Empire*. He is widely recognized for composing some of the most iconic scores for the medium. Wall created the distinctive musical signature for Bio-Ware's sci-fi epic *Mass Effect*. The soundtrack won numerous accolades, achieving cult status with fans. In 2011, he received British Academy (BAFTA) and Spike TV VGA nominations for his work on *Mass Effect 2*. Wall is cocreator of *Video Games Live* and served as its music director and conductor from 2005 through 2010, performing with more than fifty of the world's finest orchestras, including the Los Angeles

Philharmonic, Hollywood Bowl Orchestra, and London Philharmonic Orchestra. He is cofounder of the Game Audio Network Guild and a frequent speaker at various educational institutions. These include the University of Southern California; the University of California, Los Angeles; Expressions Center for New Media; and the Los Angeles Recording School. He is currently an online faculty member of Berklee College of Music in Boston, Massachusetts.

AUSTIN WINTORY

www.austinwintory.com

In March 2012, the PlayStation3 game *Journey* instantly became Sony's fastest-selling PlayStation title, and the soundtrack album debuted on the Billboard charts higher than any original score in gaming history. In December 2012, more history was made when it was announced that Austin Wintory's soundtrack for *Journey* had become the first-ever Grammy-nominated video game score. The score subsequently won an Academy of Interactive Arts and Sciences DICE Award, two British Academy Awards, a Spike TV VGA award, and IGN's "Overall Music of the Year" Award, along with six GANG nominations and host of other honors. Wintory's previous PlayStation3 game, *flOw*, made him the youngest composer to receive a British Academy Award nomination, and it also won him a wide variety of other game industry accolades, including the Game Audio Network Guild's "Rookie of the Year." Furthermore, Wintory has scored more than forty feature films, and his first major film score, for *Captain Abu Raed*, which won an award at the Sundance Film Festival, was short-listed for the 2009 Academy Awards for Best Original Score. Shortly thereafter, the *Hollywood Reporter* named Austin "One of 15 Composers Primed to Join the A-List."

INDEX

ABOUT THE AUTHOR

www.jeremyborum.com

Jeremy Borum is a film composer, orchestrator, and music engraver. Among the first wave of working composers to see the digital demonetization of music as a piece of history, not an ongoing process, he built a successful music career in an uncertain industry that is reinventing itself. He currently has credits on fifteen features, two network television shows, seventeen shorts, and thirty-five albums. An active member of the Society of Composers and Lyricists, Borum is a contributing author to their quarterly journal, the *Score*. He has worked globally with many major orchestras and studios, recording or performing in about thirty countries to crowds as large as 80,000. He teaches a biannual intensive film scoring seminar at Citrus College in Glendora, California. A do-it-yourself guy to the core, he has also built two studios and custom gear.

Borum is a founding member and coowner of the digital sheet music publisher ZMX Music. Prior to his time with ZMX, he prepared music engravings for many of the largest print music publishers, including Hal Leonard, EMI, Edition Peters, Alfred, Morning Star, and others.

Thousands of his music engravings are available both digitally and in print worldwide.

He studied music at The Colburn School in Los Angeles, California; Berklee College of Music in Boston, Massachusetts; Australian National University in Canberra; and the University of California in Davis, California.